WINES & VINEYARDS

OF SOUTH AFRICA

WINES & VINEYARDS

OF SOUTH AFRICA

WENDY TOERIEN

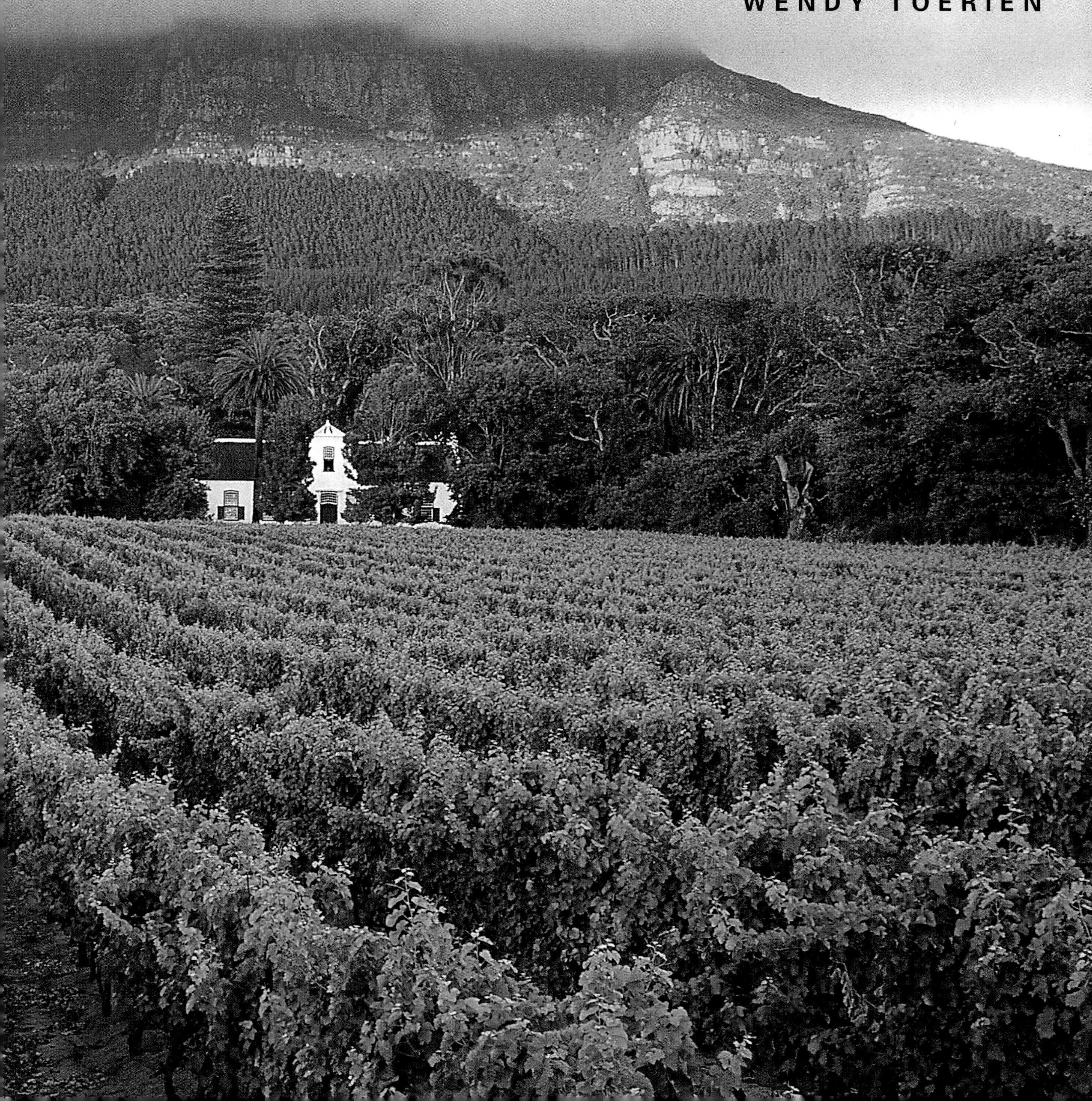

AUTHOR'S ACKNOWLEDGEMENTS

To all those winemakers and viticulturists who give so liberally of their time to share their expertise, knowledge and love of wine with us writers. All we do is try to spread the message. For myself, an opportunity, at last, to especially thank Johan Malan of Simonsig, Nicky Krone of Twee Jonge Gezellen, Carl Schultz of Hartenberg and viticulturist Johan Pienaar for their open doors and minds.

Struik Publishers (Pty) Ltd
(a member of Struik New Holland Publishing (Pty) Ltd)
Cornelis Struik House
80 McKenzie Street
Cape Town 8001

Reg No.: 54/00965/07

First published in 2000
10 9 8 7 6 5 4 3 2 1

ISBN 1 86872 437 9

PUBLISHING MANAGER: Linda de Villiers
EDITOR: Gail Jennings
CONCEPT DESIGNER: Petal Palmer
DESIGNER: Beverley Dodd
ILLUSTRATOR: Dave Snook
PROOFREADER: Sally D Rutherford
INDEXER: Mary Lennox

Reproduction by Hirt & Carter Cape (Pty) Ltd
Printed and bound by Craft Print (Pte) Ltd, Singapore

PHOTOGRAPHIC CREDITS

SHAEN ADEY/SIL: cover (front); title page; pages 5 (third from bottom), 19 (below), 24–25, 118, 121 (below), 124, 127, 133, 153, 168.
MIKE ALLWOOD-COPPIN/NDWP: pages 40–41. PAT DE LA HARPE/AFRICA IMAGERY: page 126.
ROGER DE LA HARPE/AFRICA IMAGERY: page 11. GERHARD DREYER/SIL: page 161. JEAN DU PLESSIS: page 160.
CHARLEY VAN DUGTEREN: pages 114–115, 157 (below), 171 (below), 172–173.
CHARLEY VAN DUGTEREN/SIL: pages 13 (top), 15, 16, 19 (top), 23 (top), 29 (top), 31, 34 (top), 37 (top), 38 (top), 39 (top), 40 (top), 43, 47 (below), 50 (top), 52 (top left and right), 55, 56 (top), 57 (top), 60 (top), 62 (top), 65 (top), 67, 69 (top), 72, 74 (below), 75 (below), 76 (below), 81 (below), 82 (below), 83 (top), 84 (top), 85 (top), 86 (top), 87 (below), 88 (top), 97 (top), 98 (top), 101, 103 (top and below), 113 (right), 114 (top), 121 (top), 122 (top), 129, 135 (below), 138 (left, right), 142 (top), 147 (top), 149, 150, 157 (top), 163 (top), 164 (left), 171 (top), 173 (top).
HEIN VON HÖRSTEN: cover (spine); pages 5 (bottom), 10, 13 (below), 14, 17, 18, 20, 21, 23 (below), 26, 29 (below), 30, 32, 45, 47 (top), 50 (below), 51, 52 (below), 53, 56 (below), 57 (below), 60–61, 62 (below), 65 (below), 66, 70–71, 74 (top), 75 (top), 76 (top), 88 (below), 97 (below), 110, 119, 122–123, 144, 145, 154, 155, 169.
LANZ VON HÖRSTEN: cover (back, back flap); half title page; pages 5 (top, second from top, third from top, second from bottom), 27, 34–35, 36, 38 (left), 39 (below), 42, 48, 54–55, 58, 69 (below), 78, 79, 81 (top), 82 (top), 83 (below), 84 (below), 85 (below), 86 (below), 87 (top), 90–91, 92, 94, 95, 99, 100, 102, 104–105, 106–107, 109, 111, 113 (left), 116, 130, 131, 132, 135 (top), 136–137, 139, 143, 147 (below), 148, 151, 163 (below), 164–165, 166.

CONTENTS

INTRODUCTION

BACKGROUND

The vine has been an integral part of South Africa's historical, agricultural and cultural landscape for more than three centuries. Now, poised on the cusp of a new century, the Cape wine industry is perhaps faced with its ultimate challenge: creating a well-organised, unified structure that will provide the support base necessary for South African wines to compete internationally with the finest in the world.

South Africa is one of the oldest of the New World wine-producing countries. However, buffeted by the political and economic travails of emerging nationhood on this large, essentially underdeveloped continent, Cape wine farmers have struggled to establish an ethos of quality and distinctive style anything like that of the other New World producers – California or Australia, even Chile – let alone the French.

In the early days, 17th- and 18th- century Dutch governors, such as Simon and Willem Adriaan van der Stel, were more intent on creating their own little kingdoms of agricultural wealth than establishing communal business interests. As a British colony during the late 1700s and most of the 19th century, the Cape, supplier of sweet and fortified wines to the colonial masters, became a pawn in the Britons' one-upmanship with the French. First it benefited from import restrictions on French wines, then virtually collapsed after an Anglo-Franco trade agreement in 1861.

Further devastation was caused by the bug *Phylloxera vastatrix*, which attacked the Cape's vines in 1885 after decimating vineyards in Europe. Large-scale replanting onto virus-immune American rootstock saw production increase, despite an already weakened market aggravated by two turn-of-the-20th-century wars fought by increasingly nationalistic Afrikaners in the north of South Africa against their British overlords.

The solution to the subsequent lake of wine in the Cape was found in the co-operative system, guaranteeing growers a market for their fruit. The resultant insidious economic culture of production of quantity rather than quality was further entrenched by the protectionist policies of the KWV (*Ko-operatiewe Wijnbouers Vereniging van Zuid-Afrika Beperkt*), founded in 1918 and subsequently granted statutory control over the entire wine industry.

Two policies were especially detrimental to the growth of wine as a market-driven, quality-oriented, competitive product: the fixing of a minimum price for wine delivered to the KWV, which undertook to buy whatever was delivered by its members; and the quota system, whereby growers were effectively licensed to cultivate wine grapes in designated areas only.

The KWV's stranglehold only began to be broken in the 1990s. After it was forced to relinquish control over the Cape wine industry after becoming a group of companies in 1997, a Wine Industry Trust was formed. Funded by the KWV to the tune of R370-million over 10 years, to be followed by a R120-million capital injection – a government litigation case found this to be owed to the industry in lieu of years of accumulated assets through its privileged position as industry controller – the Trust is supposed to take over the regulatory role so long fulfilled by the KWV. It is run by 13 government-appointed trustees representing all power players within the industry, including the KWV, producer/ wholesalers, private cellars and labour unions.

'Vision 2020', a think-tank involving various interest groups in Cape wine, is working out an agenda for the development of the industry over the next 20 years or so.

Based on a similar '2025' plan implemented by the forward-thinking Australians, the project has drawn together government representatives, training and research institutions, producer/ wholesalers, winemakers, marketers and commentators to give direction to future viticultural development. Researchers are drawing up accurate statistics reflecting the current state of the industry, from the number, age and types of vines, production figures and market size to expenditure and controls.

While the Trust takes time finding its feet (and the finances it is owed), smaller organisations continue to go about their business of encouraging and promoting their own specific interests. These include self-help groups such as the Cape Estate Wine Producers Association, the Pinotage Producers Association, the Port Producers Association, the Cape Independent Winemakers Guild and the South African Wine & Spirit Exporters Association. Viticultural services traditionally provided by the KWV are now being handled by VinPro, a service organisation operating independently but still effectively under KWV directorship. And Winetech, the Wine Industry Network for Expertise and Technology formed in 1996 with representatives from the KWV, SFW, Distillers and estate and private cellars and co-ops, continues to co-ordinate research in the wine industry.

There still appears to be far too many disparate groups with overlapping concerns fragmenting the control and development of Cape wine. And the KWV and traditional producer/wholesalers such as Stellenbosch Farmers' Winery and Distillers still seem to have too great a balance of power compared with the many independent producers out there. Yet individual, privately owned cellars and new-look co-operative wineries with efficient business structures are at the vanguard of viticultural initiatives and quality wine production in this country, as well as putting so-called 'farmworker empowerment' into practice. And it is they, with their quick market responses and quality drive, who are proving that Cape wine can, indeed, count among the world's finest.

Upon re-entering the world markets in the early 1990s, South African wine experienced a boom period, riding the wave of interest created by 'Mandela magic'. Exports leaped from 20-million litres in 1992 to 116-million in 1998 and currently account for about 25% of total production. In the first four months of 1999, there was an 18% increase in white wine exports compared with the same period the previous year. And the high demand for reds is being answered by a concerted effort to increase plantings of noble red varieties.

VITICULTURE

Viticulture is finally receiving the recognition required of an aspect of wine production most acknowledge as integral to quality. The Cape, with its mild Mediterranean climate, influenced by maritime conditions and mountainous terroir, is viticulturally ideal for growing good grapes. Mid-year winters are cold and rainy, giving the dormant vine time to marshal its resources and store water. Spring is usually mild and sunny enough for good budding and berry set. Summers are warm to hot, with long, sunny days to facilitate optimum ripeness of the fruit. Excessive heat is often tempered by the prevailing south-east wind and breezes off the cold Atlantic Ocean on the southern and western coasts. There is seldom a bad vintage in such conditions, unlike in Europe where summer rain, cold and severe frost can hamper ripening and wreak havoc during harvest.

South Africa's winelands are made up of three major soil types: granite, shale and sandstone. Valley-floor and river-side soils are invariably sandy or alluvial, fairly deep, with the latter marked by a dark brown, almost blackish colour and containing nutrient-rich organic matter. Vines grown here tend to bear heavily, which is not conducive to quality. Yet traditionally, because of the accessibility of water and ease of cultivation, these were the areas where grapes were grown in abundance, resulting in vast quantities of mediocre wine.

Viticultural expertise gained over the past few decades has, however, taken serious growers up into the foothills, seeking out the better soils (typically types such as Tukulu, Hutton, Clovelly and Glenrosa) and cooler meso-climates required for the slow ripening of fruit for concentrated flavour. This is occurring in both the traditionally fine-wine areas and the hot hinterland, home of the former bulk-wine, co-op producers.

But what is creating the excitement are the new areas being opened up following the long-overdue abolition in the early 1990s of the KVW's protectionist quota system, whereby wine grape cultivation could only take place on existing farming units in historically demarcated regions, many of which encompassed areas vastly unsuited to quality wine production.

Vineyard management has also become a prime consideration. Together with scientific analysis of soils to identify type and match it up with suitable grape varieties, growers now employ equipment such as neutron probes to monitor ground moisture content. Spray irrigation, once widely and randomly used in the hotter regions, resulting in large crops of dilute juice, is now frowned upon. Drip irrigation is *de rigueur* as growers familiarise themselves with concepts such as vine stress levels and are able to carefully mete out water just to tide the vine over a particularly hot period. While many believe dryland vineyards still produce the best fruit – if they're planted in the correct spot – a heatwave during the 1999 vintage reminded them that nature's vagaries allow farmers no certainties.

Canopy management has become more than just good housekeeping among Cape wine growers, largely influenced by the successes of the Australians, headed by viticultural guru Richard Smart. It is now seen as integral to the development of good-quality fruit and can determine formation of specific varietal characteristics that ultimately affect wine style. To this end, winemakers are either spending more time in their vineyards, hiring dedicated viticulturists or calling in consultants. Fruit 'ripeness' is the new buzzword.

Most South African vineyards are trellised, despite a certain school of thought that bush vines acquire a natural balance that contains vigour and concentrates flavour. Trellising gives the vineyardist greater control, allowing for pruning that can either expose fruit to the sunlight necessary for optimum ripening or protect the berries from excessive heat. Bunches can be 'dropped' to curb yield and enhance fruit concentration. Trellising and correct canopy management help to aerate the vines, both as coolant or deterrent to diseases such as rot. And they give pickers and machinery such as mechanical harvesters easy access to the bunches, with minimal damage to the fruit.

Varietal selection is increasingly geared towards producing the best quality wine and, at the same time, keeping up with market trends. The move is towards the majors. In the 1990s, what is touted as the 'big six' group of varieties – Sauvignon Blanc, Chardonnay, Cabernet Sauvignon, Merlot, Shiraz and Pinotage – was identified as being integral to the improvement of the Cape's reputation as an internationally recognised quality wine-producing region.

Grape growers are being encouraged to increase plantings at the expense of the many ill-chosen, unsuitable and unmarketable varieties that still occur in vineyards. The focus in the main wine regions is on red varieties, both for premium labels and fruity, easy-drinkers for which the Cape's warm, temperate climate is so suitable. Less than 20% of local vineyards are devoted to red. Cabernet Sauvignon, Pinotage, Merlot and Shiraz already occupy the top spots as the most widely planted reds, with the lesser Cinsaut caught amidst them but being uprooted and replaced by the nobles at a steady rate (plantings fell by nearly five per cent between 1985 and 1997).

Greater international exposure through South Africa's entry into the world wine markets during the 1990s is sparking interest in varieties new to the Cape. Overseas travel and working trips by local vintners are also broadening horizons, as is the exchange of students. The influence of 'flying winemakers', mostly Australians and New Zealanders linked to UK-based International Wine Services who travel the world making wine to retail buyers' specifications, is also noteworthy. And top cellars are hiring world-renowned viticultural consultants such as Californian Phil Freese to advise on new vineyard development.

Thankfully, when it comes to the selection of varieties, much more attention is paid to local adaptability and market trends than in the past. While still committed to the basic Bordeaux classics Cabernet Sauvignon, Merlot and Cabernet Franc, introduced in the 1970s and '80s, vintners are intent on refining their wines with the addition of more specialist Médoc varieties such as Malbec and Petit Verdot. The

Rhône is a new sphere of inspiration, with Shiraz now being joined by Mouvèdre, Grenache and the white, Viognier varieties at home in more rugged terrain and hence deemed especially suited to South Africa's warmer, drier conditions.

Similarly, Italian varieties such as Sangiovese and Nebbiolo are being tested, the latter at higher altitudes and cooler climes as is its preference. And the specialist Champagne grape, Pinot Meunier, has also been introduced here by Cap Classique makers, again in the quest for improved quality.

Careful clonal selection is now common practice. Today's vintners are far more in touch with what they and their consumers want in a style of wine, and are actively seeking out the finer nuances provided by specific clones: Sauvignon Blanc from the Loire, Sémillon from Australia, Chardonnay from both Burgundy and California. The old BK5 Swiss Champagne clone of Pinot Noir is being replaced by fine Burgundian material. The 'Schleipp' clone, popular among New World wine producers, has introduced a new flavour profile to Cabernet Sauvignon.

Despite its ideal climate, South Africa does experience problems with vine diseases, the most common being powdery and downy mildew. The major scourge of the Cape winelands, though, is the leafroll virus.

South African researchers, through the Vine Improvement Association, have found ways of containing the virus by propagating 'cleaned-up' material, but although being supplied with so-called 'virus-free' stock, growers report that the virus invariably returns in time. This problem, compounded by delays in acquiring new plant material, has led to a few leading producers (such as Rustenberg) embarking upon a private importation arrangement with the Department of Agriculture. A chronic shortage of material, as well as unreliable supplies from commercial nurseries, has also spurred private producers on to establish their own nurseries.

According to the latest statistics available, by the end of 1997 South Africa had nearly 100 000ha under wine grape vines, with a substantial increase of over 4 000ha recorded in the three years prior to that. There are more than 4 600 primary wine-grape growers, including (by the end of 1999) some 287 wine producers comprising 95 estates, 125 private cellars and 67 co-ops (excluding the handful of producing wholesalers).

The winelands are divided up into demarcated areas according to the Wine of Origin (WO) scheme, introduced in 1973 to classify wine-producing areas with some semblance of homogeneity of character and quality, as well as to guarantee accuracy of claims to origin, variety and vintage to protect the consumer. Officially, the 'Cape Winelands' is sub-divided into four wine regions: the Coastal region, the Breede River Valley, the Klein Karoo and the Olifants River Valley.

Each wine region is further divided into districts, the eight most important being Stellenbosch, Paarl, Robertson, Worcester, Swartland, Tulbagh, Overberg and Calitzdorp. Cape Point is a recent addition, as yet still being developed but promising great potential for quality wine.

Within these districts are wards, comprising a group of farms that share a similar terroir. But recent demarcations have proved fraught, primarily because the Demarcation Board is lagging behind progressive farmers developing new terrain. There is the prospect of existing wine farms now being cut in two by demarcation lines that adhere stringently to homogeneity of soil, climate and topography.

The smallest 'production unit' in the WO scheme is the estate, made up of one or more adjoining properties, which has its own cellar and bottles its own wines. Previously confined to using only home-grown grapes, estates have since 1995 been allowed to buy in grapes, so long as quantities do not exceed 45% of their total annual crush and the wine is bottled under a second, 'non-estate' label.

With exports booming, several have subsequently chosen to 'deregister' and operate as 'private cellars' with no restrictions on sourcing fruit. Alternatively, some former 'private cellars' who bought in grapes while establishing their vineyards have gained 'estate' status, which they believe is integral to promoting their terroir-specific style and the quality of their wine.

THE FORMAT OF THIS BOOK

With the number of Cape wineries nearing the 300 mark, boosted by a bevy of new names each year, highlighting the most important of them is a difficult task. The selection of 'main producers' in this book is therefore based on several criteria.

Wine quality is among the most relevant of these selection factors, as is a track record of consistently high standards. Intellectual application, dedication and passion by both owner and winemaker should also convince of a commitment to ongoing viticultural development and continued striving for quality.

Those featured as important producers are all wineries worth visiting also for the charm and character of the place and its people, be it a historic homestead, designer cellar or visitor-friendly venue. All have their own cellars, which are open to the public, even if by appointment only. Strong ties, often emotional, between the wine growers and their piece of land, whether over generations or newly established, augur well for wise long-term cultivation. Within their designated area, the wineries highlighted stand out as being most reflective of the style and substance of quality winemaking there and are invariably the most innovative.

These major producers feature at the beginning of each section, along with details of their key wines.

All the other producers are listed alphabetically after the featured wineries. Some of the latter may fulfil most, if not all, of the 'major producer' criteria, but are in a state of flux, albeit temporary, due to ownership or winemaker changes. Several new stars merely need time to assure us that their latent potential is lasting.

Space constraints also limit the number of cellars highlighted, particularly in the chapters about Paarl and Stellenbosch, which offer an embarrassment of riches to the wine lover and winelands visitor.

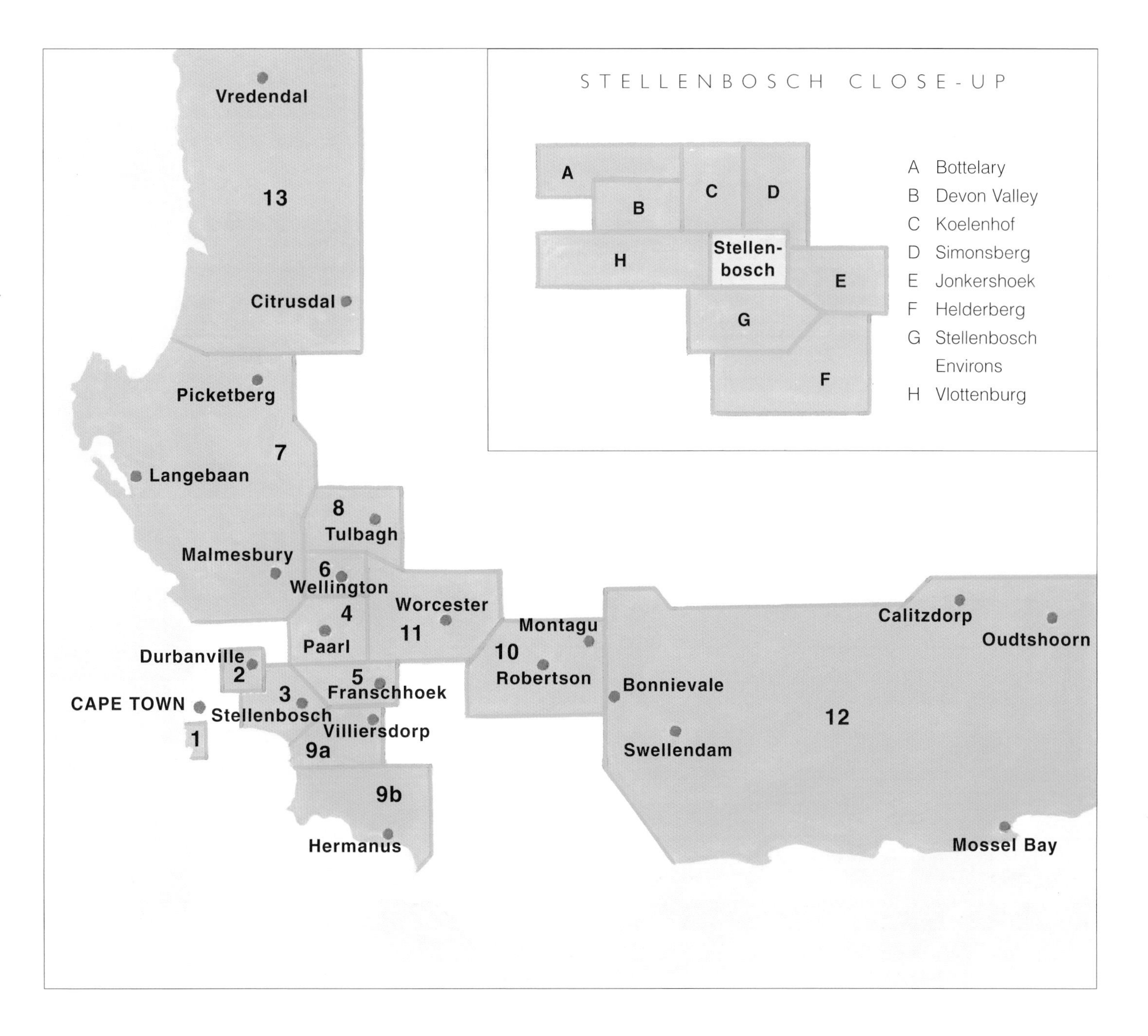

THE CAPE WINELANDS

1 Constantia
2 Durbanville
3 Stellenbosch
4 Paarl
5 Franschhoek
6 Wellington
7 Swartland
8 Tulbagh
9 Overberg
9a Elgin
9b Walker Bay
10 Robertson
11 Worcester
12 Klein Karoo
13 Olifants River

C O N S T A N T I A

Officially, Constantia is one of the wards within the Coastal region. And it is one that can truly lay claim to a climate influenced by maritime conditions, for the bench of vineyards sloping up the south-facing Constantiaberg has sweeping views of False Bay towards Muizenberg.

Stately gabled manor houses such as 17th-century Groot Constantia add a unique character to local wine farms.

Historically, Constantia is the seat of the Cape wine industry, the chosen spot for the autocratic 17th-century governor of the Cape, Simon van der Stel, to establish his own little kingdom, a model agricultural enterprise in which vines, by chance, found their place. They flourished here in the mild, temperate climate with its ample winter rainfall, and subsequent owners of the rambling estate, notably the Cloetes, crafted sweet dessert wines hailed by European royalty (Napoleon) and British writers (Dickens and Jane Austen) alike. Today, Constantia is still green and verdant, but it is the upper-crust suburban gardens, the grassed and treed public commonage and the horse paddocks that provide the lushness. Vines have had to fight for survival and valuable ground has been lost to housing development.

But, at the same time, there has been a renaissance of the core historic Cape Dutch heritage sites, in tandem with the development of a handful of prime wine farms. It has taken money – overseas, private and corporate. But the excellence of Constantia's viticultural potential has made it worthwhile. And success is leading to the exploration of new areas with a similar profile, such as the Hout Bay Valley across the Constantiaberg. And soon there will be Wines of Origin Cape Point, following the designation in 1998 of the new Cape Point district, running roughly from Chapman's Peak along the perimeter of Silvermine Nature Reserve to Kalk Bay on the False Bay coast. Developer Sybrand van der Spuy, together with former Steenberg winemaker Emmanuel Bolliger, is clearing some 15ha of virgin land and planting Sauvignon Blanc, Sémillon, Chardonnay, Cabernet Sauvignon and Merlot on the new Noordhoek Estate.

1. Ambeloui
2. Buitenverwachting
3. Constantia Uitsig
4. Groot Constantia
5. Klein Constantia
6. Steenberg

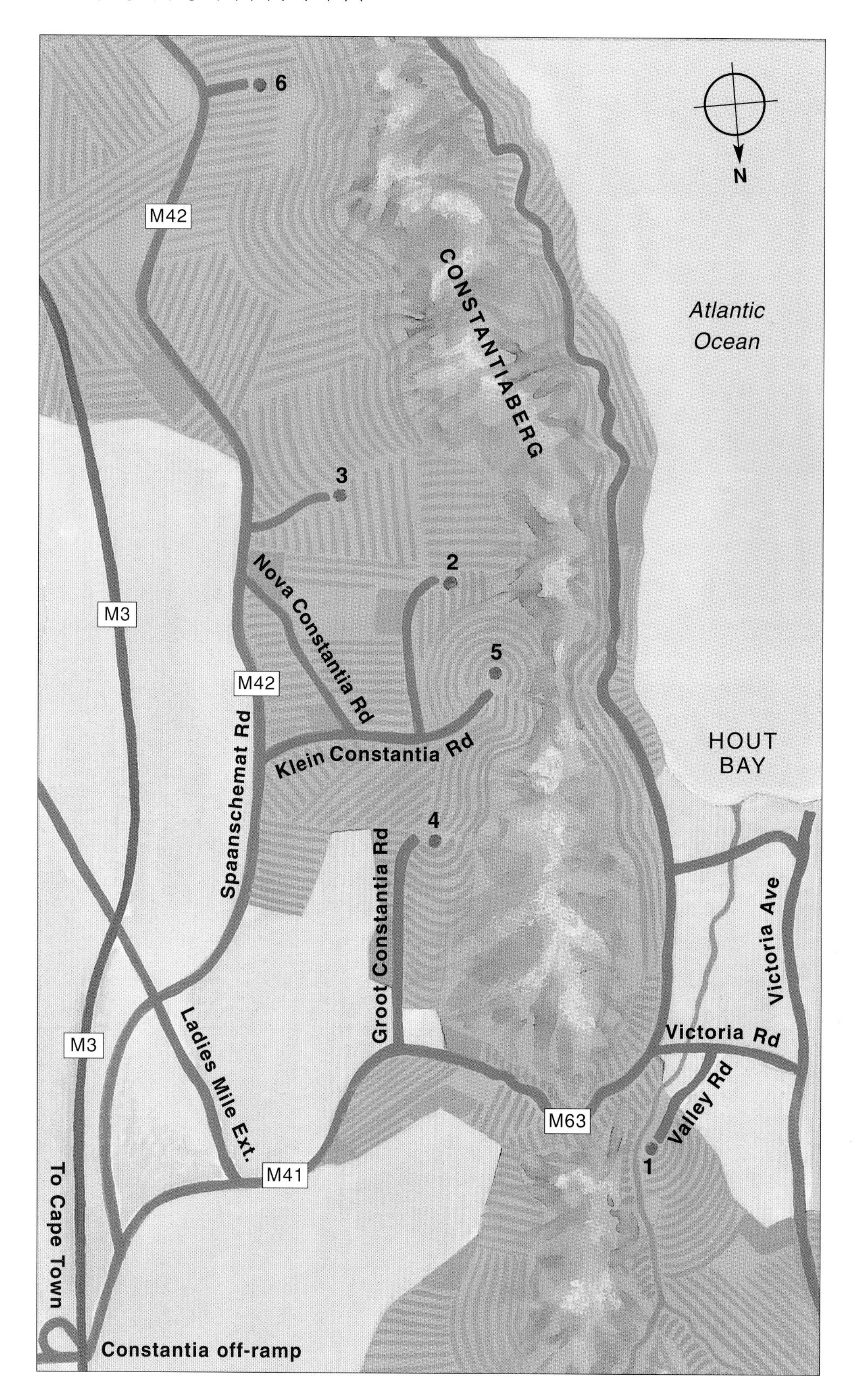

OPENING PAGE: The cool-climate vineyards along the Constantiaberg produce some stunning Sauvignon Blanc, while reds such as Cabernet and Merlot have a distinctive elegance.

BUITEN-VERWACHTING

OWNERS
Christine Müller and Lars Maack

KEY WINES
Christine, Cabernet Sauvignon, Sauvignon Blanc, Chardonnay, Rhine Riesling, Buiten Blanc, Buiten Keur, Brut Cap Classique, Noblesse Noble Late Harvest

A last-minute adjustment to building plans in 1988 saw the Buitenverwachting cellar doubled in size. This was an unintentional foresight, because demand for this estate's fine wines continues to outstrip production, which is currently close to capacity at 50 000 cases from about 100ha (which includes some 20ha leased nearby and devoted solely to Sauvignon Blanc). 'This is Sauvignon Blanc and Cabernet territory,' aver winemaker Hermann Kirschbaum and owner/manager Lars Maack.

Maack is the son of German Christine Müller and her husband Richard, who in 1981 bought a run-down Buitenverwachting, complete with Cape Dutch manor house, and turned it into a property that, as the name implies, 'exceeds expectation'. A large, modern and functional cellar was built and vines re-established on selected sites.

Admitting to being a 'conservative' and a 'traditionalist', Kirschbaum has nevertheless changed the style of Buitenverwachting's wines. His predecessor's award-winning Merlot formed the backbone of the consistently fine, beautifully balanced, classic flagship red blend Christine in the early '90s. This wine has more recently been based on Cabernet. The varietal Cabernet, discontinued for a few vintages, is now back: elegant, yet full of flavour and firm, ripe tannins. The Merlot, meanwhile, has gone towards the perennially popular, easy-drinking 'second' red blend Buiten Keur. New plantings also include some Cabernet Franc and a touch of Malbec 'for colour'.

The farm is predominantly Sauvignon Blanc, made in a Loire-like fresh and flinty style and a late developer. The variety has replaced Rhine Riesling as the main ingredient, together with increasingly more Chenin Blanc, of Buitenverwachting's best-selling Buiten Blanc. The Riesling, too, has undergone a facelift. Quite unlike its terpeney Cape counterparts; it is a lovely, light, scented, dryish German look-alike. Buitenverwachting's Riesling tends to be susceptible to botrytis and the result is one of the Cape's nicest Noble Late Harvests, a rich yet not overly sweet wine given complexity by partial oak fermentation à la Sauternes. The Chardonnay is full and creamy, becoming deliciously limey in maturity.

Old Swiss BK5 Pinot Noir clones are being pulled up and replaced with a recognised Burgundian clone, expected to do well in the cool climate.

TOP: Owner and general manager Lars Maack with winemaker Hermann Kirschbaum.
BELOW: Buitenverwachting's vineyards include Pinot Noir for a fine bottle-fermented bubbly.

GROOT CONSTANTIA

OWNER
Groot Constantia Trust

KEY WINES
Gouverneurs Reserve, Cabernet, Shiraz, Shiraz/Merlot (Heerenrood), Constantia Rood, Pinotage, Chardonnay Reserve, Chardonnay, Sauvignon Blanc, Weisser Riesling, Gewürztraminer, Chardonnay Noble Late Harvest, Natural Sweet, Tawny Port

GROOT CONSTANTIA
ESTATE WINE
WYN VAN OORSPRONG CONSTANTIA
GOUVERNEURS RESERVE
VINTAGE 1995 OESJAAR
12,5% VOL
750ml A332
LIMITED RELEASE

Historic Groot Constantia seems to have finally found its place on the cusp of the millennium, with new winemaker Bob de Villiers presiding over a revamped cellar, which includes an investment in small oak barrels.

Some 45 000 cases are produced from vines that have been scientifically replanted over the past decade of what is earmarked as a 15-year vineyard replanting programme. While production has nearly doubled since the mid-'90s, the vast Groot Constantia range has been trimmed. Total vineyard space is being cut from about 100ha to an eventual 88ha of mostly classic varieties.

But the farm will still produce fair quantities of various 'Blanc de Blanc'-type whites and dry red blends. Says general manager Danie Appel: 'We have a dual purpose on the winemaking side alone – to produce the top-quality wines for which Constantia has the potential and which serious wine lovers expect from us, and to educate all sorts, from the brandy-and-Coke drinker to the Japanese tourist who has never tasted South African wines. These are the guys who are looking for an uncomplicated, often slightly sweeter wine; they buy a bottle to try and, hopefully, will like it enough to come back for more, and so develop their taste for fine wine.'

It is only since 1993, when this government-owned property was handed over to a trust, that it has been operated as a strictly commercial venture, with all costs having to be covered by profits. After a century of being constrained by typically bureaucratic considerations and run more as a popular tourist destination than a fine-wine estate, Groot Constantia now concentrates on its wines.

Much of the farm's 100ha of vineyards cover the south and south-east slopes of the Constantiaberg up to about 220m above sea level, overlooking nearby False Bay. Soils are mostly Table Mountain sandstone-derived, with granitic clay-based Hutton and Clovelly types on the hillside and sandier, warmer soils lower down. Classic cool-climate wines are emerging. The Sauvignon Blanc is a fine, full-bodied and fruitful wine. The Weisser Riesling, often picked with some botrytis to give it extra complexity, is rich, with plenty of ageing potential. The Chardonnays, both standard and Reserve, also show evidence of fruit that has had the advantage of slow ripening, obtaining greater concentration that, with subtle wooding, results in what are usually extremely elegant wines.

But some swear by the farm's reds. Groot Constantia Cabernets, Shirazes and Pinotages from the '60s are still full of life, complex and balanced. Today, the French classics (Merlot, Cabernet Sauvignon, Cabernet Franc and Shiraz) and local hero Pinotage make up most of the 60% of plantings devoted to red varieties. The Gouverneurs Reserve, a traditional Bordeaux-style blend of Cabernet Sauvignon, Merlot and Cabernet Franc, has never been a heavyweight but, while drinkable quite young, has surprised with a lovely, rounded elegance after 10 years in bottle. Groot Constantia's Shiraz, successfully blended with Merlot and variously labelled as Heerenrood or simply Shiraz Merlot, has produced a delicious wine and may yet find its way into the Gouverneurs Reserve.

OPPOSITE: The 17th-century Groot Constantia homestead is managed by Danie Appel (**BELOW**), here with winemaker Bob de Villiers in front of the historic cellar.

KLEIN CONSTANTIA

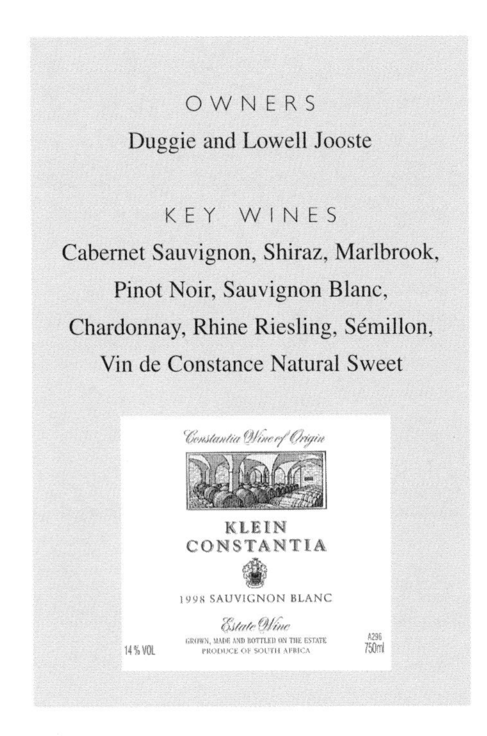

Klein Constantia's father-and-son team of Duggie and Lowell Jooste with their winemaker, Ross Gower.

The Joostes bought this dilapidated historic property, once part of Van der Stel's 17th-century Constantia, in 1980. The impetus was the farm's terroir. The south and south-east aspects up to 300m above sea level offer the coolth ideal for Sauvignon Blanc, Chardonnay and Pinot Noir, while lower, north-facing slopes down to about 90m are exploited for reds. Accompanied by deep, moisture-retaining Hutton and Clovelly soils, the generally cool conditions mean that the fruit ripens almost two weeks after Stellenbosch, resulting in greater flavour concentration.

Jovial winemaker Ross Gower bottled the estate's first vintage, after a 50-year hiatus, in 1986. Still a bold, beautiful wine, the Sauvignon Blanc bucked some trends when the incorrigible Gower let some botrytised fruit slip into his *encépagement* in vintages such as '87 and '93. Sauvignon Blanc remains the most widely planted variety on the 75ha farm, which has a 70:30 white to red wine ratio. The very fine Noble Late Harvest is also made from Sauvignon Blanc. Gower has provided similar excitement recently with a stunning grassy, figgy, fruity Sémillon. His lovely sweet/sour Rhine Riesling, again sometimes fleshed out with botrytised fruit, is one of the Cape's best.

Klein Constantia's wines, typified by their high alcohols, have always been robust. Says Gower, whose personal taste tends towards full, rounded wines: 'We want to make heavyweights; it is the big wines that bring out more character.' But the fruits of Gower's recent attempts to match New World richness with Old World elegance are never more apparent than in the latest vintages of the still-concentrated yet supremely balanced and supple Marlbrook, the estate's flagship red blend of the two Cabernets with Merlot.

The varietal Cabernet has that distinctive mintiness and has recently assumed a less heavy, more classical guise. The warm, peppery Shiraz, with the sweet and spicy notes imparted by American oak, is made in tiny quantities. Shiraz production will be bolstered over the next five years by new plantings on a recently acquired prime red-wine property in the warmer Helderberg area of Stellenbosch. From here too comes Cabernet Sauvignon and bush-vine Merlot; this new source of grapes may also lead to a second label in time. Back at 'KC', the Burgundian PN113 clone has recently produced a delicately berried and balanced Pinot Noir.

The marriage of tradition and modern know-how is also embodied in Klein Constantia's greatest success: Vin de Constance. This old-wood-matured natural sweet wine, made from Muscat de Frontignan grapes in emulation of the old 17th-century sweet Constantia wines, has wowed the world's most discerning palates and been presented at international wine events alongside Château d'Yquem.

OPPOSITE: The top vineyards of Klein Constantia are being planted to more Sauvignon Blanc and a Burgundian Pinot Noir clone.

STEENBERG

OWNER
Johnnic Industrial Corporation

KEY WINES
Merlot, Cabernet Sauvignon, Sauvignon Blanc, Chardonnay; Motif Blanc Sec, Rosé Sec and Rouge Sec

STEENBERG
ANNO 1682
1999
SAUVIGNON BLANC
ALC 13.0% VOL
produced and bottled
at *STEENBERG*
product of SOUTH AFRICA
WINE OF ORIGIN CONSTANTIA A530 ℮750 *ml*

Wine is thought to have first been made on this historic Cape Dutch property in 1695. Nearly three centuries later, major Johannesburg-based industrial holdings and property group Johnnic stepped in to save the farm from rack and ruin. Now a golf estate, with a restaurant and luxury country hotel in the 1740 manor house, wines are once more being produced.

The 70ha of vineyards are ideally situated on cool south- and east-facing slopes, made up of six different types of soil generally lighter and more friable than that of the neighbours. And they're devoted solely to the classics: Pinot Noir on the stony ground, low-lying decomposed granite for Cabernet, Merlot and Cabernet Franc, and the Chardonnay, Sémillon and prize Sauvignon Blanc on the higher slopes. Newer plantings include Shiraz.

Since 1990, GM Herman Hanekom has been overseeing the viticultural development. Winemaker Nicky Versfeld works in a state-of-the-art cellar with a 1 200-barrel maturation cellar. His shy, self-deprecating demeanour is perhaps indicative of his essentially gentle approach in the winery. He, like Hanekom, believes that good fruit is integral to wine quality and attributes Steenberg's success to the terroir. Cellar manipulations are kept to a minimum, with as little fining and filtering as possible, no doubt an approach reinforced by recent trips to Sancerre and Graves, home of some of France's finest Sauvignon Blancs and Sémillons.

It is fruit, pure and simple, that distinguishes all Steenberg's wines – the result, Hanekom believes, of slightly more sunshine hours and open sites than the rest of Constantia. The

The historic Steenberg wine farm has been newly restored, with its 18th-century buildings now housing a luxury hotel and restaurant and its vineyards replanted to modern classics such as Sauvignon Blanc, Chardonnay, Cabernet and Merlot.

Steenberg winemaker Nicky Versfeld is a dab hand at Sauvignon Blanc, drawing on fruit-rich grapes from vineyards expertly managed by Herman Hanekom.

Sauvignon Blanc is typically pungent, full of grassy, nettley, capsicum aromas and juicy, supple fruit flavours. The Sémillons are full-bodied but zesty, with the wooded version showing greater concentration and a distinctive nuttiness on top of the limey, citrus fruit. The Chardonnay is improving as the vines mature.

As for the reds, they are probably the most fruit-driven of all the Constantia contenders. The Merlot is a wonderfully soft, silky wine, combining a creamy, chocolatey character with a spicy, minerally bite and firm but ripe tannins. The Cabernet has all the variety's typical fragrance of cigarbox and tobacco, underpinned by rich, ripe cassis fruit. A combination of new and used oak barrels is employed for both. Adding extra interest is a block of Nebbiolo, an important variety in Italy where it thrives on the cold, misty high ground. Hanekom figures Steenberg's proximity to the sea may give the variety the chilly off-shore breezes it needs.

AMBELOUI

Former Pretoria assurance executive Nick Christodoulou and wife Anne bought their 'little vineyard' (the meaning of Ambeloui in Cypriot) in 1990. Four years later, they planted just less than a hectare of Chardonnay and Pinot Noir on this Hout Bay Valley property. A small winery was built under the house and equipped with basic, mostly manual equipment from France, and the whole family (including four children) jumped in to harvest the first grapes for vinification in 1998.

'Our wines will always be truly handcrafted,' says Anne. With help from nearby Buitenverwachting vintner Hermann Kirschbaum, they have produced about 1 300 bottles of Lisa Brut MCC, a classic, biscuitty bottle-fermented bubbly named after their oldest daughter.

CONSTANTIA UITSIG

The smallest of the vineyards along the Constantiaberg 'bench', Constantia Uitsig is a historic Cape Dutch property renovated by businessman and game lodge owner Dave McCay and wife Marlene.

With expert advice from manager André Badenhorst, who was born on Groot Constantia and helped re-establish neighouring Buitenverwachting, the McCays started planting vineyards in 1990. A cellar is still in the pipeline (the historic original was demolished by previous owners). Wines are made for them by Nicky Versfeld at nearby Steenberg. Among these, the soft, supple, easy-drinking Merlot – different from the richer, more classic Merlots of its neighbours – is probably the finest of the reds. The Sémillon Reserve, big and tasty, fruity yet racy, is very Sauvignon Blanc-like in style. Current production from just over 30ha is around 14 000 cases.

Big money has gone into the re-development of Constantia's historic wine farms over the past two decades, with a newcomer like Constantia Uitsig beginning to make aromatic Sauvignon Blancs and juicy Merlots.

D U R B A N V I L L E

Cool granitic soils help retain moisture in Durbanville's vineyards, where water-sapping alien eucalyptus trees provide unwelcome competition.

A ward within the Coastal region, Durbanville is set among the rolling green hills of the Tygerberg, the little-known source of some of the premier wines produced by the big guys in more renowned wine regions: Nederburg and the KWV in Paarl; Distillers and SFW in Stellenbosch.

The hilly countryside provides slopes of varying aspects and altitudes, allowing for the cultivation of both red and white grapes of excellent quality. Durbanville is 15km from the sea: the Atlantic Ocean in the south with False Bay to the south-east. Between September and March, those cool sea breezes keep the temperature down to a temperate 19°C, while the notorious south-east wind tempers the humidity in which vine diseases flourish. Though the average rainfall is relatively low (300–400mm), the deep, cool, granitic soils, with a fair clay content, help retain moisture.

Growing wine grapes was one of the early farming activities in the area, together with wheat and vegetables. But the names of some of the 17th-century estates (Altydgedacht, Diemersdal and Meerendal) have only become known among wine lovers over the past decade or so, with the decision by new generations to bottle produce for sale from the cellar door.

The selection is classical as a result of replanting programmes. At a public tasting-cum-workshop, speaker Trevor Mast of top Australian producer Mount Langhi Ghiran encouraged local vintners to exploit the cool climate for specialisation in his style of rich yet restrained and elegant Shirazes – instead of the 'blockbusters' made world famous by wineries in warmer territories.

There is a passionate concern among these independent wine farmers about the future of the Durbanville hills. The area is under siege by the Cape Peninsula's expanding northern suburbs. Fresh impetus to preserving this rural enclave by exploiting its value as a commercially viable viticultural producer and tourist destination has been provided by new arrivals. Distillers, long a recipient of grapes from Durbanville, has developed a modern winery among the Tygerberg foothills. Savanha Wines of Paarl has snapped up Doordekraal and Springfield to pin down a supply of premium red varieties for its new ranges.

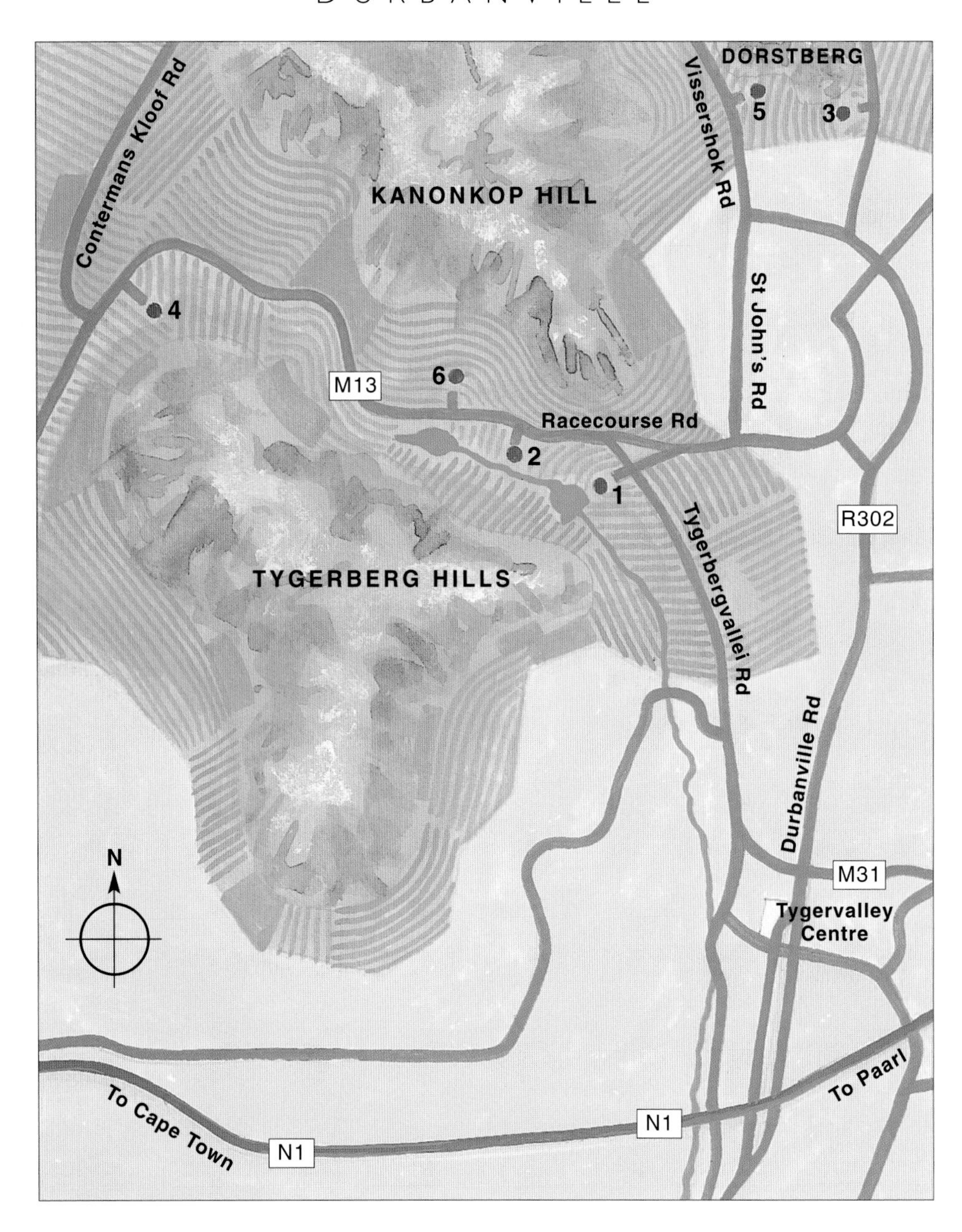

1. Altydgedacht
2. Bloemendal
3. Diemersdal
4. Durbanville Hills
5. Meerendal
6. Nitída

OPENING PAGE: Durbanville's vineyards face constant threat from encroaching suburban development as Cape Town's northern suburbs stretch out across the Cape Flats to the distant Hottentots Holland mountains.

NITÍDA

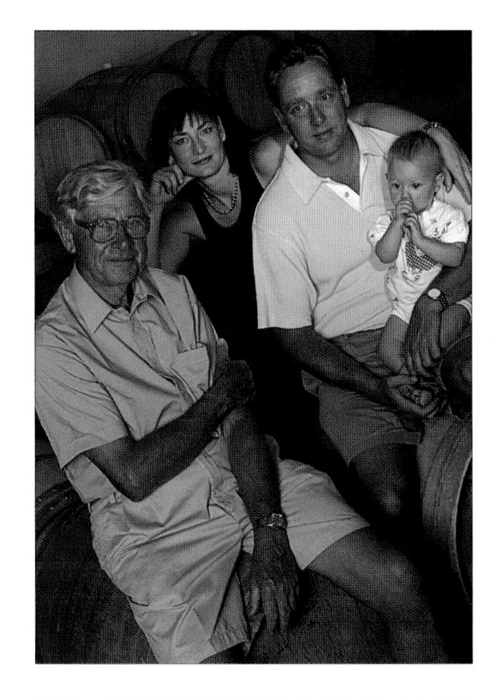

OWNER
The Veller family

KEY WINES
Cabernet Sauvignon, Merlot/Cabernet Franc, Pinotage, Shiraz, Sauvignon Blanc, Chardonnay

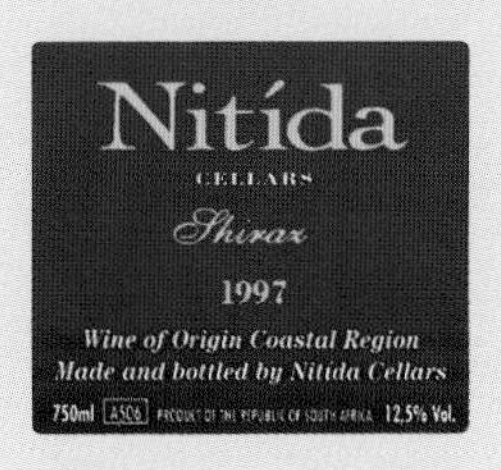

This former sheep and cattle farm found its way into the hands of a young wine lover looking for a rural retreat in the late 1980s. Metallurgist Bernhard Veller decided to make his own wine after time spent helping brother-in-law Richard Friedman develop Môreson in Franschhoek and establishing that his property had good clay-based Hutton soils and cool south-facing slopes.

Veller now has about 13ha under vine, all new-clone material: predominantly Cabernet Sauvignon and Sauvignon Blanc, Merlot, Cabernet Franc, Pinotage and Chardonnay, and some Ruby Cabernet. Production in the new little hi-tech cellar is limited to around 5 000 cases a year. Veller and winemaker Riaan Oosthuizen want to keep things hands-on. 'It's the only way to produce top quality.'

Nitída's maiden Sauvignon Blanc caused quite a stir in 1995, with its fully fruited and typically grassy nose and delicious flavour. The grapes were from bush vines grown by Jackie Coetzee on Bloemendal. Subsequent vintages from Veller's own fruit have cemented the reputation of Nitída, further enhanced by an elegant, gentle Chardonnay combining lemony freshness and butterscotch creaminess.

But Nitída's reds have proved even more exciting. The Shiraz is the star, a new-wave Cape example of a ripe, rich, spicy wine, robust and structured, with prominent oak, though with elements of the traditional earthy, smoky character of the variety. The Cabernet is a similar combination of ripe, plump fruit and savoury spice, with a meaty texture, yet elegant. New is a Pinotage and an easy-drinking Merlot/Cabernet Franc blend.

ALTYDGEDACHT

Winemaker Oliver Parker surprised everyone with his award-winning 1995 Pinotage. Perhaps not so astonishing, given this tough variety's favourable response to traditional methods of vinification, to which the Parkers of Altydgedacht are stubborn adherents. They use open cement fermentation tanks; wooden spatulas for punching down the cap of skins; sloping, gravity-fed chutes instead of pumps;

TOP: The Vellers of Nitída – Gerhard, son Bernhard and grandson Pier, with Bernhard's wife Peta.
ABOVE: The Nitída range of wines is named after the *Protea nitída* growing prolifically on the farm.

copper coils containing chilled spring water to cool the must. The estate has an unbroken tradition of winemaking stretching back more than two centuries and spanning five generations of Parkers, now represented by brothers Oliver and John, the vineyard manager. A small range of whites and reds, including the Cape's only bottled wild and earthy Barbera, are made in a cellar dating back to 1710. Grapes are supplied to SFW for its Nederburg range.

BLOEMENDAL

Farming is fun for laid-back Jackie Coetzee, a keen board-sailor and horse-rider and now restaurateur – Bloemendal restaurant, set among newly planted vines on nearby Kanonkop, boasts wrap-around views of Table Mountain, Table Bay and across Durbanville towards the Hottentots Holland mountains.

Yet Jackie is totally committed to Bloemendal, bought by his great-grandfather at the turn of the 19th century, with much of its good-quality 150ha of vines established by his father. Only some 5 000 cases are bottled – the rest is snapped by wine producer/wholesaler Distillers.

But these are delicious wines on occasion, particularly the lovely smooth, chocolatey Merlot and a distinctive Cabernet, usually quite minty and firm. His Sauvignon Blanc can also surprise with unexpectedly pungent asparagus and gooseberry aromas and flavours.

DIEMERSDAL

One of the old, historic wine farms in Durbanville, Diemersdal was granted in 1698 and bought in the 1920s by the great-grandfather of current owner/winemaker, Tienie Louw. Long a supplier of the KWV, Louw has thrown in his hat with Swiss consortium SAVISA, which has been doing big business in South African wine overseas since the latter part of the '90s. SAVISA handles all Diemersdal's white wines and most of the reds, with Louw retaining about 10% of his crop from some 170ha for his own bottlings. It is red-wine territory, capable of fine Pinotages and particularly Shirazes.

DURBANVILLE HILLS

This modern slate-stone and glass-walled cellar is a new venture between large wine and spirits producer/wholesaler Distillers and several of its grape growers in Durbanville. The R68-million development gives Distillers a 55% share and the farmers (including Bloemendal and Altydgedacht) a 40% stake, with the balance allotted to the farm and winery workers. The 8 000-ton cellar is manned by former Groot Constantia winemaker Martin Moore. Only about 30% of the wines vinified here will go towards an own range, comprising 'fruity, New World, easy-drinking' styles from the Cape's 'big six' varieties: Sauvignon Blanc, Chardonnay, Cabernet Sauvignon, Merlot, Shiraz and Pinotage. The rest will be blended into the existing premium Distillers labels such as Fleur du Cap and Stellenryck, handled at The Bergkelder cellars in Stellenbosch.

MEERENDAL

This is one of the area's original farms, planted to wheat and wine in the 18th century and boasting a beautiful, thatch-roofed and gabled Cape Dutch manor house. Meerendal was the first in Durbanville to produce wine under its own label, with owner William Starke focusing on port varieties after World War II. In the 1970s, son Kosie made Meerendal famous for its Shiraz and Pinotage. The Pinotage remains good, made in a more juicy, modern style than before, as is the Shiraz and the new releases of Cabernet and Merlot. Also new is a delicious Natural Sweet. The farm is now run by Kosie Starke's widow Christa and right-hand man, winemaker Soon Potgieter, who are planning a new pressing and barrel cellar to handle the 1 000 tons from about 130ha.

RIGHT: The Altydgedacht homestead epitomises Durbanville's wine-farming fraternity: laid-back growers of some of the Cape's finest fruit, yet only now gaining public recognition after having to fight urban development to maintain their rural lifestyle and natural riches.

S T E L L E N B O S C H

The Stellenbosch district, with a history of winemaking stretching back to the early days of the 17th century, is one of the largest, most intensively farmed viticultural areas in the Cape. It is framed by mountains: the Simonsberg in the north-west, the Jonkershoek peaks and Stellenbosch Mountain and the Helderberg range which abuts onto the craggy Hottentots Holland. These sun-warmed south-, south-west- and south-east-facing slopes are in turn cooled by the chilly Atlantic Ocean, as they look out over False Bay.

The gable of the Lanzerac manor house reflects the contours of the Jonkershoek peaks behind it.

In between, the land gives way to undulating slopes and valleys formed by the Bottelary hills to the north-west and the Papegaaiberg on the south-western outskirts of the town. This varying landscape gives the district the vast array of soils, climatic conditions, aspects and altitudes that make it the richest, most diverse of all the Cape's wine-producing areas, covering nearly 16 000ha.

As a distinctive 'Wine of Origin' appellation, Stellenbosch is world-renowned. But the diversity and sheer scale of winemaking activities have led to the division of the district into viticultural wards, such as Simonsberg-Stellenbosch, Jonkershoek, Bottelary and Devon Valley. Areas of homogeneity such as Helderberg, Koelenhof and Vlottenburg help carve up the vast Stellenbosch district into manageable entities, whether from a visitor's or viticulturist's point of view. Similarly, the wineries and wine farms on the outskirts of Stellenbosch, along the Eerste River and in Paradyskloof between the Stellenbosch and Helderberg mountains, can be grouped in a Stellenbosch Environs unit, as they either don't fit in anywhere else or wish to retain a broader Stellenbosch identity.

STELLENBOSCH ENVIRONS

As the core of one of the Cape's greatest wine-growing districts, the town of Stellenbosch is home to most of the major large wine and spirits producer/wholesalers. But many are downscaling or making way for dynamic new large-scale ventures.

Gilbeys, for example, with its multi-national International Distillers & Vintners links, has sold off its Devon Valley production facilities and handed over wholesale activities to a specialised agency, the new African Wine & Spirits. Distillers is redesigning its operating structure, separating its own-brand production from the marketing and distribution of traditional 'member' estates. It is also linking up with independent producers such as the Hygrace Farms of Hans Schreiber, owner of Neethlingshof and Stellenzicht, to boost production and exports of the new Lusan Premium Wines properties that include its own wholly-owned wine estates. Stellenbosch Vineyards, a public company now running the affairs of four Stellenbosch co-ops, represents the new market-driven, quality-orientated wine production venture that will compete with the traditional producer wholesalers. In the meantime, established, much-loved old wine farms such as Alto, Rust en Vrede and Blaauwklippen are taking on a new lease of life.

STELLENBOSCH ENVIRONS

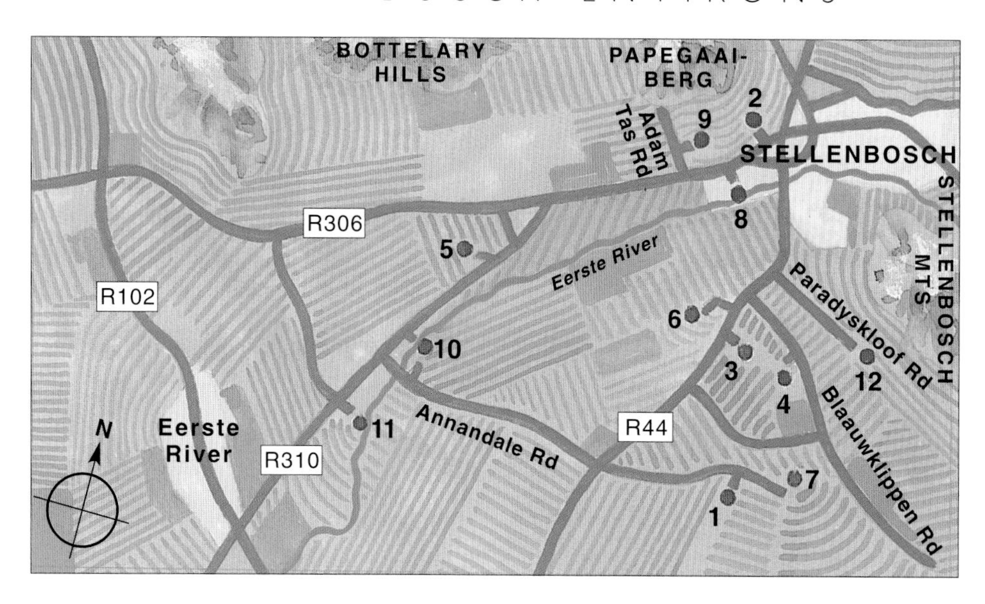

1. Alto
2. Bergkelder
3. Blaauwklippen
4. Blue Creek
5. Eersterivier
6. Kleine Zalze
7. Rust en Vrede
8. SFW
9. SFW (Oude Libertas)
10. Spier
11. Stellenbosch Vineyards (Welmoed)
12. Vriesenhof

OPENING PAGE: Many of the Stellenbosch district's quality wine-growing properties, such as Vriesenhof, lie along the slopes of the numerous outcrops that dominate the local landscape.

ALTO

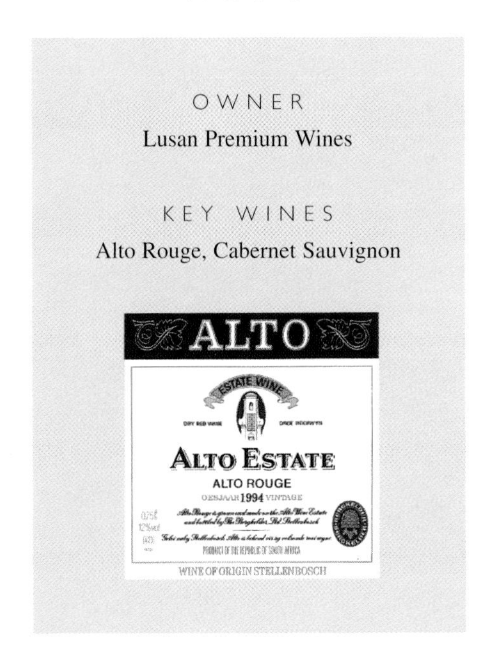

OWNER

Lusan Premium Wines

KEY WINES

Alto Rouge, Cabernet Sauvignon

The key to Alto's success lies in the early recognition of its viticultural strengths and the commitment by its custodians not to deviate from the path. The 100ha of vines lie in a narrow strip running up the Helderberg peaks just before they link up with Stellenbosch Mountain. Altitudes vary from 120m to 500m, soils are good, clay-based granite and vines benefit from cooling breezes off False Bay.

Originally part of the farm Groenrivier, first settled in 1693, Alto was the result of a division by early 20th-century owner Hennie Malan. Malan decided upon Cabernet Sauvignon, Shiraz and Cinsaut to create the more immediately accessible red blend named Alto Rouge – sold to a London merchant for a decade before release onto the local market in 1933.

In 1959 Alto fell into the hands of former farm manager Piet du Toit, who handed it over to his son Hempies in 1983. Du Toit Junior has remained as custodian winemaker, even though the farm now belongs to the new Distillers/Hans Schreiber joint venture, Lusan Premium Wines.

Du Toit is a traditionalist. 'We just do what we have believed in for a 100 years,' is how he has explained away his many successes. Yet he has replanted spent old vines to virus-free, new-clone Cabernet and, since the '84, increased the content of newcomer Merlot in his Rouge at the expense of Shiraz and Cinsaut to the extent that Merlot has dominated some recent vintages. The modern Rouge is a mix of Bordeaux classics Cabernet Sauvignon, Merlot and Cabernet Franc, though a dash of Shiraz 'for Cape flavour' has been re-introduced. Small French oak barrels have replaced old vats, though Alto's smooth, drinkability must come with the use of second- and third-fill barrels.

TOP: Winemaker Hempies du Toit, who also grows proteas along the higher reaches of Alto on the slopes of the Helderberg.

ABOVE: Alto's red wines are marked by a smooth drinkability enhanced by second- and third-fill small French-oak barriques.

RUST EN VREDE

OWNER
Jannie Engelbrecht

KEY WINES
Rust en Vrede Estate Wine, Cabernet Sauvignon, Shiraz, Merlot, Tinta Barocca

This fine red-wine property, which grew vines in the 1700s, has emerged from its brief hiatus after the departure of vintner Kevin Arnold in 1997 with a whole new perspective.

Former Springbok rugby player Engelbrecht has handed over the reins to son Jean, an airline pilot. New in the cellar is promising winemaker, former Saxenburg assistant Louis Strydom. And to match the recent surge in the rejuvenation of the vineyards – now up to more than 40ha of virus-free plant material, which is beefing up the already good quality of Rust en Vrede's wines with an exciting new fruit concentration to match their classic elegance – the cellar has been revamped and expanded. Annual production should soon double to around 24 000 cases. But the 'estate' guarantee of quality remains. Says Engelbrecht: 'Anywhere in the world, owners come and go. So do winemakers. But there's one thing that remains: origin. Stellenbosch, and Rust en Vrede.'

Rust en Vrede's Estate blend has always maintained a Cape identity with its primarily Cabernet Sauvignon and Shiraz make-up while many others were going the Bordeaux route with Cabernet Sauvignon, Merlot and Cabernet Franc. Merlot has played a role, albeit a minor one, in more modern vintages. But it is still a wine that encapsulates the power and structure of Cabernet and the sweet mulberry fruit, spiciness and pepperiness of Shiraz.

The varietal Shiraz is also a show-stopper, with new-clone fruit and sweet American oak vanillins joining the smokiness that is a trademark of Rust en Vrede. The Cabernet Sauvignon is typical of its variety. The Merlot is soft, supple and mouthfilling, given gentler oak treatment than its stablemates, and the rare varietal Tinta Barocca shows a fresh new fruitiness.

TOP: Rust en Vrede owner Jannie Engelbrecht and new winemaker Louis Strydom, overseeing the rejuvenation of this venerable estate (**OPPOSITE**) with its classic Cape Dutch buildings.

BLAAUWKLIPPEN

This historic wine farm, dating back to 1692, is entering a new era after being bought in 1999 by German businessman Stephan Schoghüber. Renovation of the large, rambling old cellars is on the cards and winemaker Hein Hesebeck's '98s and '99s already reflect an invigorated touch. The emphasis on Blaauwklippen's 100ha will be increasingly on reds. A new varietal Merlot and Cabernet Franc both exhibit a freshness of fruit, softness of tannin and ease of drinking. The renowned Shiraz has a rare richness. Hesebeck's treatment of the farm's trademark Zinfandel is novel: no wooding, concentrating on the variety's characteristic brambly, wild berry flavours, with a special Reserve bottling from old bush vines.

BLUE CREEK

The rustic Voorspoed mountainside fruit-and-wine farm has been committed to Cabernet Sauvignon by father-and-son team Rabie and Piet Smal. Jacques Kruger made the first ripe '96 and '97 vintages while still cellarmaster at nearby Blaauwklippen, but Piet Smal, a dentist, has now taken over.

KLEINE ZALZE

The 30ha Kleine Zalze vineyards and cellar were sold by Gilbeys in 1996 to Wellington grape grower Jan Malan and brother-in-law Kobus Basson. Modernisation of the old winery allows for the handling of 3 000 tons of grapes and room for 1 000 barrels. Providing back-up for new cellarmaster Willem Loots and assistant Andries Eygelaar is an impressive team of consultants including Vriesenhof's Jan Boland Coetzee and Yves Barry of Domaine la Chevaliére in the Languedoc and Domaine Laroche in Burgundy. Grapes will be sourced from Kleine Zalze, Malan's three Voëlgesang wine farms in Wellington and growers in Franschhoek, Durbanville and Stellenbosch. Early releases of reds show promise, with a Vineyard Selection range featuring a fine Cabernet Sauvignon and Shiraz from old vines, and a good Merlot and Pinotage.

SPIER

This winery forms part of the fairly glitzy wine, food, entertainment and conference complex developed by Dick Enthoven on the old Cape Dutch homestead he bought from the Joubert family in 1993. About 60ha of undulating vineyards on the 400ha spread are being replanted. More Chardonnay, Shiraz and Merlot will increase vineyards to about 120ha. Cellar capacity will double to around 1 000 tons. Winemaker Frans Smit makes a particularly good Chardonnay and Sauternes-like, oak-fermented Noble Late Harvest under the IV Spears label (pending legal pronouncement on opposing claims to the rights of the Spier brand name by Enthoven and Hydro Holdings, owner of the other 'Spier' cellar at Goedgeloof).

STELLENBOSCH FARMERS' WINERY (SFW)

Major producer/wholesaler SFW is situated on the original Oude Libertas wine farm, first granted in 1689. Founded in 1935 by an American, William Charles Winshaw, SFW established famous brands that are still widely enjoyed, including the red blends Château Libertas and Tassenberg, La Gratitude dry white, Grand Mousseux sparkling wine and others. It is also the home of pink bubbly Fifth Avenue Cold Duck, popular off-dry white quaffer Graça and Lanzerac Rosé. The flagship range is Zonnebloem, headed by the Lauréat Bordeaux-style red blend with some consistently good varietal Cabernet Sauvignon, Merlot, Shiraz and Pinotage.

Cellarmaster is veteran Wouter Pienaar.

STELLENBOSCH VINEYARDS (WELMOED)

At home at what was Welmoed co-op (the Welmoed name is now confined to a wine brand), Stellenbosch Vineyards is a modern version of the traditional producer/wholesaler that dominated the Cape wine scene into the second half of the 20th century.

Though still bottling specific wines under their own labels, the four Stellenbosch co-ops – Welmoed, Eersterivier, Bottelary and Helderberg – joined forces and formed a public company in 1996. The primary aim of the 150-odd growers is to initially invest in the 'big six' premium varieties to produce internationally marketable wines. The total 3 500ha involved occupies some of the best viticultural land in Stellenbosch.

In charge of winemakers is Chris Kelly, a New Zealander trained at Australia's Roseworthy institute and a former 'flying winemaker' for the UK's International Wine Services. Assisting him is Mike Graham, who makes the Welmoed wines and helps with the new, three-tier Stellenbosch Vineyards portfolio, including the Genesis range of premium wines and the new, all-purpose dry-white blend Versus. Innovations include a Shiraz Cap Classique called Infinity. At Bottelary, Elizabeth Augustyn concentrates on Cabernet Sauvignon, Merlot, Shiraz and Pinotage. At Eersterivier, Herman du Preez is allowing the Cabernet Sauvignon and Merlot to gain pre-eminence. Winemaker Mark Carmichael-Green handles Helderberg whites and reds.

THE BERGKELDER

The wine-production arm of the mighty Anton Rupert-owned wine and spirits producer/wholesaler Distillers Corporation formed in 1945, The Bergkelder was built in 1968. Carved into the Papegaaiberg hilltop, it houses the premium reds from the company's own brands and the estates it owns with Hans Schreiber under Lusan Premium Wines. It also markets and distributes, through SA Wine Cellars, wines from leading independent farms such as Allesverloren, Meerlust, Jacobsdal and La Motte.

The company's own brands cover the full quality spectrum. Only selected varieties and vintages appear under the Stellenryck label – the Sauvignon Blanc can be very good, as can the bottle-aged Cabernet Sauvignon and a weighty Chardonnay. The Fleur du Cap wines are wider ranging, encompassing some fine premium varietal reds. Cellarmaster Callie van Niekerk has also introduced special 'unfiltered, unstabilised' bottlings of an excellent Cabernet Sauvignon and Merlot, as well as a Sauvignon Blanc. The Fleur du Cap Noble Late Harvest is a consistently good value-for-money treat.

VRIESENHOF

After buying the 25ha Vriesenhof in 1980, establishing new vines, building a winery and then taking over the nearby tiny Talana Hill vineyard and cellar, former Springbok rugby player Jan Boland Coetzee is now replanting more than 50ha of the existing 70-odd ha of land he either owns or leases. He has long-term contracts with several private growers along the Blaauwklippen River – and he still finds time to consult for wineries such as Kleine Zalze, Lanzerac and Yonder Hill. All this keeps him engrossed in the study of specific vineyard sites, clones and barrels, ever searching for cause and effect regarding wine style and quality.

After an illustrious career with Kanonkop, Coetzee followed his red-wine métier on his own turf. The Vriesenhof Kallista Bordeaux-style blend is muscular, in the vein of the more traditional Cape reds. But recent vintages of this and his lean, firm Vriesenhof Cabernet Sauvignon and Pinotage are showing greater fruit depth to match tannins that cry out for bottle-ageing. The Talana Hill Royale blend is gentler. Chardonnay is Coetzee's specialist white, again a broad, generously oaked wine bottled under both labels in the tiny, underground Talana Hill cellar. The remainder of his fruit, including some Sauvignon Blanc, goes into the value-for-money Paradyskloof range.

Vriesenhof wines are muscular, made for the long haul, with more recent vintages showing greater fruit depth to balance that early leanness and firmness.

HELDERBERG

This area consists of two different viticultural terroirs. The bench of south-facing slopes along the Helderberg mountains offers soils that are deep and well drained, with a moisture-retaining clay-substructure typical of the Hutton, Clovelly and Tukulu types. Overlooking False Bay, these high-lying areas are cooled by the south-easter, producing particularly rich, powerful reds.

Then there are the undulating lowlands closer to the sea, ideally temperate but with sandier soils. Here the reds are less powerful, more elegant, like the Meerlusts and Vergenoegds, and one finds a greater proliferation of whites, from Chardonnay to Chenin Blanc. The wonderful potential of the Helderberg is encouraging investment in a number of new wineries, large and small, dedicated to producing prime-quality wine. Round the corner, in the basin formed by the Helderberg and Hottentots Holland mountains, are monied developments galore.

JP Moueix, the family-run firm with the largest land ownership in Pomerol (including Château Pétrus), has bought 40ha near Vergelegen. In partnership with Savanha Wines, Moueix will be replacing existing vines with Cabernet Sauvignon, Merlot, Shiraz, Chardonnay and Sauvignon Blanc – he's already released an Ingwe Chardonnay/ Sauvignon blend – and may build a cellar once the vines are mature and the quality has been assessed. Local banking phenomenon Christo Wiese, owner of Lanzerac, is developing the historic Lourensford estate. He's planting around 100ha on the 'back' slopes of the Helderberg opposite Vergelegen.

Though further removed from the Helderberg, yet sharing its overall viticultural and climatic profile, the next little valley just below Sir Lowry's Pass is quietly undergoing a renaissance. Vineyards in the area known as Knorhoek, historically a source of grapes for some of Nederburg's finest old reds from the '30s and '40s, are also being rejuvenated.

HELDERBERG

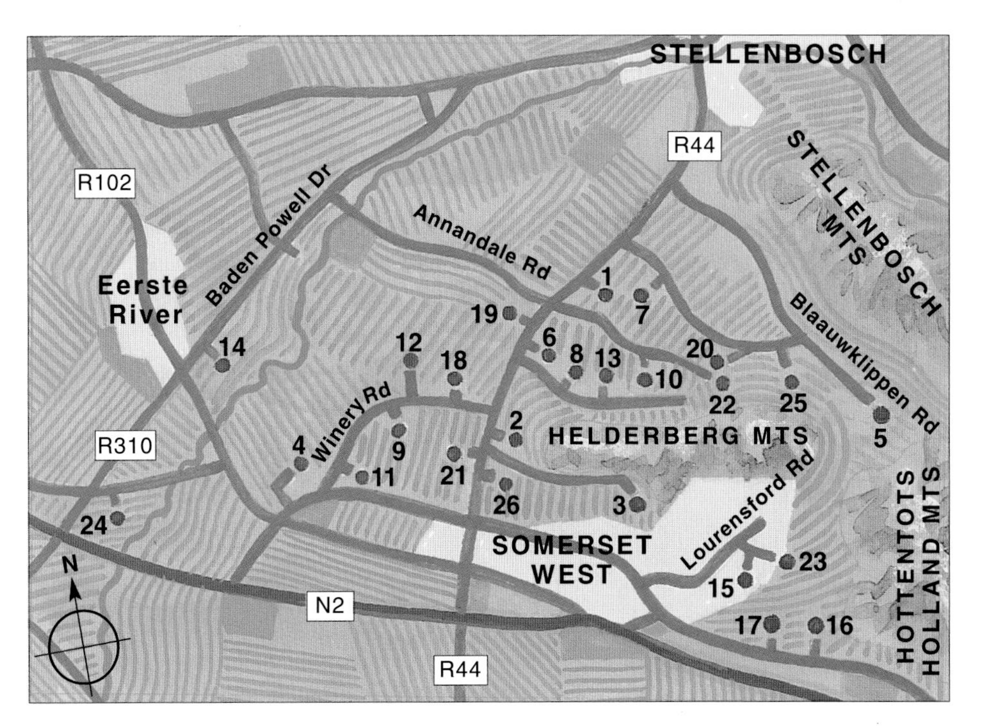

1. Audacia
2. Avontuur
3. Cordoba
4. Dellrust
5. De Trafford
6. Eikendal
7. Graceland
8. Grangehurst
9. Helderberg
10. Helderkruin
11. JP Bredell
12. Ken Forrester
13. Longridge
14. Meerlust
15. Morgenster
16. Mount Rozier
17. Onderkloof
18. Post House
19. Somerbosch
20. Stellenzicht
21. Stonewall
22. Uva Mira
23. Vergelegen
24. Vergenoegd
25. Waterford
26. Yonder Hill

CORDOBA

OWNER
Jannie Jooste

KEY WINES
Cordoba Crescendo,
Cabernet Sauvignon, Merlot,
Shiraz, Chardonnay, Sauvignon Blanc;
Mount Claire Mountain Red,
Mount Claire Mountain White

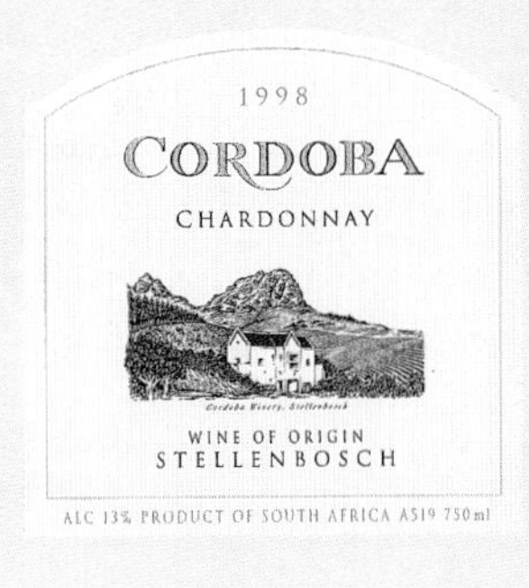

Winemaker Christopher Keet is the beaming face of this state-of-the-art, low-key, emerging winery on the Helderberg (it turns out about 7 000 cases, the target being around 12 000). Somerset West businessman Jannie Jooste has seldom been seen since assigning Vriesenhof's Jan Boland Coetzee the task of revitalising and replanting the 30ha of vineyards, some as high as 600m up, in the late '80s.

Some of the vines retained are more than 20 years old, and this prime red-wine site, known as De Helderenberg farm, used to provide fruit for Vriesenhof until the newly named Cordoba's maiden vintage handled by Keet in 1994. First came the whites: a crisp, reductively made Sauvignon Blanc that drinks well after a year in bottle; and a Chardonnay, whole bunch-pressed, barrel-fermented, quite oaky. A second label called Mount Claire, comprising a Mountain White and Mountain Red blend, was established to absorb wine not deemed quite the quality a fussy Keet is looking for.

The reds have always been in another league, deeply coloured and richly flavoured, but invariably with firm tannin structure. Merlots, Cabernets and Cabernet Francs, vinified and bottled separately, show structure, elegance and fruit richness. The Cabernet is pure cassis and the Merlot plummy, though both are firm, with the Cabernet carrying a fair whack of wood (and asking to be laid down).

The flagship, a blend of the three, is the Cordoba Crescendo. It surprised with its final make-up: as much as 70% Cabernet Franc, with just 20% Cabernet and 10% Merlot. But the Cabernet Franc has been outperforming all its stablemates, with its rich, peppery, spicy character. With recent vintages fleshed out with a dash of Merlot, the Crescendo is a full, complex wine with plummy, blackcurrant fruit, firm, dry tannins and solid, French oaking that recommends it for bottle-ageing.

TOP: Chris Keet, winemaker at Cordoba, with faithful companion Della.
RIGHT: Cordoba boasts some of the highest vineyards along the Helderberg Mountain, where some serious reds are made.

GRANGEHURST

OWNER
Jeremy Walker

KEY WINES
Pinotage, Cabernet Sauvignon/ Merlot, Tribute

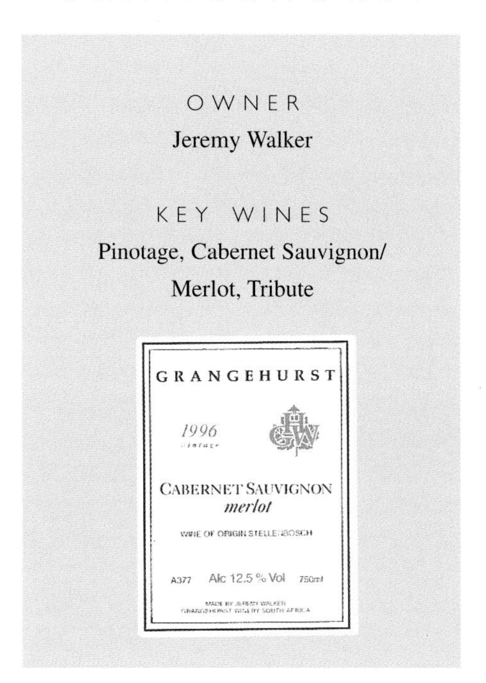

Jeremy Walker, always intrigued by the world of winemaking, armed himself with an oenology and viticulture degree, followed by an MBA and a stint in property broking before joining Seymour Pritchard in establishing Clos Malverne in the Devon Valley from 1986 to 1991. He then embarked on his own venture, Grangehurst, on the family smallholding. His first wines, from grapes carefully selected from prime spots all over Stellenbosch, were made in an old squash court, using second-hand equipment.

Through a system of debentures, regular customers helped him extend his négociant-style grape purchases. Now, nearly a decade later, he's graduated to a new stainless-steel tank and underground barrel maturation cellar, while the defunct squash court still provides space for blending and storage. The old basket press, bought in 1982 when Walker was already envisioning his own winery, worked well enough to persuade him to stick with basket presses, albeit some very smart-looking, automated Italian versions.

For all the new expansions, Grangehurst will remain a small, hands-on winery – annual production is close to the ultimate target of just 9 000 cases. Walker sources his grapes from four vineyard areas, all prime red-wine sites: Helderberg, Firgrove, Devon Valley and Stellenboschkloof. Ideally, he would like to be in charge of a site in each area, ensuring top quality from vineyard management right through to the bottle. Much like his arrangement with friend Dave Hidden, whose 7ha Pinotage vineyard in Devon Valley produced the award-winning '97 Hidden Valley Pinotage. Some of the fruit also goes towards Grangehurst Pinotage, one of the leading new-wave Cape Pinotages – a serious, robust, barrel-matured wine made to last for up to 10 years.

Walker's Cabernet Merlot blends are similarly full-bodied, opaque, densely fruited, richly oaked and firmly structured. They are wines that need at least five years, sometimes longer, to come into their own. His varietal Cabernet is tighter and leaner, but Reserve bottlings and special barrels are always stunners – chewy, meaty wines with classic structure.

TOP: Vintner Jeremy Walker with his daughter Hayley, alias 'Princess Pinotage'.
LEFT: Walker's *négociant* winemaking business is based at the family home, set among others' vineyards, with Longridge Winery behind.

JP BREDELL

OWNER

Anton Bredell

KEY WINES

JP Bredell Cape Vintage Reserve and Cape Late Bottled Vintage ports; Shiraz, Merlot, Pinotage, Chardonnay

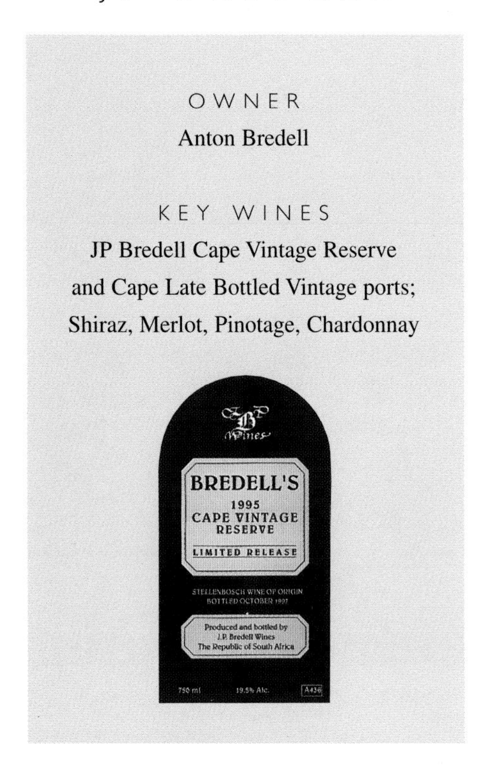

Anton Bredell is giving the Nel brothers of the 'South African port capital', Calitzdorp, a run for their money, with a port voted SA Young Wine Show Champion Wine in 1998.

Helderzicht and its neighbouring Onder-Rustenberg make up the family wine business JP Bredell, the biggest single private producer of port in the country. The total production of some 1 800 tons of mostly port and red varieties flowed into the monolithic cellars of KWV in Paarl, renowned for its fine ports, until 1989, when the experts exhorted young Anton Bredell to bottle his own. His father Koos (JP) had made champion reds and ports in the '60s and Anton grew up on the farm imbued in port wine production. He committed himself to traditional Portuguese techniques in the rambling old farm cellar, now spruced up.

The varieties he uses are the port classics: Tinta Barocca and Souzão. Sandy soils with a gravel layer for good drainage and a clay substructure for water retention, plus hot summer days cooled by a southerly breeze off nearby False Bay, provide ideal conditions for these two varieties chosen from among nine grown here since the mid 1900s.

Anton Bredell (**TOP**), owner of JP Bredell, has spruced up the old Helderzicht farm cellar (**ABOVE**), where he makes his definitive Cape ports and some new-wave classic varietal reds.

JP Bredell ports are handcrafted wines. Older blocks of vines, yielding marginal crops, are nurtured. Open concrete tanks are used for fermentation, the cap of skins is punched down manually every three hours during the 48-hour fermentation period. 'It's the personal touch – you can see what's happening and you're more in control.' He is similarly dedicated to the strict Portuguese style guidelines. His heavyweight wines are fermented much drier than the earlier, sweet Cape ports, and more heavily fortified to around 20% A/V. The authentic premium Vintage Reserve is bottled after the requisite two years in 300 litre oak barriques, whereafter it should be kept for at least five or more years in bottle before opening.

By comparison, his Late Bottled Vintage, if not deemed of Vintage quality, is left in wood for a further two to three years. The lighter, purely fruity Ruby, previously bottled as Helderzicht, will in future appear under the JP Bredell label.

These successes have spurred him on to vinify varietal reds such as Merlot, Cabernet Sauvignon, Shiraz and Pinotage, some snapped up for the KWV's prestige Cathedral Cellar range, others bottled under JP Bredell.

MEERLUST

OWNER

Hannes Myburgh

KEY WINES

Rubicon, Merlot, Pinot Noir (Reserve), Chardonnay

One of the Cape's 'First Growths', Meerlust has an aristocratic history and a continuity of tradition that is nevertheless seamlessly blending into the New World of wine. This is largely due to long-time winemaker, the redoubtable, Italian-born Giorgio Dalla Cia, and his close, almost paternal relationship with owner Hannes Myburgh. Myburgh, who took over the running of the farm in 1986 upon the death of his father Nico, is the eighth generation on Meerlust, which he has lovingly restored; it is the only wine estate declared a national monument.

Dalla Cia has been here for over 20 years. An advocate of enduring, classic wine styles in the face of the onslaught of easy drinkability, he has kept a steady course with the flagship Rubicon, first bottled in 1980. Through changes from large old vats to small, new French-oak barrels and the replanting to new virus-free clones, the recipe is a constant. And the wine is always a study in elegance and balance.

The Merlot is moving with the times, becoming big and bold. Dalla Cia has also rung the changes with the truffley Pinot Noir, which shows deeper colour and more fruit sweetness from a new Burgundian clone and serious oaking. He has also introduced a Chardonnay: full bodied, well-oaked, barrel-fermented and left on the lees for many months. It is styled on Burgundy's Meursaults and Montrachets. 'I believe in getting rid of all that fruitiness that disguises the true structure of Chardonnay.'

Dalla Cia makes no bones about following the French style. 'Rubicon is our interpretation of the Bordeaux style,' he asserts. 'We're using the best from France as our benchmark, not the best of the New World.' Assistant Chris Williams has been dispatched to France for experience, and new plantings include Gallic classics Petit Verdot and Viognier, as well as more Cabernet, on 40ha of newly acquired land.

ABOVE: The classic Cape Dutch homestead of Meerlust, now home to Hannes Myburgh (**TOP**), eighth generation Myburgh on the farm. With him is cellarmaster Giorgio Dalla Cia and assistant winemaker Chris Williams.

VERGELEGEN

OWNER

Anglo American's Amwines

KEY WINES

Sauvignon Blanc, Chardonnay, Sémillon, Vin de Florence, Vergelegen, Vergelegen 'Show Special', Cabernet Sauvignon, Merlot, Pinot Noir, Mill Race Red

VERGELEGEN
SAUVIGNON BLANC
1999

This 3 000ha farm in the basin formed by the northern slopes of the Helderberg and the majestic Hottentots Holland mountains has been the property of diamond and mining corporation Anglo American's Amfarms since 1987. Amfarms (now called Amwines) will now be concentrating on its wine business after recently selling off all its other agricultural interests here and on sister farm Boschendal.

Vines were planted on Vergelegen in 1700 by the owner, Cape governor Willem Adriaan van der Stel, who set about establishing a model estate much as his father, Simon, had done at Constantia. A succession of landlords followed, right up to 20th-century incumbent Tom Barlow, who uprooted much of the vineyards from the '60s. Yet it gave viticulturist Gerrie Wagenaar a clean slate upon which to plan the new-look Vergelegen. Starting in 1989, he has cultivated just over 100ha of classic varieties: high-lying, south-facing Sauvignon Blanc, Chardonnay, Sémillon on the low-lying slopes, Cabernet Sauvignon, Merlot and Cabernet Franc on both high, cool aspects and warmer, lower hillsides.

Already right at home in the 1 200-ton, French-designed, multi-levelled, octagonal cellar sunk into a hilltop, former Stellenzicht star winemaker André van Rensburg took over from talented Martin Meinert in 1998, improving even further on Vergelegen's excellent reputation. Top of the list is the Sauvignon Blanc, with the full varietal gamut of classic fig, gooseberry, greenpepper and grassy aromas and flavours. The outstanding Reserve is a special vineyard selection from the Schaapenberg hill, some 400m high overlooking False Bay, and is hailed by its maker as the epitome of what Vergelegen's terroir is capable of.

The same goes for the embryonic flagship red, probably to be known simply as Vergelegen. A blend of 75% Cabernet, 20% Merlot and 5% Cabernet Franc, all from the lower-lying Rondekop vineyards just below the hilltop winery, the maiden '98 shows a beautifully soft, rounded, elegant mouthful, with plenty of ageing potential. Joining this red blend at the tip of Vergelegen's pyramid of quality will be a white, which at this stage may be a Sauvignon, or even a Sémillon. As for the Chardonnay, while the 'standard' bottling is quite toasty – from the '99 vintage it will be 100% barrel-fermented and all from own grapes – the single-vineyard Reserve from lower Schaapenberg is simply gorgeous.

From the '98 vintage, all the reds are from Vergelegen's own grapes. While the Merlot has impressed with its stunning structure and rich fruit since the maiden '94 vintage, the Cabernet is coming into its own with a fully fruited, coffee and cigarbox nose and palate.

TOP: Award-winning winemaker André van Rensburg surveys his new domaine from the hilltop cellar at Vergelegen. The farm (**RIGHT**) is a must for visitors, with its immaculate Cape Dutch architecture and gardens.

VERGENOEGD

OWNERS
John Faure and Haydn Wright

KEY WINES
Reserve, Cabernet Sauvignon, Merlot, Shiraz, Cape Vintage Port

VERGENOEGD
ESTATE WINE
STELLENBOSCH
Cabernet Sauvignon 60%
Merlot 35% Cabernet Franc 5%
1995 RESERVE

Well-loved Vergenoegd, with its rural atmosphere and 18th-century cellar, has been revitalised in recent years, under management of a new partnership: owner/winemaker John Faure and his cousin-by-marriage Hadyn Wright, who looks after the vineyards and marketing. The Faures have been making wine on this 1696 Cape Dutch homestead, one of the oldest viticultural properties in Stellenbosch, since 1820; winemaking dates back to at least 1788.

The farm has had a longstanding relationship with the KWV, which takes its white grapes and bulk red wine for blending. But since 1972 around five per cent of the crop from 120ha has been bottled under the Vergenoegd label. John, who took over the winemaking from his father Jac and uncle Brand in 1983, retained the traditional use of open concrete tanks and large old vats to make the farm's trademark medium-bodied, savoury reds.

But the trend towards fresher, fruitier New World styles persuaded Faure to re-evaluate Vergenoegd's character. Experimentation with longer maceration, roto-tanks and small oak barrels has had pleasing results, though he has not foregone the traditional ways. He still uses his *kuipe* for fermentation and cellar techniques are kept simple and natural, with minimal fining (only with egg white) and a single filtration.

'Young, fruity wines are not for us,' he says. But a new ripeness of fruit, easy drinkability and elegance run like a theme through all his reds. Wines are still bottle-aged for at least a year before release. The Reserve, a classic blend of Cabernet Sauvignon, Merlot and Cabernet Franc, is full of mulberry, plummy fruit and a slight mintiness, with a dry finish. The Cabernet is slightly leaner, more herbaceous, while the Merlot is the most modern, soft, rounded and sporting a greater percentage of new oak.

TOP: John Faure, with children Chris and Abigail and vineyard manager Haydn Wright.
OPPOSITE: The Vergenoegd manor house, home to several generations of Faures.

AUDACIA

This is an old wine-growing property, resurrected by insurance man Trevor Strydom and wife Diane. A cellar, last used in the 1970s, is back in operation, and small quantities of single-varietal wines have been bottled since 1997. Former Elsenburg cellar technology lecturer Elsa Carstens is the winemaker.

AVONTUUR

Racing stud owner Tony Taberer's Avontuur re-established its 60ha of vineyards in the late '70s and the first wines were bottled in 1987. Premium varieties are carefully sited along south-west-facing Helderberg slopes, and Jean-Luc Sweerts (now with Agusta) produced some broad Chardonnays and a very drinkable, value-for-money Avon Rouge Cabernet Merlot blend. Reserve bottlings of the odd varietal Pinotage, Merlot and Cabernet Franc have rated highly, as has the Bordeaux-style Baccarat. Lizelle Gerber is the new winemaker.

DELLRUST

Albert Bredell, younger brother of top port producer Anton Bredell of JP Bredell Wines, has established his own label on the family's second property, Onder-Rustenberg. He's restored the old cellar, where wine was made from 1917 to 1970. Consultant Eugene van Zyl has helped with a Sauvignon Blanc, an unusually off-dry Chardonnay and Chenin Blanc. A Tinta Barocca Cinsaut blend drinks most easily among premium varietal reds, and there's a Ruby Port.

DE TRAFFORD

Architect David Trafford and his late father first planted Cabernet Sauvignon, Merlot, Cabernet Franc, Pinot Noir and Chardonnay on inaccessible grazing land on Mont Fleur farm in 1983. Grapes were hand-pressed and wine was made in plastic containers for home consumption until '92, when some 3 000-odd bottles of De Trafford varietal reds were sold commercially. Maximum production is still just 3 000 cases, handcrafted in a tiny cellar.

Trafford uses indigenous yeasts, allowing malolactic fermentation in small French oak barrels, racking the wine over about 20 months, lightly fining with egg whites and bottling without filtering. Both the Cabernet and Merlot are exceptionally rich, deeply fruited, powerful wines with ripe tannins to last. A blend, called Collage, was previously lighter, more herbaceous, but is intensifying. A new Shiraz and Shiraz Reserve are richly flavoured, bold wines. More recently he has produced some serious Chenin Blancs from mature vines. And he's pioneered a new style of sweet wine in the Cape, based on the French Vin de Paille (straw wine): a naturally full-sweet, wood-aged Chenin made from grapes air-dried to almost raisin-like concentration on racks (or straw).

EIKENDAL

Owned by Swiss company AG für Plantagen since 1982, this modern, 30 000-case winery on two old farms dating back to the late 18th century, maintains a low profile under shy Austrian manager/vintner Josef Krammer and winemaker Anneke Burger. One of Vriesenhof's Jan Boland Coetzee's consulting projects, Eikendal's 60ha carries noble whites and reds. The citrussy, elegant Chardonnay is a favourite, and with the smooth, tasty Merlot makes up a great value-for-money duo. Reserve bottlings of wines such as the Cabernet Sauvignon and the Classique Bordeaux-style blend show good balance between power and elegance.

GRACELAND

In 1991 this brand-new boutique cellar launched two French-oak-matured '98 reds. Just a few hundred cases of a soft, rich and ripe but well-structured Cabernet and a slightly more immediately accessible, herbaceous, coffee-like Merlot were produced in '98. Quantities doubled in '99 but will remain limited. Financial man Paul McNaughton and wife Susan bought the 18ha farm in 1990. Martin Meinert made the first vintages, but New Zealand consultant Rod Easthope is now in residence.

HELDERKRUIN

Neil du Toit's two properties, Brandwag and Helderkruin, comprising some 100ha, have been replanted to red varieties such as Cabernet, Merlot and Shiraz, as well as some award-winning Pinotage and Pinot Noir. Ultimately reds will take up 80% of vineyard space. All are French-oak matured. Whites include Sauvignon, Chardonnay and Sémillon, while some old Chenin Blanc and a 30-year-old Shiraz block still yields riches.

Du Toit, an SFW supplier, built his own winery in 1997 and former SFW winemaker Koos Bosman presides over a range of easy-drinking wines under the Yellow Door label, as well as premium varietal wines (including a good Pinotage) under the Helderkruin name.

KEN FORRESTER

Top Gauteng restaurateur Ken Forrester renovated dilapidated Scholtzenhof farm and has been producing some innovative wines over the past few years. His full, wood-matured Chenin helped blaze the way for serious varietal attempts from the mid-'90s. He is now exploring a Rhône-style red, using some rare, established Devon Valley Grenache with his home-grown Shiraz for an increasingly substantial but easy-drinking mouthful. Martin Meinert makes the wines at his Devon Crest cellar in Devon Valley.

LONGRIDGE

Conceived in 1992 by wine *négociant* Johann Laubser, Longridge has joined forces with two other large wineries with similar ideals of marketing good-quality, big-brand wines. While maintaining their separate identities and brand names, Longridge, Savanha Wines and Spier Cellars now operate under ownership of Trylogy Wine Corporation, with Laubser as CEO. Young Aussie winemaker Ben Radford of Longridge oversees winemaking at all three, assisted in the Longridge cellar by Kirstin Katzenberg. The winery handles up to 2 000 tons of grapes from half-a-dozen-or-so Durbanville and Stellenbosch growers. There's also its own 80ha next to Meerlust, with most of the fruit earmarked for the premium Longridge and excellent value-for-money Bay View ranges. The concentration is on classic varieties. A close working relationship with Burgundian vintner Martin Prieur is immediately evident in the stylish, subtle, long-lived Chardonnay.

MORGENSTER

Since 1992, Giulio Bertrand, a semi-retired Italian businessman, has been amalgamating what is now a 200ha piece of property originally part of Vergelegen. Virgin north-facing slopes were planted to Cabernet Sauvignon, Merlot and Cabernet Franc, for a 'St-Emilion-style red blend' vinified by Lanzerac's Wynand Hamman in consultation with Pierre Lurton of top Bordeaux Château Cheval Blanc. A Sauvignon Blanc under second label Lourens River Valley is pleasant. Newly appointed winemaker Marius Lategan is helping set up a cellar.

MOUNT ROZIER

Myrtle Grove Farm, hidden among the foothills of the Hottentots Holland mountains just below Sir Lowry's Pass, is where former engineer and Franschhoek fruit farmer Dave Lydell tends some 45ha of vineyards in granitic and sandstone soils on cool, high-lying south- and south-east-facing slopes. In just two years, Lydell, brother-in-law and Cape Town architect Gert Loebenberg and Gauteng businessman Michael Rubin have spruced up neglected vines, planted new clones and plan more Sauvignon Blanc and some Pinot Noir. The small, functional, red-wine dedicated cellar where consultant Ernst Gouws of Hoopenburg makes Mount Rozier wines will not exceed 5 000 cases. Initial offerings have been well fruited, elegant and immediately drinkable, with the Cabernet the pick of the bunch.

ONDERKLOOF

On Onderkloof the French oak-matured Pinotage and Cabernet Sauvignon are looking good, with new Shiraz and Merlot plantings in the wings. A Chardonnay, Sauvignon Blanc and off-dry white blend called Floreal from the maiden '99 vintage heralded veteran winemaker Danie Truter's new-found freedom in his own winery, in partnership with Beat Musfeld and John Harrison. Truter, who helped build up Hartenberg, will concentrate on reds.

POST HOUSE

The Gebers' family farm bottles a few hundred cases of fruity Chenin Blanc and two very drinkable reds, a Cabernet and Merlot. An old barn, plus borrowed and converted equipment (including a former tobacco press) is used by Nicholas Gebers. Most of the grapes from the Post House's 30ha go to Longridge.

SOMERBOSCH

Die Fonteine, home to Somerbosch Wines, has been farmed by the Roux family for more than 50 years. Supplying fruit to nearby Helderberg co-operative winery for years, Wally Roux and his sons Wrensch (now fully occupied in the L'Ormarins cellar), Japie and Marius decided to bottle wine under their own label in 1995. Production is around 13 000 cases. Replantings over the past 15 years have replaced old Chenin Blanc and Cinsaut grapes with noble reds. The farm's sandy soils and warm climate augur well for fruity Cabernet, Cinsaut and Pinotage, with Merlot showing particularly well.

STELLENZICHT

Owned by German banker Hans Schreiber since 1981 and guided to superstardom by outspoken, talented winemaker André van Rensburg from 1994 to 1997, Stellenzicht is now the domain of Guy Webber. Webber can rely on expertly planted vineyards as well as a massive hi-tech cellar. Current production is around 60 000 cases from 140ha. The stars have been a gooseberry-rich Sauvignon Blanc and a benchmark, new-wave South African Shiraz. The Merlot, Cabernet and Bordeaux-style red blend, known as Stellenzicht, all exhibit enormous depth of flavour and texture. Then there is the creamy, citrussy Chardonnay and a full-bodied, leesy and lemony Sémillon, as well as gorgeous Noble Late Harvests.

STONEWALL

Happy Vale Farm, with its 1828 gabled cellar and 1858 manor house, has been given a new lease of life by De Waal Koch, whose great-great-grandfather bought the farm in 1873. Koch renovated the original cellar in 1996, having already started replanting much of the 80ha of vineyards. Many of the grapes go to SFW, but top consulting winemaker Martin Meinert produces just over 2 000 cases, which include a most impressive Merlot Cabernet blend and a single-varietal Cabernet, both delicious, complex, juicy reds.

UVA MIRA

Acquired by retired mining executive Des Weedon in 1994, Uva Mira is supplementing existing 10-year-old Sauvignon Blanc and Chardonnay vines with Merlot and Cabernet Sauvignon, with 45ha as the ultimate goal. Some 12ha are currently in production, with wines made by Jan Boland Coetzee at his Vriesenhof winery until the Uva Mira cellar is completed.

A Sauvignon Blanc and a Chardonnay will soon be joined by a Merlot and a novel varietal Roobernet, but Cabernet promises to be the farm's speciality.

WATERFORD

A star in the making, given the passion and dedication of go-ahead winemaker Kevin Arnold (formerly with Rust en Vrede) and financial clout of owner, Gauteng information technology whizz Jeremy Ord. Of the 120ha, some 50ha of prime, virgin vineyard land have been earmarked. About 14ha are planted to Sauvignon Blanc, Chardonnay and Cabernet, with another 13ha being cultivated for more red, including Arnold's speciality, Shiraz. They'll also be experimenting with Bordeaux niche varieties Petit Verdot and Malbec, as well as the Rhône's Mouvèdre and Italian heavyweight Barbera. The Kevin Arnold Shiraz from Overgaauw grapes is dark and vibrant, a rich, sweet and spicy wine with great ageing potential. The Waterford Cabernet, like the Chardonnay from carefully selected vineyards leased nearby, is downright gorgeous.

YONDER HILL

This small wine farm was bought in 1997 by Cape businessman Frikkie Naudé from Rob Mundell, former tobacco merchant and Rhodesian rugby player. Jan Boland Coetzee of Vriesenhof helped establish the 10ha of prime reds, including Cabernet Sauvignon, Merlot and Cabernet Franc, as well as Chardonnay.

New onboard is self-taught winemaker David Lockley. He will oversee major expansions to the cellar – plans include an 800-barrel-maturation facility, a tasting room and a vinoteque. Current production of just over 2 000 cases will increase to 14 000. The plummy, smooth Merlot is the signature variety, while the Cabernet Sauvignon and Cabernet Franc join it in the solid iNanda blend.

The Helderberg peaks overlook top-quality winelands with clay-based soils and temperate climes.

JONKERSHOEK

The Jonkershoek Valley is probably one of the most beautiful little enclaves in the Stellenbosch wine district. It is a deep, narrow cleft between the north-eastern slopes of the Stellenbosch range and the fissured peaks of the Jonkershoek mountains on the south-eastern end of the town. Now the high-lying slopes of decomposed granite, mainly on the southern and south-eastern slopes, are being exploited for their viticultural potential, albeit it on a small scale.

The recognition in recent years of the potential for classic varieties, mainly reds such as Cabernet and Merlot, is seeing some good-quality wines coming out of what is officially one of the Wine of Origin wards of the Stellenbosch district. Capital injection by the more wealthy businessmen and bankers turned wine producers has rejuvenated some long-established cellars, such as Lanzerac and Oude Nektar. But, whether monied or not, the wine farms in the area remain small, hands-on, quality-driven endeavours.

JONKERSHOEK

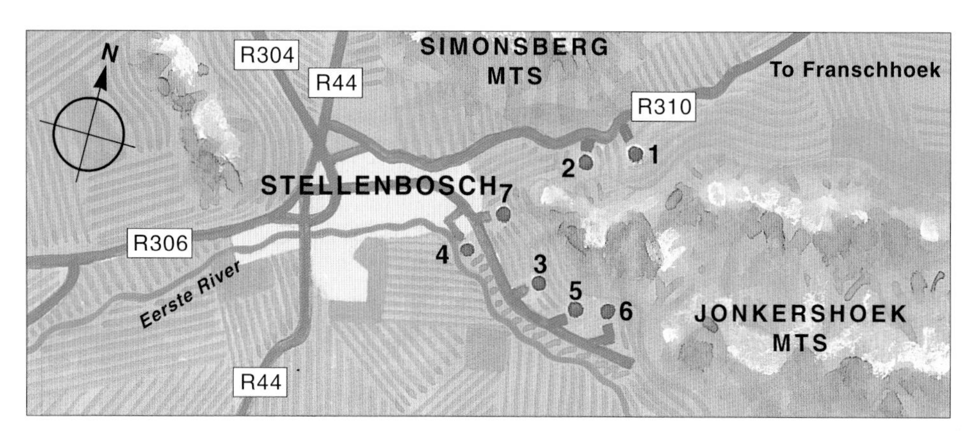

1. Camberley
2. Delaire
3. Klein Gustrouw
4. Lanzerac
5. Le Riche (Leef Op Hoop)
6. Neil Ellis
7. Rozendal

NEIL ELLIS

OWNERS
Neil Ellis, Hans-Peter Schröder

KEY WINES
Groenekloof Sauvignon Blanc, Elgin Chardonnay, Stellenbosch Cabernet Sauvignon, Jonkershoek Shiraz, Elgin Pinot Noir

ABOVE: Oude Nektar, the modern new winery built by Hans-Peter Schröder (**BELOW**) for his business partner, Neil Ellis, who now has the help of talented red winemaker Louis Nel.

After some 25 years, itinerant winemaker Neil Ellis has finally found a 'home' in the narrow, mountain-ringed Jonkershoek Valley. Armed with viticulture and winemaking training at Elsenburg College as well as a Stellenbosch University degree in chemistry and microbiology, Ellis did stints in the cellars of the KWV, Groot Constantia, Zevenwacht and Louisvale during the '70s and '80s, before finally bottling wine under his own label in 1989 (while still at Louisvale).

Putting his name on the label is no ego trip for Neil Ellis. 'It is the best guarantee of quality I can give,' says the man who is one of the Cape winemaking scene's quietest, yet most commanding personalities.

His new set-up at Oude Nektar, with its state-of-the-art, partly underground 500-ton cellar, allows him the freedom to best follow his particular modus operandi: identifying the variety and style of wines he wants, finding the right pockets of land in which they will thrive, and then seeking out the growers with whom he can work to nurture the vineyards and grow the quality of fruit he requires. He is particularly excited about the potential for red wines and Chardonnay on the 250ha mountainside slopes of Oude Nektar, where he is in partnership with businessman Hans-Peter Schröder.

Schröder bought the struggling property in 1989 and called viticulturist Prof Eben Archer who identified some 40ha as prime vineyard land. Cabernet Sauvignon, Merlot and Shiraz make up 70% of the total. The rest is under Chardonnay and some Sauvignon Blanc. Soils are decomposed granite, with the Cabernet settled in warmer, lower-lying sandy, alluvial soils around the lake next to the winery. The vineyards are all on the cool south-facing slopes of the towering Jonkershoek peaks, which derive extra benefit from a cooling early-morning mist bank.

The quality of the Shiraz and Cabernet specifically gave rise last year to the first bottling of Oude Nektar vineyard-designated wines from the superior '97 harvest. Labelled as Neil Ellis Jonkershoek Valley wines, these top-of-the-range wines are French-oaked and show a lovely ripeness of red berry fruit, giving them instant palatability, yet reveal an intensity and complexity that should reward with bottle-age.

The Groenekloof Sauvignon Blanc is a regular star performer in the Neil Ellis portfolio; it is probably one of the Cape's most varietally expressive, full of pungent guava, nettle and ripe fig aromas and flavours. This wine comes from the West Coast vineyard of Contreberg, where Ellis has been in another *négociant*-style partnership with third-generation grape grower Alex Versfeld since 1991. Chardonnay lovers will be equally enamoured of the barrel-fermented Neil Ellis Elgin Chardonnay. Asked to define the sort of wine he's striving to make, Ellis chooses the words 'stylish' and 'classy'.

His third label is Inglewood, reserved for wines not quite meeting his high expectations for the Neil Ellis and vineyard-designated ranges. But they're fruity, eminently drinkable and priced for everyday enjoyment.

CAMBERLEY

Home of Cape Town quantity surveyor John Nel and wife Gael, the small property sports a small basement cellar from whence comes a very fine Cabernet Sauvignon, filled out by Merlot: full of cassis and vanilla oak flavours with a dry, classic finish. The fruit comes from just 2ha of vines planted in 1991 on prime red-clay soils. Friend Kevin Arnold of Waterford helps out in the cellar.

DELAIRE

These cool, high-lying, decomposed granite vineyards were planted to mainly Chardonnay, Cabernet and Merlot by wine writer John Platter in the '80s. Now owned by Iranian businessman Masoud Alikhani, young winemaker Bruwer Raats follows in the footsteps of Mike Dobrovic (Mulderbosch) and Chris Keet (Cordoba). He produces some pleasant Sauvignon Blanc and Chardonnay, and is doing good things with the Merlot. Total annual production is just over 7 000 cases.

KLEIN GUSTROUW

After restoring the 1817 Cape Dutch homestead and converting an old farm building into a cellar, retired Gauteng financial director Chris McDonald and wife Athalie have turned their 4ha of Cabernet Sauvignon and Merlot into a muscular, meaty, mouthfilling blend since the maiden 1993. The self-taught winemaker sticks to a recipe: 65% Cabernet, 35% Merlot. Only about 1 250 cases are made and, after a year in small French oak, the wine is given two to three years in bottle before release.

LANZERAC

The historic Cape Dutch farm Lanzerac (circa 1692) is once again producing wine, thanks to maverick banker and business magnate Christo Wiese, who bought it in 1991. Former owner SFW had managed the vineyards and used the grapes mainly for its Lanzerac Pinotage and Rosé until the '70s, when the Lanzerac range was all but phased out. Some 50ha of premium red and some white have been planted and winemaker Wynand Hamman works in a spanking new 600-ton cellar. Cabernet Sauvignon and Merlot predominate, supported by Cabernet Franc and Malbec. Shiraz and Pinot Noir will offer something different, while 3ha of Pinotage may see the farm's own Pinotage soon. (The current Lanzerac Pinotage is still made by SFW.)

The vines are relatively young, so, while the fruit is there, the maiden '96 Chardonnay, Cabernet and Merlot were closed, reserved, almost stern. Subsequent vintages have shown richer, riper fruit to balance the tannin and wood. Although the Cabernet is regarded as the flagship, the fuller, more rounded Merlot has performed better to date.

Long a supplier of grapes to SFW, Lanzerac now bottles the cream of its crop under its own exclusive label.

LE RICHE

After more than 20 years with high-profile Rustenberg, veteran winemaker Etienne le Riche struck out on his own in 1996. Helped by Leef op Hoop farm owner Kobus Marais, from whom he leases an old cellar, Le Riche has epoxy-coated the old *kuipe*, fitted good second-hand equipment and installed a small bottling line. His first few Le Riche Cabernets from the '96 and '97 vintages, from grapes bought in from the Helderberg, Jonkershoek and elsewhere in Stellenbosch, have been solid, structured, ripe and powerful wines. This regal grape will be his métier and he is now concentrating on Cabernet, vinifying parcels from Bottelary, the Helderberg and Jonkershoek separately 'to familiarise myself with the character of each area'.

ROZENDAL

Once a part of Lanzerac, Rozendal is the domain of Swiss-German chef Kurt Ammann. He bought the 25ha property, complete with historic homestead and a cellar built in 1864, in 1981, producing his first wine in 1983: a Cabernet Sauvignon Cinsaut blend from bought-in grapes. After resurrecting the cellar and planting some 7ha of his own Cabernet and Merlot, his Rozendal blend has become synonymous with elegance and balance and a wonderfully smooth drinkability. Bought-in grapes, including Cabernet Franc, are also sometimes used in the mix. This self-taught winemaker fines only with egg white, and neither stabilises nor filters, relying on good fruit for his 3 000 cases.

SIMONSBERG

This is one of the main wards of the Stellenbosch district, encompassing prime viticultural land along the south and south-west flanks of the Simonsberg Mountain looking towards False Bay some 15km away. These slopes offer a range of sites ideal for fine white and red wines: from the warmer north and north-west aspects to the cooler south and south-east. The soils up here are mainly granitic – red clay Hutton and Clovelly types – ideal for the classic red varieties. But some good whites, such as Sauvignon Blanc, Chardonnay and Rhine Riesling, also do well in selected vineyards.

Along these mountains lie some of the Cape's most historic wine farms, established in the late 17th century, from the regal Rustenberg to the romantic Muratie – both are currently being rejuvenated.

Then there are the old stalwarts, from Delheim to Kanonkop to Lievland. Across the R44 (Klapmuts road) are some exciting, newer farms, all producing prime reds: L'Avenir, Laibach, Warwick. Some have vineyards on the Simonsberg slopes, others running up Klapmutskop hill. Brand-new boutique wineries, like Remhoogte, are popping up too.

The area boasts some of the Cape's highest, coolest vineyards, previously dedicated to fruit farming but now being given over to viticultural development. Thelema is one example, where star vintner Gyles Webb is now helping neighbour, Rand Merchant Bank chairman GT Ferreira, with his 40ha of new vineyard and state-of-the-art cellar.

SIMONSBERG

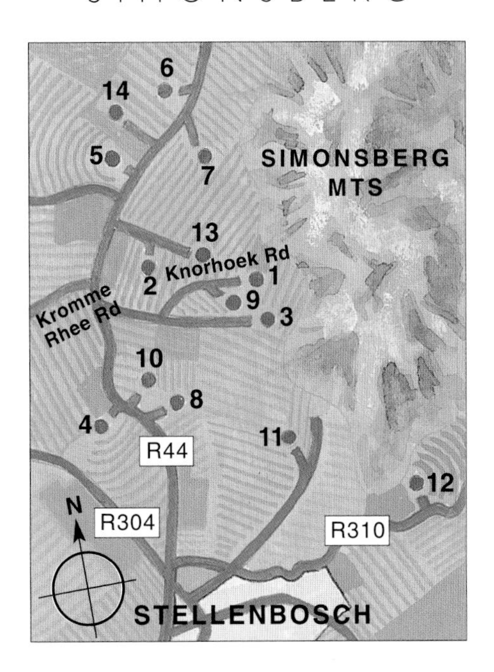

1.	Delheim	8.	Morgenhof
2.	Kanonkop	9.	Muratie
3.	Knorhoek	10.	Remhoogte
4.	L'Avenir	11.	Rustenberg
5.	Laibach	12.	Thelema
6.	Le Bonheur	13.	Uitkyk
7.	Lievland	14.	Warwick

KANONKOP

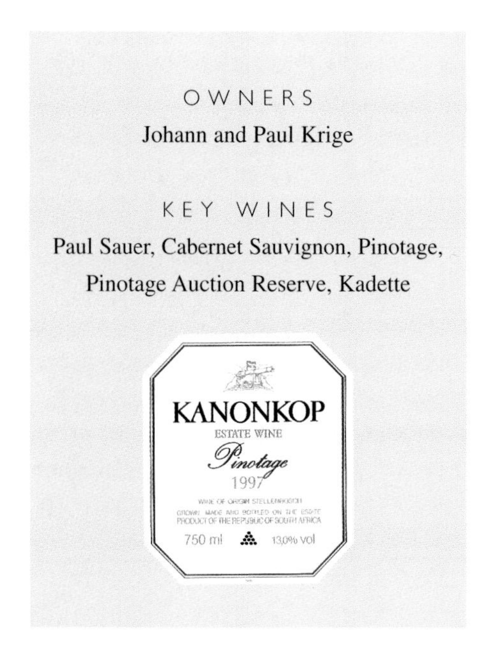

OWNERS
Johann and Paul Krige

KEY WINES
Paul Sauer, Cabernet Sauvignon, Pinotage, Pinotage Auction Reserve, Kadette

This is one of the Cape's most high-powered wineries, whose international accolades have single-handedly placed South Africa among the quality wine producers of the world. In the last decade, vintner Beyers Truter has been voted Winemaker of the Year at the International Wine & Spirits Competition and his Paul Sauer Bordeaux-style blend has twice won the Château Pichon-Longueville Comtesse de Lalande trophy for 'best blended red wine worldwide'.

Kanonkop has been producing a trio of top reds for the past three decades. The Paul Sauer blend of Cabernet, Cabernet Franc and sometimes Merlot, the varietal Cabernet and the Pinotage are all marked by the pure power of fruit and oak, neither noticeably New World nor elegantly Old World. These are Cape reds at their best, with the Pinotage being a

TOP: The winning team of proprietors – Johann and Paul Krige and their internationally acclaimed vintner Beyers Truter have established Kanonkop (**ABOVE**) as one of the Cape's 'First Growths', renowned for Pinotage, Cabernet and a classic red blend.

standard bearer for the full-bodied rich and robust style many see as establishing this home-bred grape among the world's more renowned varieties. The secret of Kanonkop's success, one suspects, lies in continuity of ownership and winemaker.

The farm, once part of Uitkyk, was owned by the Sauer family from early in the 20th century. It was second-generation Paul Sauer, a national cabinet minister, who starting growing wine grapes in the 1930s. The farm was later taken over by son-in-law Jannie Krige, whose two sons are in charge today: Johann (business manager) and Paul (vineyard manager). More than three decades have seen just two winemakers in the cellar: Jan Boland Coetzee (now at Vriesenhof) and Beyers Truter, who celebrated his 20th vintage in 2000.

A strong, outspoken character, Truter is the Cape's champion of Pinotage. Trained in chemistry, he is critical of complacency in his craft, constantly analysing the effects of viticultural and oenological techniques on wine quality. Vineyard renewal at Kanonkop is ongoing on the 140ha of vineyard land, comprising both high-lying stony, pebbly, granite soils and lower, sandier soils that were intensively prepared during the '80s before planting. Bush vines, mostly Pinotage, are being replanted, but some 50ha of old vines are being replaced by virus-free, trellised vineyards.

He is also constantly studying and refining vinification techniques, from length of skin contact to the number of times a day the skin cap is punched down during fermentation. He remains a proponent of open-tank fermentation. The first Cape winemaker to treat Pinotage to new, small-oak maturation on a commercial scale, he is a traditionalist, favouring Vicard medium-toasted French oak in a combination of new and used barrels. He eschews the modern trend towards American oak which, he believes, may initially seduce with its strong, sweet vanilla flavours but does not stay the pace. 'Aged Pinotage can become so smooth, so delicate, so Burgundian.' And he firmly believes it capable of producing wines of French First Growth status.

L'AVENIR

OWNER
Marc Wiehe

KEY WINES
Pinotage, Pinotage Reserve, Cabernet Sauvignon, L'Ami Simon, Chardonnay, Chardonnay Special Cuvée, Sauvignon Blanc, Chenin Blanc, Vin d'Erstelle, Rosé Maison, Special Late Harvest, Vin de Meurveur Noble Late Harvest

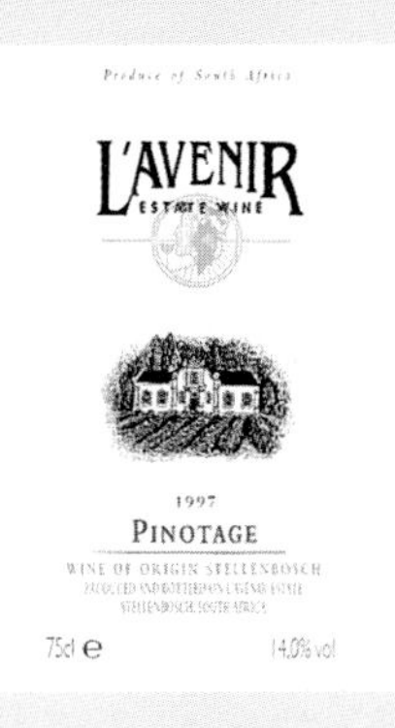

An unlikely pair, the smooth, suave, French Mauritian sugar merchant and the voluble, bespectacled Afrikaner. But Marc Wiehe and Francois Naudé share a passion for wine that has set this relatively new estate on the fast track to becoming as highly vaunted as its neighbours in the prime Simonsberg-Muldersvlei bowl.

Wiehe bought the farm in 1992, taking over some excellent raw material formerly delivered to Nederburg. Some 45ha of vines are planted on varying slopes facing north to south to south-west, most of which catch the cool maritime breezes off False Bay. These provide for a fairly eclectic range that will be maintained with new plantings of bush vine Pinotage and regrafting of a new, virus-free clone onto Weisser Riesling rootstock. Sauvignon Blanc is replacing Cinsaut.

The idea is to remain small; the winery produces around 20 000 cases, but includes something for most tastes. It is bound up in a shared philosophy between owner and vintner that 'wine is for drinking'; therefore tasting is not an intellectual exercise – it is simply a means to find out what wines you would like to drink.

ABOVE: L'Avenir is one of the promising new wine estates in Stellenbosch, set on the road to success by talented winemaker Francois Naudé (**OVERLEAF**) and his boss, urbane French Mauritian Marc Wiehe.

MORGENHOF

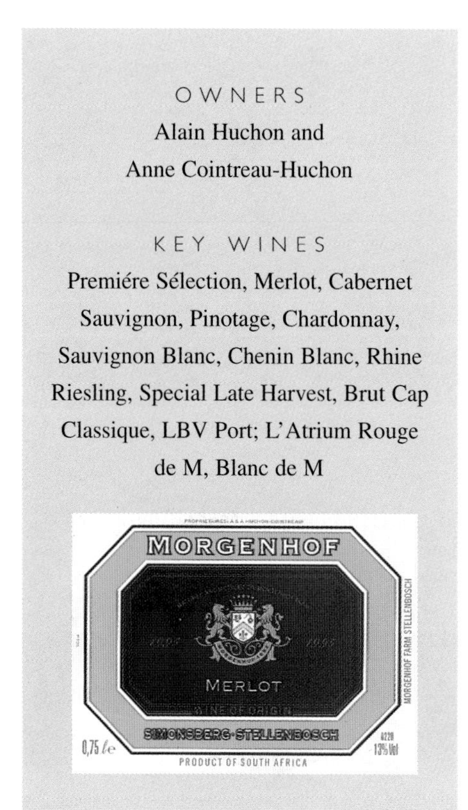

OWNERS

Alain Huchon and Anne Cointreau-Huchon

KEY WINES

Premiére Sélection, Merlot, Cabernet Sauvignon, Pinotage, Chardonnay, Sauvignon Blanc, Chenin Blanc, Rhine Riesling, Special Late Harvest, Brut Cap Classique, LBV Port; L'Atrium Rouge de M, Blanc de M

Naudé came to winemaking as a rookie. A pharmacist by profession, he moved from Pretoria to the Cape winelands to try to find his niche, experimenting with a Cabernet Sauvignon for own consumption. Its bold flavours and density of both fruit and tannin caught the attention of Wiehe, who was looking for a winemaker. Naudé rose to the challenge with skillfully made, easy-drinking blends of Merlot and Cabernet (L'Ami Simon) and a very tasty, off-dry blend of the farm's minor whites Colombard and Crouchen Blanc, touched up with some Rhine Riesling. Then Naudé hit the headlines with a Pinotage, his favourite variety, made in what was already his recognisably bold style from 30-year-old vines. The fruit was wonderfully rich and sweet.

Next up were some winning whites: a very Burgundian-style Chardonnay showing the winemaker's skill with oaking, more subtle here than with his robust reds. And again with his award-winning Chenin Blanc, where he challenged the new convention that Chenin needed to be wooded to be regarded as 'serious' by coming up with an incredibly rich, off-dry, unwooded Chenin. His secret lay in the use of very ripe grapes, slightly affected by botrytis.

A historic Cape Dutch farm imbued with French flair by Alain and Anne Huchon, who bought the property in 1993, Morgenhof has built up a solid line-up of notably rich reds, recently topped by the release of a flagship Bordeaux-style blend called Premiére Sélection, a mature, meaty, savoury wine. Though the best Cabernet goes into this carefully bottle-aged blend, the farm's varietal Cabernet is equally substantial, while the Merlot is one of the most opulent in the Cape.

The hilly vineyards of up to 450m above sea level offer a range of aspects and granite, shale and sandstone soils, ideal for both white and red premium varieties. Morgenhof's wines have a distinctly French elegance as a counterpoint to their lush fruitiness. This style is echoed in a very fine Chardonnay, subtly oaked and fresh yet with a degree of buttery smoothness. Similarly the Sauvignon Blanc, from newly planted Loire clones, while Morgenhof's Chenin Blanc, one of the new-wave, serious, wooded

The designer circular underground barrel-maturation cellar at Morgenhof, like Vergelegen, is reminiscent of that of Château Lafite-Rothschild in Bordeaux.

ABOVE: The new tasting room at Morgenhof, a combination of restored Cape Dutch architecture with elegant French style.
OPPOSITE TOP: The dynamic Morgenhof duo of winemaker Rianie Strydom and owner Anne Cointreau-Huchon.

Cape versions, also proves that French flair provides a fillip for our most ordinary whites.

A pretty good Cap Classique and one of the Cape's rare Late Bottled Vintage ports, predominantly Tinta Barocca, give an indication of the scope of the quality possible from this newly registered estate. Currently around 60ha of vineyards are still being replanted and forested land cleared for new vines. Ultimately, nearly 85ha will be devoted primarily to premium varieties, as well as selected Chenin Blanc vines and port classic Touriga Naçional. The best will carry the Morgenhof Estate and Simonsberg Wine of Origin label; anything not meeting very exacting standards will be bottled as L'Atrium Wine of Origin Stellenbosch.

Backed by the able and enthusiastic Huchons – the canny Anne Huchon is a member of the famous Cointreau family of Cognac and the Champagne House of Gosset – new winemaker Rianie Strydom (married to Rust en Vrede's new winemaker Louis Strydom) is faced with the challenge of filling former winemaker Jean Daneel's sizable shoes. But working stints in St-Emilion and a long apprenticeship under Daneel, familiarising herself with the vineyards and the sophisticated 25 000-case winery and awesome circular underground barrel-maturation cellar, have equipped her well.

RUSTENBERG

OWNER
Simon Barlow

KEY WINES
Five Soldiers Chardonnay; Peter Barlow Cabernet Sauvignon; Rustenberg Stellenbosch (red blend), Rustenberg Stellenbosch Chardonnay; Brampton Chardonnay, Cabernet Merlot

Simon Barlow inherited Rustenberg from his father, the late Peter Barlow, who helped build up the mighty industrial multi-national Barlow-Rand. The 1 000ha mixed dairy, fruit and wine farm was a hobby. But to his son, the historic property, with its classic Cape Dutch buildings and a tradition of winemaking that spans three centuries, was home. 'And now it's my business.'

LEFT: The Schoongezicht manor house, behind which a spanking new cellar complex has been built by Rustenberg owner Simon Barlow (**ABOVE**), here pictured with his wife Rozanne.

In 1996 Barlow embarked on a multi-million-rand transformation of the farm: a 1 000-ton fermentation cellar, complete with stainless-steel fermentation tanks suspended from the thatch-covered rafters. Adjoining is the underground vaulted 900-barrel maturation cellar linked by underground passage to a Cap Classique production facility in the 18th-century cellar.

Vines are being shifted to higher ground on the Simonsberg slopes behind. Here cool, deep, well-drained decomposed granite soils will be planted to Sauvignon Blanc, Chardonnay, Cabernet Sauvignon, Merlot, Cabernet Franc. Those 'hotspots' are earmarked for Rhône varieties – Shiraz, Grenache, Mouvèdre – a new direction for Rustenberg. This will take the current 60ha under vine up to 120ha. Grapes also come in from 45ha of Chardonnay and Sauvignon Blanc on the Helderberg slopes of Nooitgedacht, the Barlows' private home.

Barlow withdrew the Rustenberg label from the market in 1995 to re-evaluate the farm's direction, which is when vintner Etienne le Riche left after 20 years in the cellar. Young Kiwi import Rod Easthope re-introduced the new-look wines and, while still consulting for Barlow, has now been replaced by young talent Adi Badenhorst, formerly at Groote Post in Darling.

The fresh-faced, value-for-money Brampton label with which Rustenberg re-entered the market in 1996 raised traditionalists' eyebrows but has since wooed all with its New World fruity friendliness. The Rustenberg name is back, but is reserved for the more subtle, serious wines, like the middle-tier Rustenberg Stellenbosch range, which will be vinified in a style that reflects a specific terroir rather than varietal character.

These wines are recognisably Rustenberg: medium-bodied and elegant, yet imbued with a new freshness and fruitiness that the last vintages under this venerable label were perhaps lacking. At the top of the heap will be single-vineyard wines, such as the Rustenberg Peter Barlow Cabernet Sauvignon and the Five Soldiers Chardonnay, naturally vinified to capture the essence of a particularly fine block of vines.

THELEMA

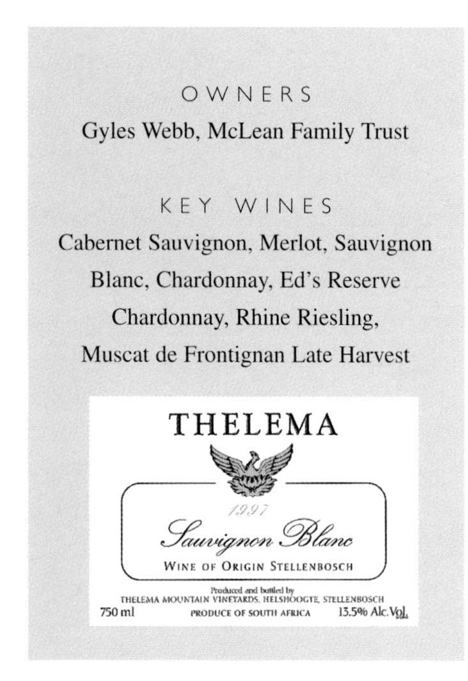

Gyles Webb came to winemaking unfettered by history and family tradition. He's an accountant who was inspired by a bottle of Burgundy to study winemaking and, in 1983, with wife Barbara and her parents, to buy a 160ha fruit farm at the top of the Helshoogte pass.

'The farm has a very strong terroir identity,' says Webb, which is probably most prominent in his minty Cabernets. At between 370m and 640m above sea level, Thelema is one of the Cape's highest and coolest vineyards with deep, decomposed granite soils. Though winter rainfall and good soil moisture retention are a given, a new dam has recently been built to allow Webb to minutely manage vine stress. Visits to California and Australia impressed him with the quality of New World fruit. 'The top guys are combining power with refinement. And that's the route I'd like to take.'

From his maiden 1988 vintage, Webb has made his mark with wines that had intensity, complexity and international appeal. Though he is not looking for 'upfront fruit that hits you between the eyes', his wines have been modern in the Cape context in that they have captured copybook varietal characteristics and good, virus-free fruit backed by the finest French oak.

The Cabernet Sauvignon and Merlot, previously combined in benchmark new-wave Cape blends, now star individually, vying with each other for lushness of fruit, intensity of flavour and that recognisable Thelema mintiness. Webb's standard Chardonnays are delicious mixtures of citrus and marmalade fruitiness and rich, toasty oak. His gooseberry-rich and racy Sauvignon Blanc is probably one of the Cape's most popular wines – it's sold out practically before release. And there's more to come, from new plantings in nearby leased vineyards of his first Shiraz, maybe some Petit Verdot, more Cabernet and Sauvignon Blanc, to special export bottlings of bought-in grapes under the Stormy Cape label.

TOP: Gyles Webb and his wife Barbara, veteran marathon runner who does Thelema's local wine deliveries ... by truck. The functional style of their barrel cellar (**ABOVE**) epitomises this down-to-earth couple's attitude to wine, too often surrounded by hype and pretension.

WARWICK

OWNERS

Stan and Norma Ratcliffe

KEY WINES

Trilogy, Cabernet Sauvignon, Merlot, Cabernet Franc, Bush Vine Pinotage, Chardonnay, Sauvignon Blanc

Warwick
ESTATE WINE
TRILOGY
1996
WINE OF ORIGIN STELLENBOSCH
12.5% vol PRODUCE OF SOUTH AFRICA 750 ml

The diminutive, outspoken Norma Ratcliffe, former Canadian champion snow-skier and self-taught winemaker, is taking a back seat in the Warwick cellar these days, having handed over to new appointee Anne-Marée Mostert, formerly of Mont Rochelle, just before the 2000 harvest. She intends spending more time in the vineyard.

There were no vines on Warwick when Stan and Norma bought the place in 1964. Their early plantings of Cabernet Sauvignon were followed by Merlot and Cabernet Franc as early as 1980, when these varieties were just beginning to show up in the Cape. From those first three tons of Cabernet in 1984, footstomped, using rudimentary, borrowed equipment and some of the Cape's first few small French-oak barrels, Warwick has grown into a 200-ton cellar, complete with extensive new maturation cellar. Red wines remain its forté and traditional clarifying methods are still applied.

All the vineyards – about 60ha of Klapmutskop slopes – have been renewed with virus-free material, with the wines showing a more modern, richly fruited accessibility without sacrificing structure. Use of new wood has been tempered. The Cabernet remains a more austere wine, classically dry. The flagship Trilogy Bordeaux-style blend shows an increase in its Merlot content. The varietal Merlot is perhaps the softest, earliest-drinking of Warwick's reds. But, despite the Trilogy's status – it has its ups-and-downs – it is the Cabernet Franc that stands out in the Warwick range. A variety that Norma helped pioneer in this country, the Warwick is a consistently rich, dense, chocolatey wine.

Ratcliffe has also shown her hand at Pinotage, exploiting some decades-old bush vines to come up with a big, plummy wine that has joined the ranks of the Cape's finest, new-wave Pinotages, with emphasis on fruit rather than tannin.

Norma and Stan Ratcliffe have introduced new blood into Warwick: son Michael and talented young winemaker Anne-Marée Mostert.

DELHEIM

German builder Hans-Otto Hoheisen bought the farm De Driesprongh in 1938 and, together with nephew Michael 'Spatz' Sperling, started developing newly named Delheim viticulturally, leaving Sperling to manage it alone from 1957.

The farm's steep, clayey, shaded slopes and high rainfall are not conducive to full-bodied reds, but the 80ha on the Klapmutskop, bought in 1975, set Delheim on the path to producing quality reds, such as the Bordeaux-style Grand Reserve in 1984. But it is the Shiraz, big, plummy and savoury, that has people taking notice. The best wines have been accorded 'estate' status under the Vera Cruz Estate label, giving vintner Philip Costandius another string to his bow.

KNORHOEK

Most of the plantings on this 125ha mountainous farm were sold as bulk wine and, more recently, as top-quality grapes to exclusive small wineries. Now brothers Hansie and James van Niekerk, fourth-generation residents, have chosen the three most promising varieties for the first 5 000 cases of Pinotage, Cabernet and Sauvignon Blanc, made at Kanonkop, Simonsig and Kleine Zalze, to whom they also sell. An own cellar is in the pipeline.

One of the Cape's early proponents of small, new-wood barrels for maturing wine, the Ratcliffes now also include used barrels in their oak mix for a more subtle, softer effect.

LAIBACH

Once part of a massive landholding including neighbouring Warwick dating back to 1818, the 50ha Laibach property was an important supplier to Nederburg until German manufacturer Friedrich Laibach bought it in 1994.

The barrel-fermented and matured Chenin is up there among the Cape's finest new 'serious' exponents of this common local variety, while the Chardonnay is a lovely, lemony, tropical fruit mouthful with the oak adding a subtle complexity. The Pinotage is a full-bodied, red berry- and banana-flavoured wine, richly endowed with French and American oak vanillins. The Cabernets, Merlots and blends of the two show a profusion of fruit and soft, ripe tannins. German consulting winemaker is assisted by Francois van Zyl.

LE BONHEUR

Owned by Distillers and now one of the Lusan Premium Wines properties, immaculately restored Cape Dutch Le Bonheur is picking the fruits of an intensive soil enrichment and replanting programme started in the '70s. Winemaker Sakkie Kotze now has 70ha of Chardonnay on the well-drained middle ground, Sauvignon Blanc and Cabernet Sauvignon on the high-lying north- and north-east facing aspects, and Merlot and more Sauvignon Blanc on the poorer, low-lying soils. All these wines show a combination of New World fruit intensity and Old World elegance. The Prima blend of Cabernet Sauvignon and Merlot is a classic of rare consistency.

LIEVLAND

'Quo vadis?' asked many when the redoubtable team of owner Paul Benadé and his vintner of over a decade, Abé Beukes, split up just before the 1998 harvest. Together they had built up the farm since Benadé took over from father Dan in 1986, replacing mostly marginal white varieties with noble reds in the decomposed granite soils and making the Rhône-like Shiraz the star of the 65ha. The estate's Bordeaux-style blend DVB, dominated by Cabernet Franc, is elegant and the everyday-drinking Cinsaut-based Lievlander a true value-for-money buy. A pioneer of delicately wooded, Sauternes-style Noble Late Harvests and a champion of characterful Rhine Rieslings, Lievland now has a young Scottish-born winemaker James Farquharson in the cellar. Recent plantings include more Shiraz and other Rhône varieties Grenache and Viognier.

MURATIE

The farm came full circle when it came back into the late Ronnie Melck's family about a decade ago. Ancestor Martin Melck and his descendants owned the property from around 1763 to 1897. The modern-day Melcks have renewed the predominantly red-wine vineyards on deep, decomposed granite soils with disease-free, new-clone Cabernet, Shiraz and Merlot, as well as Pinot Noir – Muratie was the first in the Cape to plant Pinot Noir in the '20s. But the essence of the farm, in the old, oak-shaded Cape Dutch homestead and dilapidated, low-ceilinged little cellar, was retained. Young Burgundian vintner Bruno Lorenzon joins the family each pressing season to turn out, among others, the stylish, elegant Ansela van de Caab Cabernet/ Merlot blend and a very fine, ripe, full-bodied Pinot Noir. A port and fortified Muscat d'Alexandrie called Amber Forever are all-time favourites.

REMHOOGTE

Former Gauteng construction engineer Murray Boustred bought this run-down 60ha property in 1994. The 40ha of vines included new-clone Cabernet, Merlot and old Pinotage, most of which had been going to Morgenhof. But Boustred, taking some on-the-job lessons from former Morgenhof cellarmaster Jean Daneel, has started bottling small quantities under his own Remhoogte label. All three varietal reds are deeply flavoured, rich, with immediate appeal, despite serious French (and some American) oaking. Vinified at Morgenhof, they are barrel-matured in an old farm building on Remhoogte.

UITKYK

With its double-storey, flat-roofed, 19th-century Cape Georgian homestead, Uitkyk was first granted in 1712. But it was 20th-century Prussian proprietor Georg van Carlowitz who established vines here. Now owned by the Lusan Premium Wines joint venture between Distillers and Hans Schreiber, the 600ha farm has been meticulously restored. The 180ha of sloping vineyards, on weathered granite and loamy Table Mountain sandstone-derived soils, have been replanted to noble varieties. Long-time winemaker Theo Brink produces the well-known Uitkyk Riesling, a Sauvignon Blanc, and the Carlonet red blend, as well as fragrant Cabernet Shiraz blend.

Underrated Le Bonheur makes a most drinkable red blend called Prima and a great Cabernet.

BOTTELARY

An official ward of the Stellenbosch district since 1996, Bottelary is centred around a series of hills separating the fringes of the northern suburbs of Cape Town around Kuils River from the Stellenbosch winelands proper. The impetus for the demarcation was the recognition of the area's potential for good reds.

South-, east- and west-facing slopes provide viticultural versatility, while the direct effects of the summer south-east wind off False Bay gives Bottelary a cooler climate than the rest of Stellenbosch. This maritime influence is a great boon to quality, as are the low-vigour, disintegrated Table Mountain sandstone-derived soils, which are well drained – the area receives plenty of winter rain driven in from the north-west.

Though not officially in the Bottelary ward, mention must be made of two new 'industrial' wine developments on the fringes. Glen Carlou's Walter Finlayson has collaborated with former engineer and marketing whizz Rob Coppoolse in a winery slap-bang in the middle of a new industrial development in Brackenfell in Cape Town's northern suburbs. The 1 000-tonner, close to major grape suppliers in Stellenbosch, Paarl and Durbanville, as well as Cape Town International airport and Table Bay harbour for transport overseas, includes an award-winning Sentinel Shiraz in its flagship range of premium varietal wines.

The Victoria & Alfred Waterfront is the site of young Bruce Jack's 'pavement' winery, Flagstone. It comprises a warehouse, open-air, jacket-cooled steel tanks and loose-standing refrigerated containers for barrel-fermentation. The South African-born oenology graduate of Australia's University of Adelaide trucks in grapes from prime areas, crosses a minefield of innovative cellar procedures and comes up with some intriguing wines, including a fruit-driven, lip-smacking old BK5-clone Pinot Noir.

BOTTELARY

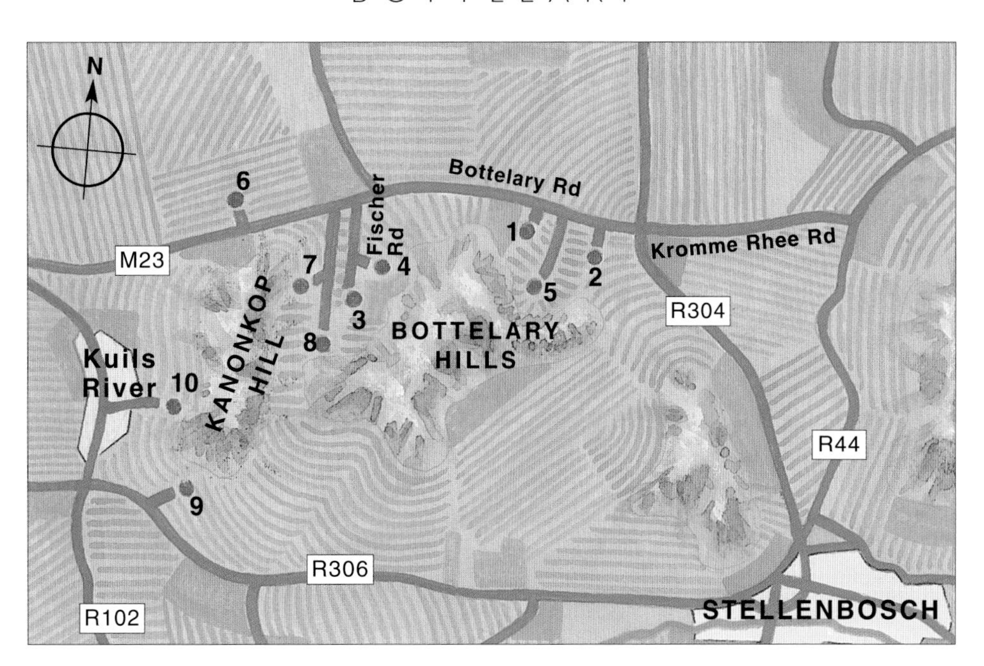

1. Bottelary
2. Bouwland
3. Fort Simon
4. Goede Hoop
5. Hartenberg
6. Hazendal
7. Kaapzicht
8. Mooiplaas
9. Saxenburg
10. Zevenwacht

OWNERS

Tanya Browne (Mackenzie) and Fiona Mackenzie

KEY WINES

Shiraz, Merlot, Cabernet, Cabernet Sauvignon/Merlot, Cabernet Sauvignon/Shiraz, Zinfandel, Pontac, Chardonnay Reserve, Chardonnay, Weisser Riesling, Sauvignon Blanc, Chatillon, L'Estreux

'We would like to be considered among the top 20 wine producers in the Cape,' admits winemaker Carl Schultz. This is neither idle fantasy nor misplaced ambition.

The estate, one of the Cape's oldest and dating back to the early 17th century, has excellent deep, moisture-retaining, red clay-based Hutton and Clovelly soils over roughly two-thirds of its nearly 100ha of vineyard land, particularly good for Cabernet and Merlot. The soils at the lower end of the east- and west-facing slopes are shallower, stonier, more humid Kroonstad and Longridge types, where the prolific growth of Shiraz and Pinotage is naturally curbed, therefore yielding fruit of greater concentration.

This is primarily a red wine farm, with some 70% planted to Shiraz, Cabernet, Merlot and Pinotage, as well as the locally uncommon Zinfandel and the rare Pontac. Hartenberg Shiraz, one of the Cape's more Rhône-like exponents with its spicy, savoury elegance, draws on vines dating back to 1974/'75. 'This is Hartenberg's heritage,' says winemaker Carl Schultz. This qualified, intellectual winemaker has been producing some fine wines, particularly Chardonnay, Merlot and Shiraz, since taking over in the 650-ton cellar from Danie Truter in 1994.

It is Shiraz, together with rarities Pontac and Zinfandel, that made a name for the modern-day Hartenberg, thanks to the talents and dedication of the Finlayson family during the 1960s and '70s and subsequent ownership by Gilbeys during the '80s. Replanting to primarily Cabernet and Shiraz had already started by the time businessman, cattle farmer and avid wine collector Ken Mackenzie took over in 1987. He has since handed over to his daughters.

In 1994 a long-term replanting programme was embarked upon. Plant material selection has been rigorous, particularly for the Chardonnay, Weisser Riesling, Shiraz and new recruit, Sauvignon Blanc. Soils dictate what varieties are planted – Rhône specialities such as Mouvèdre and Grenache, Cabernet Franc and Pinotage will soon be added. In tandem with the replanting programme came a major investment in up to 1 000 small oak barrels. And there's a new cellar due to be built, necessitated by a sizable increase in annual production from just 12 000 cases in 1994 to 50 000 cases once the farm is fully productive.

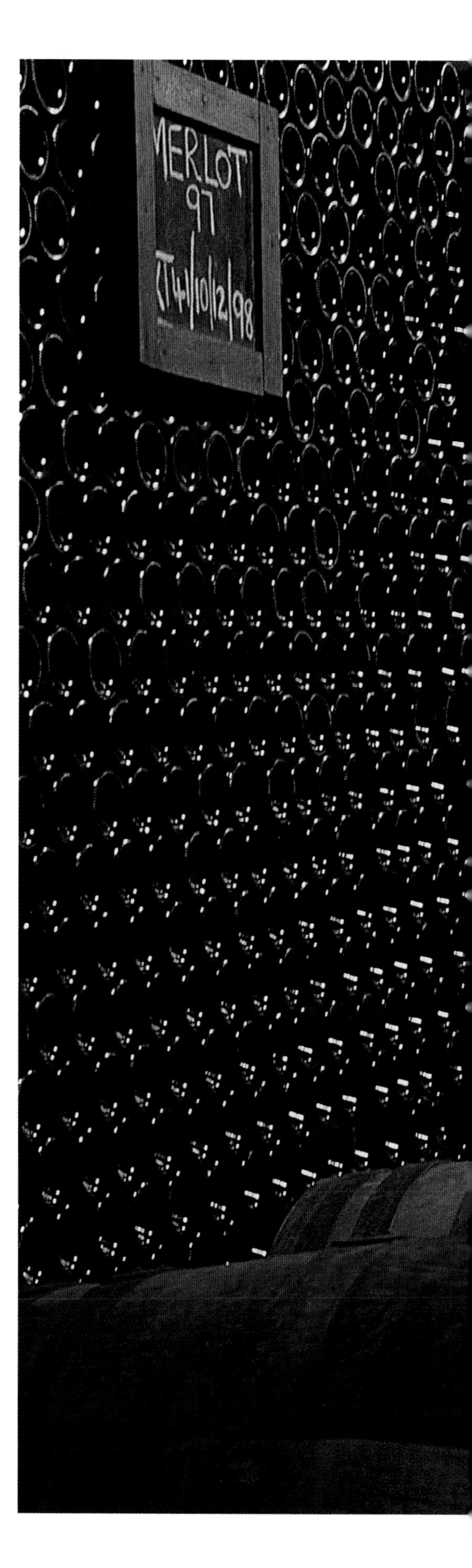

TOP: Tanya and James Browne now run Hartenberg with Tanya's sister Fiona Mackenzie, while winemaker Carl Schultz works on his classic Shirazes and Merlots in the cavernous underground cellar (**RIGHT**).

SAXENBURG

OWNER
Adrian Bührer

KEY WINES
Private Collection Cabernet Sauvignon, PC Merlot, PC Pinotage, PC Shiraz, Saxenburg Cabernet, Merlot, Pinotage, Gwendolyn, Manuel, Vin Rouge, PC Chardonnay, Sauvignon Blanc, Grand Vin Blanc, PC Le Phantom Brut Cap Classique, PC Le Rive de Saxenbourg Natural Sweet

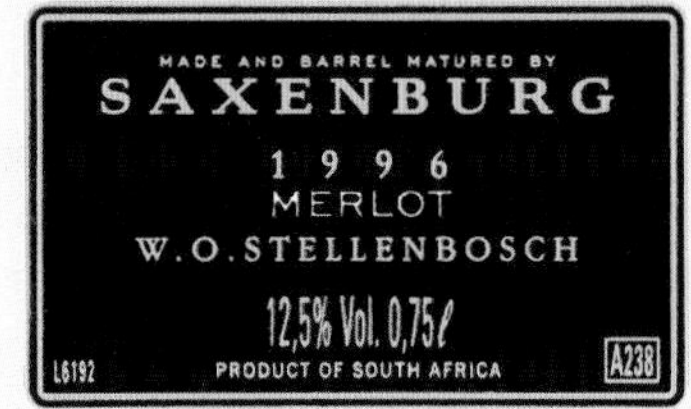

Despite a strong Saxon background, Saxenburg's modern viticultural bent lies towards France. Ownership has passed from 1693 free burgher Joachim Sax through two Swedes to its present-day Swiss proprietor Adrian Bührer, who bought the farm in 1989. Bührer's subsequent acquisition of Château Capion in the burgeoning French winelands of Languedoc-Roussillon has led to a novel, cross-viticultural venture between his two properties. And the gregarious, enormously competent winemaker Nico van der Merwe is happily working two vintages in two different hemispheres each year.

The marriage of Cape and French fruit has produced two interesting, very drinkable blends: the Grand Vin Blanc, combining Chardonnay and Chenin, and the Vin Rouge, a melange of Cinsaut, Carignan, Grenache, Cabernet Sauvignon, Cabernet Franc and Tinta Barocca.

One step up in the Saxenburg portfolio are classic blends, introduced by the fruity, spicy, smooth and elegant Gwendolyn Shiraz Cabernet blend and the Manuel Cabernet Merlot. But it is

Saxenburg's Private Collection range, made in small quantities, that has placed this winery among the Cape's top echelon of new-wave producers. Van der Merwe first worked with different clones through bought-in grapes,

ABOVE: Saxenburg's vineyards overlook the distant False Bay and the northern suburbs of greater Cape Town. **TOP:** Winemaker Nico van der Merwe.

selected and harvested by him, while getting to know the Saxenburg vineyards. Only after about four vintages in the cellar did replanting of some 100ha on Saxenburg begin, the concentration on Cabernet Sauvignon, Cabernet Franc, Merlot and Shiraz, and Pinotage to capture exports.

Reds are fermented in open cement tanks and pumped over. Traditionalist Van der Merwe tries to avoid filtration, cold stabilisation and pre-fermentation sulphuring, fining only with egg white and only if necessary. His wines are wooded in either French Nevers or American oak, the latter specifically for the Pinotage and Shiraz. And the Shiraz, pure fruit mixed with herbs, pepper and sweet vanilla oak, is unequivocally the farm's flagship, though the Cabernet, with its leafy, capsicum aromas and rich, ripe and juicy fruit, is right up there.

Balance marks the whites as well. The Chardonnay is a blend of mostly oak-fermented and matured wine, with a dash of unwooded Chardonnay to add typical freshness and elegance. The Sauvignon Blanc can be a stunner, made in the softer, to many more drinkable, style by bringing out the variety's tropical fruit character.

BOUWLAND

This is a new wine farm, purchased by Kanonkop's Johann and Paul Krige and winemaker Beyers Truter, in 1997. The 130ha already had 60ha of vines comprising mostly white varieties with some Merlot, but the trio is replanting to red, predominantly their speciality Pinotage, but also Cabernet Sauvignon which, together with the Merlot, will be used for blending. An interim Merlot Cabernet Sauvignon blend, vinified at Kanonkop, is an accessible and affordable wine. A new cellar is 'on the cards'.

FORT SIMON

Renier Uys' new 650-ton winery is a massive brick-walled fort, complete with parapets, moats and drawbridges, built on the farm Hou Moed bought by his father in 1961. Most of the farm's 60ha of vines are white varieties (Sauvignon Blanc, Chardonnay and Chenin Blanc) bought by Distillers. But with winemaker Marinus Bredell now bottling wines under the Fort Simon label, Renier and brother Petrus are banking on reds, particularly Cabernet Sauvignon and Shiraz. To date, the Merlot, Pinotage and Shiraz have produced fruity, easy-drinking wines.

GOEDE HOOP

Once a predominantly white wine farm, Goede Hoop became known for its reds during nearly 20 years as a member of The Bergkelder. But over the past five years since going solo, former teacher turned winemaker Pieter Bestbier is re-establishing Goede Hoop whites: a softly fruity, crisp Sauvignon Blanc and his first Chardonnay both show great promise. Meanwhile, his Vintage Rouge has shed its Pinotage and Shiraz components to become a classic Merlot Cabernet blend, fruity and elegant, as are the varietal Cabernet and Shiraz. Bestbier, the third generation farming on these steep, gravelly slopes, still relies on old-fashioned open-tank fermentation.

HAZENDAL

This historic Cape Dutch wine farm may finally fulfil its potential under ownership of wealthy Russian-born entrepreneur Mark Voloshin with winemaker Ronell Wiid in the cellar.

Voloshin bought the rather run-down property in 1994 – it had been in the Bosman family since 1831. He has restored the 1764 national monument manor house and old cellar and built a new, hi-tech, 800-ton winery. Nearly 70ha of white varieties are being replanted, concentrating on Merlot, Cabernet Sauvignon, Shiraz, Pinotage and Pinot Noir. The latter, together with new Chardonnay material, is earmarked for a Cap Classique. The first young Cabernet and Shiraz vinified for the second label, Kleine Hazen, show concentrated fruit and soft tannins, and a subsequent similar blend under the premium Hazendal label won Wiid the prestigious Diners Club Winemaker of the Year award in '99.

KAAPZICHT

The farm Rozendal came into the Steytler family in 1946 and supplied bulk wines, grapes and concentrates to wholesalers. But by the 1980s, winemaker Danie and brother George, the vineyard manager, started bottling up to 75% of the total 1 300-ton crop. Kaapzicht Pinotages rate among the Cape's benchmarks, with their typical cherry and banana aromas, juicy fruit and ripe tannins complemented by spicy new oak. Kaapzicht Cabernet has always been a fine example of this variety. But it is Shiraz that gets Steytler's vote as a future star.

MOOIPLAAS

This picturesque, Cape Dutch farm, bought by Nicholas Roos in 1963 and a supplier of quality bulk wine through Vinfruco to the UK market, recently acquired estate status and bottled three wines under its own label. The Sauvignon Blanc has done well, but son Louis, the winemaker, believes the future of the farm lies with reds: the Pinotage, from mostly 25-year-old bush vines, with classic cherry fruit and banana flavours; the Cabernet with the typically minty character of new clones. Merlot is used as a blending ingredient, a Pinot Noir is in barrel and newly planted Shiraz should find its way into bottle within the next few years.

ZEVENWACHT

Bought in 1992 by Johannesburg businessman Harold Johnson, Zevenwacht's cool climate produces generally elegant wines. Some 200ha are planted to premium white and red varieties. Winemaker Hilko Hegewisch makes a champion wooded Chenin Blanc and a still white blend of Pinot Noir and Chardonnay. Zevenwacht reds are also improving steadily, combining fruitiness with finesse. Merlot does well here and more is being planted for a Reserve bottling and a Cabernet blend. Shiraz is another star, brilliantly blending sweet fruit, Rhône-like pepperiness and French-oak toastiness. The Zevenrivieren premium range, from Johnson's Jonkershoek property, is being rejuvenated.

DEVON VALLEY

One of the newer wards in the district of Stellenbosch, Devon Valley was established in 1997. The area has long been a source of top quality fruit for nearby Distillers' cellar, The Bergkelder and Stellenbosch Farmers Winery. It also used to be the home of Robert Fuller, an exclusive range of reds made on-site by liquor and wine wholesaler Gilbeys, which has recently handed over its wine portfolio to newly formed African Wine & Spirits, based in Constantia, which bottles Robert Fuller, Bertrams, as well as mass-marketed Craighall and Mondial wines.

The Devon Valley flag is kept flying by some fine, small independent cellars, as well as JC Le Roux (owned by Distillers), whose top sparkling wines are made in what is the Cape's first 'House' of sparkling wine. They have banded together to form the Devon Valley Vintners Association, with the intention of marketing the ward as a distinctive, top-quality wine area.

The valley is formed by a natural watershed on the south-eastern side of the Bottelary hills, fed by the Veldwagters River and encompassing about 1 300ha of vineyard land, with mainly south-, east- and west-facing aspects, sharing similar red, clay-based Hutton soils and a mild climate. The area is 5°–6°C cooler than Koelenhof just over the rise, not quite as warm as some of Stellenbosch. The south-easter off nearby False Bay is funnelled up into the Koelenhof area, making a slight angled detour into and over the Devon Valley hills, where the funnelling effect drops the temperature even further. One can see it in the depth of flavour, and also in the overall elegance of the wines.

DEVON VALLEY

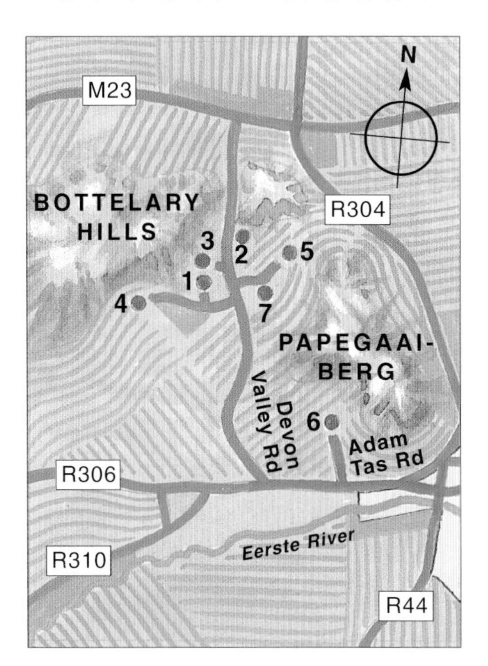

1. Clos Malverne
2. Devon Hill
3. House of JC Le Roux
4. Louisvale
5. Meinert/Devon Crest
6. Middelvlei
7. Sylvanvale

JC LE ROUX

OWNER
Distillers Corporation

KEY WINES
JC Le Roux Pinot Noir Cap Classique, Chardonnay MCC, Pongrácz MCC NV, La Vallée MCC, Sauvignon Blanc Sparkling, La Chanson, Le Domaine

This dedicated 'Champagne House' is a first for South Africa, established in 1998 in the former Bertrams cellars, owned by wine and spirit producer/wholesaler Gilbeys and sold to competitor Distillers in 1996. Over R50-million was spent on the project. The 14 000m² complex was rebuilt and revamped, offering wine lovers a rare opportunity to view every step of the process from a series of public walkways throughout the massive building.

Between five-million and six-million bottles of bubbly are to be produced here each year, under the keen eye of young oenologist Melanie van der Merwe. Besides about five years of experience in the Distillers' Bergkelder cellars, where she specialised in sparkling wine, this capable young woman has worked at the Champagne House of Roederer and explored both the Veuve Clicquot and Moët & Chandon operations.

The House of JC Le Roux, ideally situated in cool-climate conditions for early pickings of tart fruit for neutral, naturally high-acid base wines, is developing some 64ha of vineyards in Devon Valley. About 30ha on the property itself is being replanted to Pinot Noir, and the rest will be leased for primarily Chardonnay and Sauvignon Blanc.

The two award-winning premium sparkling wines, JC Le Roux Pinot Noir and JC Le Roux Chardonnay, spend over four and five years respectively on the lees, and many more months in the bottle before release. Current vintages on sale still include an '89 and '90. It is the use of reserve cuvées held in massive 7 200 litre wooden vats and the extended bottle maturation which give these wines their wonderfully evolved biscuity aromas and flavours. By comparison, the Pongrácz, a popular non-vintage blend of Chardonnay and Pinot Noir, usually has just more than two years on the lees, providing a fresh, fruity but still complex mouthful.

Spanning the divide between these classics and JC Le Roux's carbonated bubblies is La Vallée. Made from Pinot Gris with 33g/litre sugar, it is the first technically sweet Cap Classique. The result is palate-pleasing smoothness rather than sickly sweetness.

ABOVE: The Cape's first dedicated 'Champagne House', JC Le Roux, in the Devon Valley, where vintner Melanie van der Merwe (**TOP**) and production chief Pierre Marais produce two benchmark, bottle-aged Cap Classiques and the everyday favourite Pongràcz, among others.

MIDDELVLEI

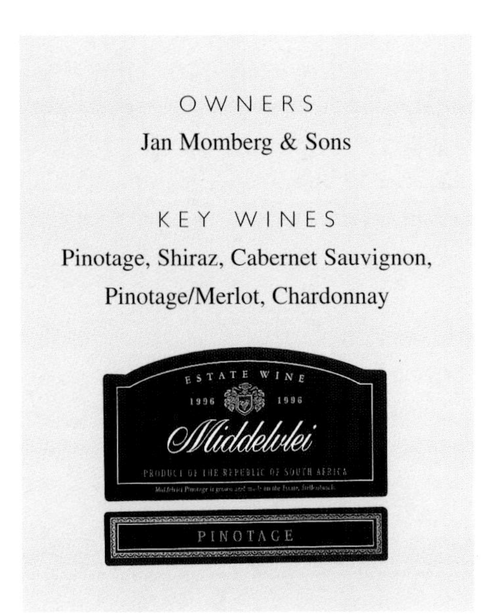

OWNERS
Jan Momberg & Sons

KEY WINES
Pinotage, Shiraz, Cabernet Sauvignon, Pinotage/Merlot, Chardonnay

Middelvlei was traditionally known for its Pinotage, later for its Cabernet Sauvignon and now a rather delicious, novel red mix of Pinotage and Merlot, one of the finest 'traditional' Cape blends. This is prime viticultural land, the last bastion against suburban Stellenbosch sprawl.

Brothers Tinnie and Niels Momberg bought the property in 1919 and pressed their first, mostly fortified wines a year later. Today, Tinnie's son 'Stiljan', though semi-retired, still takes an active interest in the farm, surrounded by family and other animals (a menagerie including dwarf Angora goats, Colbrook pigs, birds, dogs and donkeys).

The 130ha of undulating vineyards face favourably south, south-east and south-west and soils are typically Devon Valley: decomposed granite with the clay-based Huttons and Clovellies. Since 1992, when 'Stiljan's' 30-odd years of gradual vine improvement was all but completed, the estate has settled on about 60% Pinotage, Cabernet Sauvignon, Shiraz and Tinta Barocca. The rest is Chardonnay, Sauvignon Blanc and Chenin.

Stiljan's eldest sons Tinnie and Ben have been winemaker and vineyard manager respectively since 1991. The deceptively large cellar, built in 1941, with its open concrete fermenters and massive cement and stainless steel tanks, has been 'stretched' to incorporate the nearly 900 new French and handful of American oak barrels the Mombergs have recently acquired.

Middelvlei bottles about 70% of its production: some 21 000 cases. The rest goes

Middelvlei makes some eminently drinkable reds, as friendly as its owners, the Mombergs, who have farmed here since the early 1900s.

The Momberg clan, headed by patriarch 'Stiljan'. Sons Tinnie, Ben and Jan are all involved in wine production at Middelvlei. supported by their family and other animals.

in bulk to Distillers. While open red wine fermenters are still used, there is greater emphasis on fruit ripeness and concentration, and generous use of new wood. Tinnie and Ben have worked overseas, at Chateau Montelana in Napa and Matanzas Creek in Sonoma respectively. So they're not shy to try new things. Like their Pinotage Merlot blend, aromatic, plummy, spicy and eminently drinkable, their biggest seller. The varietal Pinotage and Shiraz follow close behind, showing the benefits of riper fruit and new oak, combining immediate charm with the promise of ageing potential. They herald a change in style from high tannins and acids to riper fruit and less pressed juice.

CLOS MALVERNE

The domain of Seymour and Sophia Pritchard produces some elegant, soft, drinkable red wines. Pritchard bought the farm in 1969, making his first commercial wines in 1988. Pinotage is the great success here, on its own and in blends with Cabernet and Merlot in the juicy, spicy Auret and with Cabernet in a new 'second-label' wine. Blends are the byword. The Cabernet Shiraz offers delicious drinkability and the Cabernet Merlot a lovely smoothness. All the reds are basket-pressed, for gentler tannins, and fermented in open concrete tanks. The 22ha have recently been extended with the purchase of two tracts of land, holding 35-year-old Pinotage vines, Sauvignon Blanc and new Merlot, Pinotage and Cabernet. Isak 'IP' Smit makes around 25 000 cases.

DEVON HILL

Now run by burgeoning but low-profile Swiss operation, SAVISA, based at Sonop in Paarl, Devon Hill is a 27ha property on the northern slopes of Devon Valley. It was bought in 1994 by the Mürset family and fellow Swiss partners in the winemaking business, who built a hi-tech, gravity-fed cellar. Pinotage is the star here, making a ripe, fleshy, fruity mouthful. An earthy Cabernet and plummy Merlot complete the predominantly red wine line-up. There is also a a crisp Sauvignon Blanc. Wines are made by Sonop's Alain Cajeux and mostly exported.

LOUISVALE

This wine farm combines classic turn-of-the-century Sir Herbert Baker architecture, colourful owners who breed champion Great Danes and miniature Schnauzers, and a tradition of excellent Chardonnays, recently joined by some very fine noble reds. Businessmen Hans Frohling and Leon Stemmet started growing wine grapes in 1988, expanding production from their first 600 cases to around 20 000 cases made by Simon Smith. Their three Chardonnays offer three distinct styles: from the big, melony, buttery, barrel-fermented mainliner to the lightly wooded Chavant to the soft, creamy, lemony new unwooded edition. Best red is the berried, spicy Dominique Cabernet Sauvignon Merlot Cabernet Franc blend.

MEINERT

Founding Vergelegen vintner Martin Meinert bought the 12ha Devon Crest in 1987, replanting to Cabernet, Merlot, Cabernet Franc and Pinotage and building a stylish, gravity-fed, partly underground winery. Having left Vergelegen in 1997, he has finally released two excellent reds under the Meinert label: a Merlot and a Cabernet Merlot blend from the highly vaunted '97 vintage. The wines show all the class and elegance with which Meinert and his cool-climate terroir have become synonymous, while the up-coming '98s promise even greater depth and concentration.

SYLVANVALE

Another new-wave Cape Pinotage has popped up in Devon Valley, this time from among 6ha of newly nurtured old vines on the rejuvenated property of the Devon Valley Hotel & Vineyards. David and Lee Ann Nathan-Maister roped in the Clos Malverne team to produce their maiden, French-oaked '98 Pinotage, an unusual dry Pinotage Rosé and an unwooded, but fully fruited, old-vine Laurie's Vineyard Chenin Blanc. New-clone Cabernet and Merlot have been planted. The wines are now made by neighbour Martin Meinert at Devon Crest.

KOELENHOF

Though not officially designated a Wine of Origin ward of Stellenbosch, Koelenhof does have a distinctive meso-climate. The hills on the south-east of the R304 (Koelenhof Rd) face north-east and south-east. And at altitudes of up to 300m and composed of mostly clay-based granitic and gravelly soils, they provide ideal viticultural land cooled by the south-east winds funnelled up the valley off False Bay.

Combined with lower-lying undulating hills, such varying terrain allows for cultivation of both noble white and red varieties, mostly Sauvignon Blanc, Chardonnay, Cabernet Sauvignon and Shiraz. Some serious Pinotages and Chenin Blancs are being made from old, rejuvenated vines, while new plantings of Pinotage promise great potential when skillfully treated.

KOELENHOF

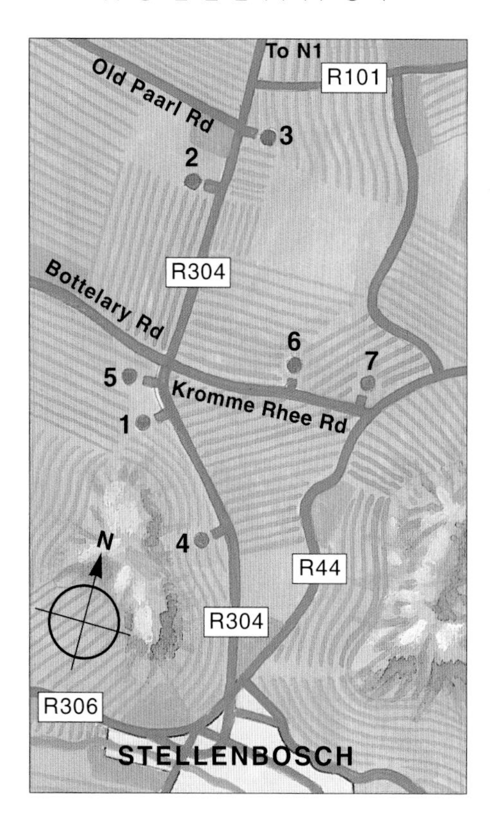

1. Beyerskloof
2. Klawervlei
3. Koelenhof
4. Louiesenhof
5. Mulderbosch
6. Simonsig
7. Slaley

MULDERBOSCH

OWNER
Hydro Holdings

KEY WINES
Faithful Hound, Millennium Cabernet Franc/Cabernet Sauvignon, Sauvignon Blanc, Barrel-fermented Sauvignon Blanc, Chardonnay, Barrel-fermented Chardonnay, Steen-op-Hout Chenin Blanc

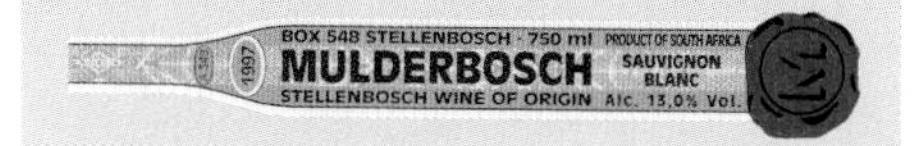

Mulderbosch may have lost a little of its charm and character with the departure in 1996 of urbane founding owner Larry Jacobs. But the other half of this sparkling team, brainy, witty vintner Mike Dobrovic, keeps the flag of fine wine and spunk flying under the new proprietorship of Pretoria-based electronics and hospital development company Hydro Holdings.

Ribald jokes, funny hats, baggy jeans and fly-away hair belie a searching mind that relishes unravelling the chemistry of turning grape juice into wine. The art of reductive winemaking and the use of ascorbic acid to fine-tune the nervousness of Sauvignon Blanc led Mulderbosch to become synonymous with this variety from the early '90s. Dobrovic's wines are ripe but racy, fresh and crisp with pungent gooseberry varietal character developing remarkable richness and fullness after a year or two in bottle.

ABOVE: Mulderbosch has established a reputation for consistently fine Sauvignon Blanc, a passion for winemaker Mike Dobrovic (**TOP**), shown here with his faithful hound.

Mulderbosch has just 20ha under vine, with slopes of between 140m and 300m above sea level facing north-east and south-east. The latter slopes host Sauvignon Blanc and Chardonnay. The former is good for reds such as the Cabernet Sauvignon, Merlot and Malbec that make up the Faithful Hound blend, which started off as a fruity, easy-drinking red and is developing into a rich and elegant, structured yet smooth classic as the vines mature. The new Millennium blend contains predominantly Cabernet Franc, its typical varietal herbaceous, leafy character fleshed out with Cabernet Sauvignon blackberry fruit and structure. Petit Verdot is also planted.

Together with nearby Simonsig, the 47ha of land bought by Jacobs in 1989 used to be part of historic 17th-century farm Nooitgedacht. Renewal of the dilapidated property included intensive soil preparation, planting and a well-equipped cellar, built on a slope to allow for gravity-fed movement of grapes and juice. 'The greatest dream of any winemaker is to plant, not inherit, vineyards,' says Dobrovic, who was involved from the start. His canopy management, especially of the sensitive Sauvignon Blanc, is based on meticulous analysis of the effects of varying levels of ripeness, sun exposure and leaf cover on berry flavour and varietal characteristics. Natural yeasts are being used on some of his barrel-fermented Chardonnay, a seamless integration of modern power with Burgundian elegance. His lightly oaked, dry Steen-op-Hout Chenin Blanc is a herby, honeyed wine from old, barely bearing vines.

OWNERS

Johan, Pieter and Francois Malan

KEY WINES

Tiara, Cabernet Sauvignon, Shiraz, Pinotage, Frans Malan Pinotage/Cabernet, Adelberg, Chardonnay, Sauvignon Blanc, Vin Fumé, Gewürztraminer, Chenin Blanc, Adelblanc, Mustique, Franciskaner, Kaapse Vonkel Cap Classique, Cuvée Royale MCC, Vin de Liza Noble Late Harvest, LBV Port; Jean le Riche Vin Doux, Vin Sec

Built up over 30 years by Frans Malan to become one of the Cape's biggest private cellars, Simonsig has earned its reputation with consistently top-quality wines, made in substantial quantities across a wide spectrum of styles. With his sons – winemaker Johan, viticulturist Francois and marketing man Pieter – involved in the farm since the early '80s, Malan founded a new Cape winemaking dynasty.

Simonsig comprises three properties: Simonsig, granted in 1682; De Hoop, a section of the original Koelenhof property and now home to the cellar and tasting room; and Morgenster, bought in 1980. The Malans also lease vineyards on adjoining Kriekbult, which are being replanted to noble varieties. This makes up some 270ha on clay-based, granitic soils. Annual production is about 160 000 cases.

Simonsig's estate comprises three farms spread across the undulating hills of the Koelenhof area, overlooked by the distant Simonsberg.

Quietly spoken winemaker Johan Malan is probably the most versatile, competent all-rounder in the Cape. His skills stretch from the elegant bottle-fermented Kaapse Vonkel Cap Classique (the first bottle-fermented SA bubbly and now the first to contain Pinot Meunier) to a creamy, nutty, toasty Chardonnay (from some of the first vines planted in this country); from one of the most delicious, rare unwooded Pinotages to a masterful 'Cape' blend, in the mid-'90s, of Pinotage and Cabernet, a benchmark on the local scene. Malan's varietal Cabernets and Shirazes are finely tuned. His Weisser Riesling, just off-dry, brings out the variety's characteristic terpeney flavours without sacrificing fruitiness.

His philosophy has always been to make good quality wines in generous quantities rather than small, show-stopping batches. Yet both the Chardonnay and the Tiara Bordeaux-style blend containing the Cape's first Petit Verdot are top performers. Other successes include a 'Red Hill' Pinotage, balancing fruit with French oak, and a 'reserve' Shiraz, a big wine doused in American wood. There's the limited-release, bottle-aged prestige '91 Cuvée Royale, celebrating 30 years of Cap Classique production, and a delicate but delicious Noble Late Harvest, named Vin de Liza in commemoration of the brothers' much-loved, late mother.

BEYERSKLOOF

Kanonkop cellarmaster Beyers Truter bought this small tract of low-yielding, gravelly land about a decade ago with the express purpose of 'working with oak to prove that we in South Africa have the fruit that can take 100 per cent new oak and produce wine to compare with the French First Growths'. He's proved his point, winning countless international awards and five-star ratings with an intense, ripe Cabernet Sauvignon/Merlot blend. Fewer than 1 000 cases are produced. The bulk of Beyerskloof's 30 000-odd cases is made up of Truter's first love, Pinotage, an intense, fully flavoured, structured wine from decades-old bush vines. The Krige brothers of Kanonkop are among the partners in this boutique venture.

KLAWERVLEI

Hermann and Inge Feichtenschlager, both Austrian-born, persist in farming wholly organically on their flatland property near Villiera. This unfortunately results in crop losses from downy mildew and other seasonal vine diseases. Practices include no chemical spraying, minimal sulphur, racking, a light filtration and fining with egg white. The 44ha of unirrigated vineyards include mostly bush-vine Chenin Blanc and Pinotage, and newly planted Merlot and Cabernet. The American-oaked Pinotage can be appealing. Winemaker Markus Sieben produces around 5 000 cases.

KOELENHOF

This co-op turned company concentrates on vineyard care and clonal selection, evident in new bottlings of a Merlot and Cabernet Merlot blend, both fairly powerful wines treated to some serious new small French and American oak treatment. Good-value quaffers carry the Koelenberg and Koelenhoffer label.

LOUIESENHOF

Stefan Smit's Louiesenhof has 95ha of vines. The Premier Collection range contains different varieties each vintage, more usually barrel-fermented. Chenin Blanc, Pinotage and Chardonnay have been joined by newcomers Cabernet Sauvignon, Cabernet Franc and Merlot. The wines sometimes show an early bottle maturation character and noticeably dry tannins. Geisenheim-trained Smit makes a Perroquet Cape Tawny port, quite dry and high-spirited, from Tinta Barocca.

SLALEY

Exciting wines continue to come out of this sophisticated new cellar, built in 1996 by the Hunting family in conjunction with Glen Carlou's Walter Finlayson and partner Rob Coppoolse, despite the termination of the relationship in 1998. New winemaker Christopher van Dieren, schooled at Simonsig, draws fruit from the Huntings' excellent 120ha of vines. The wild, smoky, plummy, chocolatey Slaley Shiraz is one of the brightest new stars, and the Chardonnay is promising. A second label, Broken Stone, offers a drinkable Cabernet Shiraz blend, Pinotage and Sauvignon Blanc.

Simonsig patriarch Frans Malan, surrounded by his sons, winemaker Johan, marketing man Pieter and vineyard manager Francois.

VLOTTENBURG

Though not one of the most renowned viticultural areas within the Stellenbosch district – it is not acknowledged as a ward – Vlottenburg has emerged in the past decade or so as one with untapped potential. Most of its vineyards occupy hillside sites, deriving benefit from cooling breezes from nearby False Bay and good, low-vigour, moisture-retaining, clay-based decomposed granite soils.

From a tradition of growing grapes for co-operatives, including Vlottenburg, Eersterivier and Welmoed, as well as supplying producer wholesalers such as Stellenbosch Farmers' Winery and Distillers, wine farmers have struck out on their own. Historic wineries with established reputations such as Uiterwyk, Overgaauw and Neethlingshof are proving they have what it takes to occupy a position among the Cape's top echelon. And the enclave of Stellenboschkloof, hidden deep in a valley on the southern end of the Bottelary range of hills, offers sites that are higher, cooler and concomitantly capable of classic wines.

VLOTTENBURG

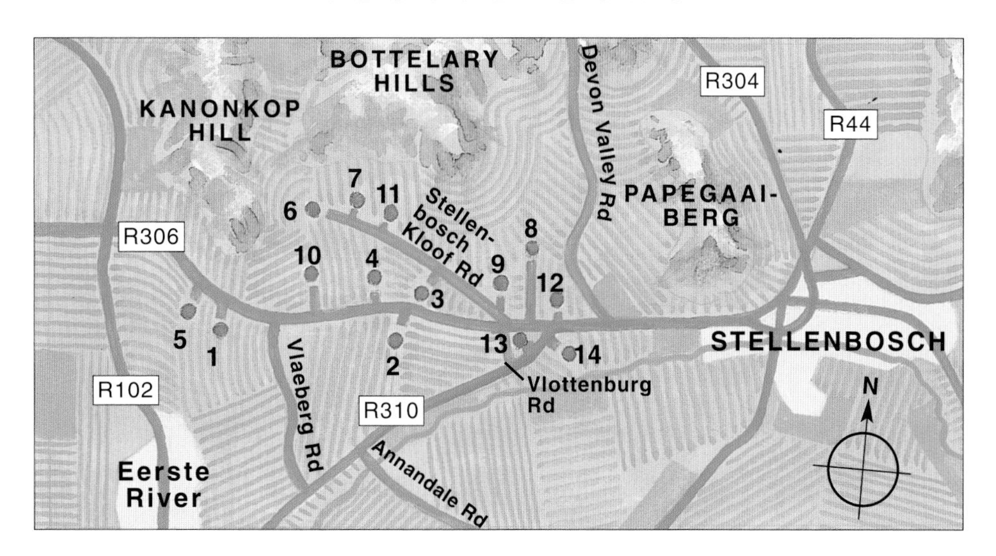

1. Amani
2. Boschkloof
3. Carisbrooke
4. Goedgeloof
5. Jordan
6. Jacobsdal
7. L'Émigré
8. Neethlingshof
9. Overgaauw
10. Reyneke/Uitzicht
11. Uiterwyk
12. Verdun
13. Vlottenburg
14. Vredenheim

JORDAN

OWNER
The Jordan family

KEY WINES
Cabernet Sauvignon, Merlot, Single Vineyard Merlot, Chameleon Cabernet Sauvignon Merlot, Chardonnay, Sauvignon Blanc, Blanc Fumé, Barrel-Fermented Chenin Blanc, Chameleon Sauvignon Blanc Chardonnay, Rhine Riesling; Bradgate Cabernet Sauvignon Merlot Cabernet Franc, Bradgate Chenin Blanc/Sauvignon Blanc

Ted Jordan of Jordan Shoes bought the dilapidated old Kanonkop and Langverwacht properties in the Stellenboschkloof in 1982. Helped by wife Sheila and son Gary, a Cape Town University geology graduate, he gradually replanted the farm, renamed Jordan, to virus-free, new-clone noble varieties and started delivering quality grapes to Eersterivier co-op. 'We were the first to deliver Chardonnay and Merlot to Eersterivier Co-op,' he says proudly.

By 1990 Gary was back from the USA, with an oenology masters from the University of California, Davis; with his wife Kathy, he also had experience at Iron Horse Vineyards in the Alexander Valley.

Vineyard siting plays a paramount role in this winery's quality drive. The 85ha are spread across slopes with a range of aspects and heights of between 80m and 310m, allowing for a variety of premium grapes. Soils are mainly low-vigour, clay-based, decomposed granite, requiring only drip irrigation in heatwaves.

The ecology-conscious Jordans have named their second-label wines Chameleon after a colony of rare Cape dwarf chameleons residing in a tree beside the farm dam.

Right from their first vintage in 1993, the wines have been well made, marked by varietal authenticity, sophistication and elegance. Their single-varietal Cabernet Sauvignon and Merlot, as well as the Chameleon red blend, are consistently full-flavoured but classy. A single-vineyard Merlot from the great '97 vintage is a superb wine, bottled both unfiltered and unfined for maximum flavour impact

The Jordans' innovative approach includes the risky use of natural yeasts. And their experimentation with different coopers and clones is ongoing. Their exceptional, always elegant Chardonnay is a case in point. They combine new and used barrels to great effect, following the philosophy that oak should merely complement the essential fruit in a wine. This is evident in the Chardonnay, and in the mix of French and American wood on one of the Cape's best wooded Sauvignon Blancs. Their barrel-fermented Chenin Blanc is emerging as one of the Cape's more serious contenders.

Kathy and Gary Jordan's success at the modern new Jordan winery has warranted the assistance of winemaker Rudi Schultz, brother of Hartenberg's Carl Schultz.

OVERGAAUW

OWNER
Braam van Velden

KEY WINES
Tria Corda, Cabernet Sauvignon, Merlot, Shiraz, Pinotage Cabernet Franc, Chardonnay, Sauvignon Blanc, Sylvaner, Cape Vintage Port

1990 1990
Overgaauw
ESTATE WINE LANDGOEDWYN
TRIA CORDA
A wood-matured, Cabernet Sauvignon/Merlot blend.
WINE OF ORIGIN STELLENBOSCH
e 750 ml GROWN, MADE AND MATURED ON OVERGAAUW ESTATE, STELLENBOSCH 12% Alc.
PRODUCT OF THE REPUBLIC OF SOUTH AFRICA

ABOVE: The Overgaauw tasting room dates back to Victorian times. Here winemakers Chris Joubert and Braam van Velden (**BELOW**), the latest in a line of Van Veldens to run the estate, produce long-lived reds.

Among the least heralded of fine-wine estates, Overgaauw produces some of the Cape's most serious reds, a fact often overlooked by wine lovers ever-eager to try out the latest trendy boutique wine.

Overgaauw has been in the family since 1784 and the cellar was built in 1909 by Braam van Velden's grandfather. The cellar still exists at the core of the modern expansions carried out by Braam and his father David since the '70s, when Braam returned from viticultural training at Geisenheim in Germany. Viticultural developments saw the large-scale replacement of some 75ha of arbitrary white varieties with the shy-bearing classics. Says Braam: 'A vineyard will be there for 25 years; you can't let short-term fashion affect your planning.'

Yet the Van Veldens proved to be ahead of their time. They were the first to bottle Merlot locally as a varietal wine in 1982. It is possibly the farm's top performer, predominating in the DC Classic blend reserved and regularly selected for the prestigious annual Cape Independent Winemakers Guild Auction. The family was also among the first to introduce whole-bunch pressing and small oak barrel-maturation in the '80s.

Red wines have made their mark here, with the top-notch Cabernet Sauvignon, Merlot and Tria Corda Bordeaux-style blend recently joined by a new-vine Shiraz, wonderfully fruit-rich, spicy and savoury. Like all Overgaauw's reds, it's made to last – they often only start peaking after at least 10 years in bottle. Another recent addition is a Pinotage Cabernet Franc blend. The Van Veldens and their 10-year-veteran winemaker Chris Joubert believe Pinotage should play an integral role in establishing a 'traditional' Cape blend.

Overgaauw remains the sole South African proponent of the little-known, floral and spicy Sylvaner. A fine limey, creamy Chardonnay and grassy, figgy Sauvignon Blanc also exhibit the trademark Overgaauw built-to-last zestiness. The Van Veldens also quietly pioneered the planting of the Portuguese port classic, Touriga Naçional, at the start of the 1990s. It has joined the estate's other traditional Portuguese varieties in its excellent Cape Vintage port.

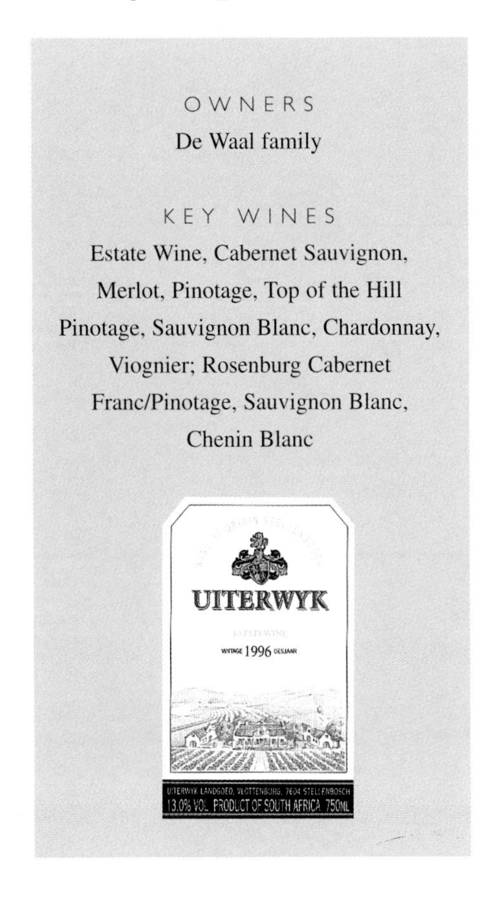

OWNERS
De Waal family

KEY WINES
Estate Wine, Cabernet Sauvignon, Merlot, Pinotage, Top of the Hill Pinotage, Sauvignon Blanc, Chardonnay, Viognier; Rosenburg Cabernet Franc/Pinotage, Sauvignon Blanc, Chenin Blanc

ABOVE: The Cape Dutch manor house of Uiterwyk, home to the De Waal brothers (**BELOW**): Chris, Daniël and Pieter. The trio has achieved major export success over the past few years.

Nineteenth-century farm Uiterwyk has been a family affair for nine generations. After four decades, owner Danie de Waal has decided to hand over the reins to his sons: Pieter (marketing), Chris (white winemaker) and Daniël, the red-wine specialist.

Among the four reds under the Uiterwyk label, Pinotage is the one that shines. It is one of the Cape's top single-varietal examples. The award-winning, big and voluptuous 1996 Top of the Hill Pinotage – so-named for the block of gnarled, nearly-50-year-old vines that bore the intensely flavoured fruit – was chosen to usher in the long-planned-for reserve range of Uiterwyk wines. Pinotage also forms the basis of Uiterwyk's Estate blend, which is still more French than New World – not surprising, given Daniël's frequent working trips to St-Emilion (Château l'Angelus) and a stint in Italy with Super Tuscan supremo, Antinori. Visits to the Rhône have borne fruit in the form of the farm's first Shiraz and Viognier.

The brothers are passionate about quality and are precise in their methods of achieving it. Secateurs are thoroughly cleaned between pruning individual blocks to combat the spread of disease. Reds are laboriously racked every three months to expose the wine to oxygen for a fuller, rounder finished product. Thin-staved imported barrels have been hunted down, providing better wood with a tighter grain.

Chardonnay most occupies Chris these days, having already established Uiterwyk Sauvignon Blanc as one of the Cape's more elegant wines, favouring the dry, aromatic, intensely flavoured

yet gentle Sancerre style. A new string to his bow is an unwooded, floral Viognier. With some 115ha under vine, Uiterwyk bottles only about 20 000 cases, selling the rest as bulk wine.

AMANI

This Afro-Tuscan winery, built by advertising executive Mark Makepeace and wife Hillary (niece of Klein Constantia's Duggie Jooste), takes in grapes from 30ha. Sandy soils on south-facing slopes offer the coolness required for racy, grassy Sauvignon Blancs. Winemaker Cathy Marshall has also introduced oaked Chardonnays and a Chenin Blanc and makes a herby, berried Shiraz and a deliciously juicy Pinot Noir for friends under the Barefoot label.

BOSCHKLOOF

Boschkloof is home to former radiologist Reenen Furter and wife Dalene, persuaded in 1995 by son-in-law Jacques Borman of La Motte to invest in 25ha (15ha are under vines) once part of the old Spier estate. Assisted by Borman, the Furters focus on Chardonnay, Cabernet and Merlot. The Cabernet is a rich red, generously oaked in all-new wood, with firm, dry tannins, made for ageing, while the Reserve Cabernet Merlot blend is more accessible.

CARISBROOKE

A neighbour of Overgaauw, Carisbrooke grape-grower Willem Pretorius has produced 2 000-odd cases of a smooth, berried Cabernet Sauvignon, with the help of Vlottenburg co-op winemaker Kowie du Toit, to whom he has supplied fruit in the past. The vineyard is just 6ha.

GOEDGELOOF

The identity of this new 'old' winery remains vague as proprietor Hydro Holdings battles it out with Dick Enthoven of Spier Home Farms to claim ownership of the Spier wine brand name. The Goedgeloof cellar, now modernised, was where the Jouberts of the old Spier Estate made their wines and, together with some 30ha of vineyard, was not included in the sale of the historic homestead to Enthoven.

Goedgeloof has since been bottling under the Kanu label. The reds have been excellent: a rich, meaty Merlot; a spicy, fruity, new-wave, new-oak Shiraz; Cabernet/Merlot and Ruby Cabernet/Cinsaut blends, all showing lovely fruit and great drinkability. Winemaker Teddy Hall presides.

JACOBSDAL

Publicity-shy Cornelis Dumas makes a Cape benchmark Pinotage. It is well priced and successfully traverses the old-style, rather tannic types and the modern, fruitier, juicier examples. Specialising in Pinotage since the '60s, when he took over the farm from his father, Dumas now has son Hannes caring for the unirrigated, bush-vine vineyards.

L'ÉMIGRÉ

Frans Gentis, a founding member of Welmoed co-op, started building his own cellar on De Morgenzon in 1993. The reds are rustic – the Cimiterre Bordeaux-style blend and Pinotage develop well in bottle – while the Azure Sauvignon Blanc and Chardonnay are zesty. Younger son Emile is the winemaker.

NEETHLINGSHOF

Bought and developed in 1985 by German banker Hans-Joachim Schreiber, this historic Cape Dutch homestead (circa 1692) is a fine viticultural property just beginning to realise its potential.

Schalk van der Westhuizen, born and bred on the farm, makes outstanding Noble Late Harvests and his new Sémillon Reserve is a barrel-fermented and matured blockbuster.

The highly vaunted '97 vintage has come up with some great reds. The new premium label, Lord Neethling, offers a Bordeaux-style blend, a Cabernet Sauvignon and a Pinotage, combining complexity and elegance.

REYNEKE

Owned by the Reyneke family for the past decade, the farm Uitzicht is managed by son Johan. Minimal intervention and eco-friendly practices in both cellar and vineyard are the philosophy here. Friend John Farquharson of Lievland vinifies a solid Cabernet Sauvignon, full-bodied oaked Chenin Blanc and Chenin Sauvignon Blanc blend.

VERDUN

Former Johannesburg Stock Exchange chairman, teetotaller and wine collector Francois Tolken bought this dilapidated property in 1995. Once famous for its Gamay Noir, Verdun had not produced wine for 15 years. A 200-ton (with expansion possibilities) modern fermentation cellar takes in fruit from some 60ha of rejuvenated vines, while the 19th-century cellar has been expanded. The Chardonnay shines among the Verdun whites and the Interlude label includes quaffers such as the Gamay. Jan van Rooyen is the winemaker.

VLOTTENBURG

The bulk of the 10 000-ton production by 21 member-growers goes to SFW, but winemaker Kowie du Toit bottles some great reds. The latest Limited Release Cabernet Sauvignon is a serious wine with ripe, sweet fruit and subtle oak, while the standard bottling is immediately accessible. A Limited Release Pinotage and regular Pinotage show ripe, plummy, savoury fruit and sweet banana flavours. The spicy Shiraz and chocolatey, plummy Merlot charm.

VREDENHEIM

Magical, mystical labels adorn the bottles of the some 8 000 cases of reds and whites made by Elzabé Bezuidenhout on her family's 17th-century Cape Dutch farm, which also supplies SFW. She's working increasingly with classic reds such as Cabernet Sauvignon, Cabernet Franc, Merlot and Shiraz. The two red blends are particularly pleasant.

P A A R L

Paarl, one of the Cape's most historic wine-producing districts dating back to the late 17th century, has long played second fiddle to the Cape Dutch charms, mountain-peaked graces and viticultural edge of Stellenbosch. Though like the scenic Stellenbosch considered part of the Coastal region, Paarl is generally a little hotter and drier than its southerly neighbour, shut off from the sea by the Simonsberg Mountain in the south, Groot Drakenstein in the south-east and, partly, by the low, centrally placed Paarl outcrop, around which many of its good vineyards are clustered.

ABOVE: Fairview's famous goat tower. **OPPOSITE:** The vineyards of Backsberg cloak the lower slopes of the Paarl side of the Simonsberg ridge.

But the western end of the valley is open to Table Bay and its maritime influence. A variety of soils, including good, clay-based granite and Malmesbury shale, are exploited for premium-quality wine grapes, though there are still substantial plantings on low-lying ground and along the Berg River, with its sandier soils originating from Table Mountain sandstone.

The district produces around 20% of the national grape crop and covers some 18 000ha of vines. Recognition of its potential has come in the form of foreign investment. A Californian couple, Simi Winery director Zelma Long and viticulturist Phil Freese, has invested in 40ha of Cabernet Sauvignon, Cabernet Franc and Merlot with Backsberg's Michael and Jill Back. Look out for the Simunye label. Top Bordeaux vintner Alain Mouiex (his family owns famous Château Pétrus) is making wine at Savanha Wines' Berg & Brook Winery. The Swiss-based Jacques Germanier Group's SAVISA (Société Anonyme de Vins Internationaux et Sud Africains) uses the local Sonop cellar as a base for its large-scale wine export business and owns Kersfontein farm in Paarl, among others.

Similar independent wholesale wine production is earmarked at the new Ashwood cellar, run by Rob Meihuizen for his Cape Town business partners. A new private cellar called Avondale is beginning to bottle premium whites and reds from its 70ha, vinified by Dewald Heyns for owner John Grieve.

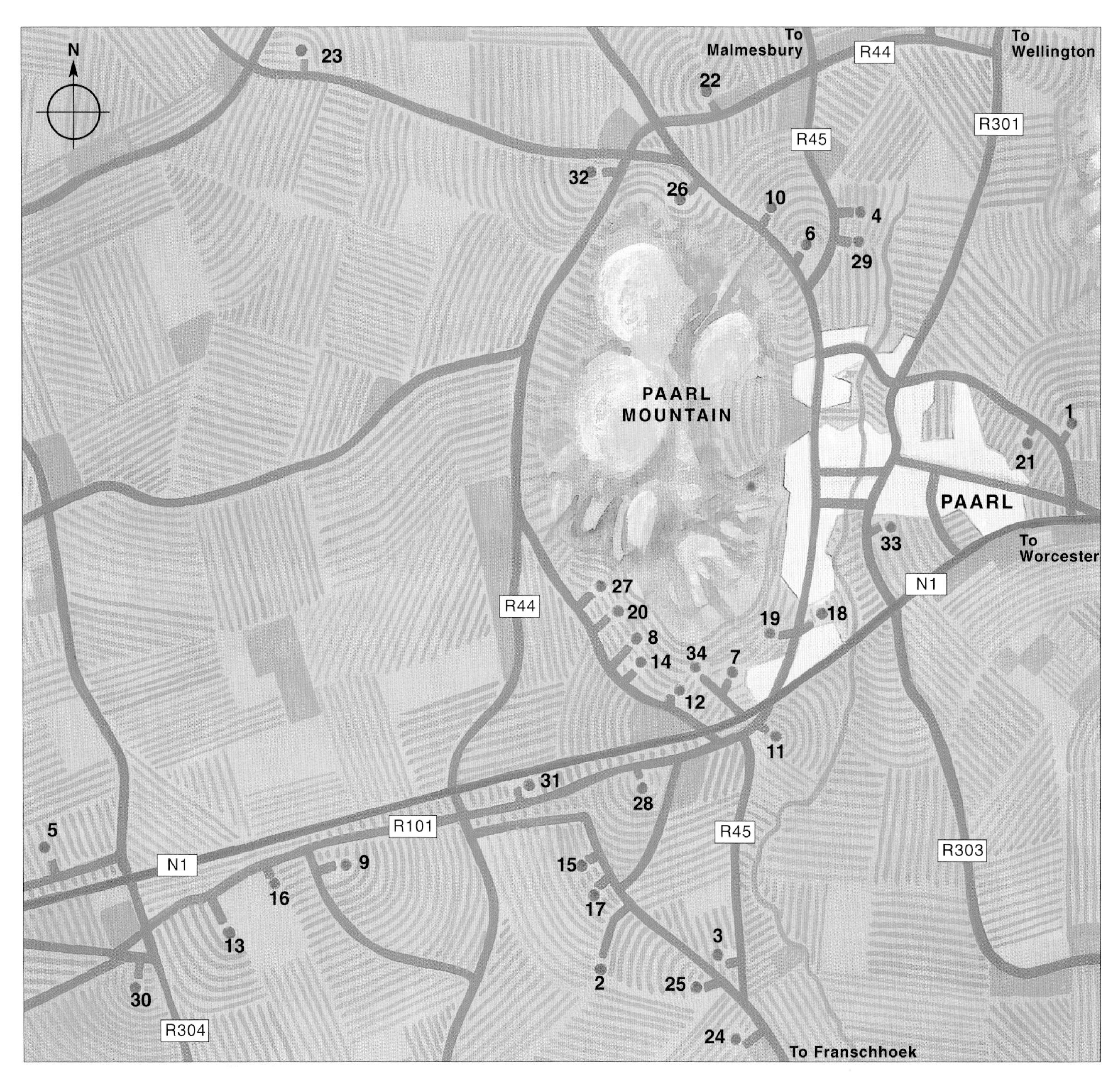

1. Ashanti
2. Backsberg
3. Berg & Brook
4. Bernheim
5. Bodega
6. Boland
7. Brenthurst
8. De Leuwen Jagt
9. De Meye
10. De Villiers
11. De Zoete Inval
12. Diamant
13. Eaglevlei
14. Fairview
15. Glen Carlou
16. Hoopenburg
17. Klein Simonsvlei
18. KWV
19. Laborie
20. Landskroon
21. Nederburg
22. Nelson
23. Perdeberg
24. Plaisir de Merle
25. R & de R Fredericksburg
26. Rhebokskloof
27. Ruitersvlei
28. Simonsvlei
29. Veenwouden
30. Villiera
31. Welgemeend
32. Windmeul
33. Zanddrift
34. Zandwijk

BACKSBERG

OWNER
Michael Back

KEY WINES
Klein Babylonstoren, Cabernet Sauvignon, Merlot, Shiraz, Dry Red, Chardonnay, John Martin Sauvignon Blanc, Sauvignon Blanc, Chenin Blanc, Sémillon, Rhine Riesling, Rosé, Special Late Harvest, Brut Cap Classique, Sydney Back Potstill Brandy

Wine bins containing bottle-ageing wines reflect Backsberg's market philosophy of ensuring an ongoing supply of wine to the public.

'We exist because we have customers. We're in the business of selling wine,' says pragmatic, bushy-bearded Michael Back of the farm's reasonable price policy – which tends to make one forget that Backsberg produces some of the Cape's most consistently elegant wines. Grandfather Charles Back, a Lithuanian immigrant, bought Klein Babylonstoren in 1916 and supplied the big merchants. Son Sydney came on-board in 1938, becoming a wholesaler and then one of the Cape's first wine farmers to sell wine to the public in 1970 under his own 'estate' label, amidst strong opposition from the large wholesale merchants. Son Michael inherited the farm in 1996.

Backsberg's 180ha, stretching from sandy flat land up to the decomposed granite and yellow and red clay of the Simonsberg slopes, have been scientifically analysed and meticulously replanted to the premium varieties: Chardonnay, Sauvignon Blanc, Cabernet and Merlot, with some Shiraz and Pinotage. Backsberg's wines have always been fruit-driven, and winemaker Hardy Laubser believes in gentle wooding. This comes through on their reds, from the elegant Klein Babylonstoren blend of Cabernet, Merlot and Cabernet Franc to the balanced Cabernet Sauvignon, minty Merlot, chocolatey Shiraz and old oak-aged Pinotage.

Among many less successful wooded Cape Sauvignon Blancs, the John Martin shows a rare complexity. The '99 standard Sauvignon Blanc is a stunner, while the Chardonnay is generally of the soft, tropical fruit variety. The Freedom Road project involves Backsberg farmworkers producing their own wine – a Sauvignon Blanc and Cabernet.

Winemaker Hardy Loubser and owners Jill and Michael Back.

OWNER
Charles Back

KEY WINES
Cyril Back Shiraz, Cyril Back Zinfandel/Carignan, Cabernet Franc, Cabernet Franc/Merlot, Gamay, Goats Do Roam (red blend), Malbec, Merlot, Pinot Noir, Mouvèdre, Pinotage, Amos Pinotage, Zinfandel/Cinsaut, Chardonnay, Barrel-fermented Chenin Blanc, Cyril Back Sémillon, Sémillon, Viognier, Sauvignon Blanc, Weisser Riesling, Rosé, Bouquet Fair, Special Late Harvest, Weisser Riesling Straw Wine, Charles Gerard Brut Cap Classique, Fortified Sweet Shiraz, Hanepoot

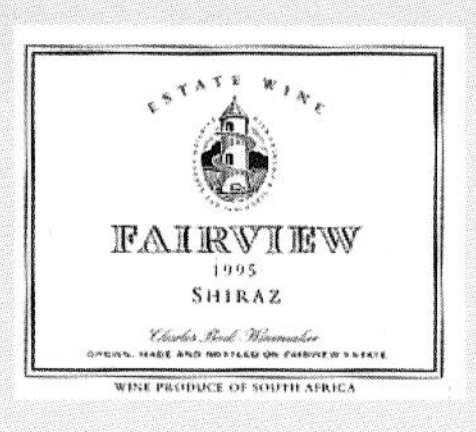

ABOVE: Fairview sports a barrel cellar and farmyard, where the goat tower (**BELOW**) signposts a successful cheese business run in tandem with wine by Charles Back, Anthony de Jager and manager Jeremy Borg.

Charles Back is one of the busiest winemakers in the business and probably the most innovative. He was the first to bottle a varietal Viognier: powerful, rich, soft and herby with typical ripe apricot flavours. He gave it the works: whole bunch-pressed grapes, fermented in barrel, softened by malolactic acid. An experimental wine from just 1ha of five-year-old vines, its success has spurred him on to plant more.

Back has also been leading the pack with exploring red varieties new to the Cape, constantly in search of those deep, drinkable, fruity wines long found at Fairview: Mouvèdre, Carignan, Grenache, also Malbec and Zinfandel. And he's fearless in his blending, turning out the most surprising combinations of the above, often grounded by Shiraz and using Cape stalwarts Pinotage and Cinsaut. Shiraz is somewhat of a Fairview speciality, peppery, spicy, sweet fruit concentration, yet always elegant. A recent visit to Rhône luminary Chapoutier will no doubt result in even more exciting wines to come.

Back is similarly brazen with his whites, turning out a big, creamy, yeasty, buttery Chardonnay, balanced with citric zest. His Sémillon, again one of the Cape's first serious attempts at bringing out the variety's true character, is a wonderfully rich, oak-fermented wine.

Bought in 1937 by his grandfather Charles, already owner of Backsberg which he left to son Sydney, Fairview was bequeathed to Cyril. Charles joined his late father in 1978. He has recently deregistered Fairview as an estate, giving him free rein to combine his Swartland Spice Route riches with those on Fairview's 320ha on Paarl Mountain's southern slopes, soon to be consigned to around 80% red varieties. Assistant winemaker Anthony de Jager helps him cope with the flood of new fruit in the revamped cellar, complete with 2 000 French and American oak barrels, while farmworker Awie Adolph makes his community's new Fair Valley wines.

GLEN CARLOU

OWNERS
Walter Finlayson, Hess Holdings

KEY WINES
Grande Classique, Merlot, Pinot Noir, Cellar Select, Chardonnay, Devereux, Cape Vintage Port

Walter Finlayson bought the 100ha farm on the slopes of the Simonsberg in 1981 and, after extensive soil preparation, started planting his

45ha spread in 1985. After more than 35 vintages, starting on his father's farm Montagne (now Hartenberg) and moving on to Blaauwklippen for its halcyon late '70s and early '80s red-wine vintages, Walter now leaves the 20 000-case production to son David.

The very New World, thatch-roofed, stone-walled cellar has a distinctly international flavour in the form of partner, Swiss businessman Donald Hess of the Napa Valley's The Hess Collection Winery. This has further cemented firm overseas contacts made by David on working trips to Australia, Burgundy and Bordeaux. It finds expression in Glen Carlou's wines, from the Devereux Chenin Blanc Chardonnay blend, one of the Cape's first seriously oaked Chenins, to the juicy, succulent Pomerol-style Merlot. Glen Carlou's flagship Bordeaux-style blend Grand Classique is similarly world class, a characterful, slow developer. As is the Pinot Noir, which has become a muscular, full-bodied, toasty mouthful, showing its warmer origins.

The Finlaysons have discontinued their varietal Cabernet, all of which goes into the Grand Classique and the new-look Cellar Select. One of the stars of this class act is the Chardonnay, the epitome of style consistency and flavour balance. Working the lees and malolactic fermentation produce a perfect combination of big, toasty, buttery, biscuitty aromas and sweet/sour citrussy freshness, with great depth and length. And the Cape Vintage Port, from traditional port varieties Tinta Barocca, Tinta Roriz and some Cornifesto, with the recent addition of the great Touriga Naçional, is one of the Cape's best.

Fine Chardonnays and Pinot Noirs are coming out of the intimate New World cellar that Walter Finlayson (TOP), wife Jill and son David have built from scratch into one of the Cape's top wineries.

HOOPENBURG

OWNERS

Ernst and Gwenda Gouws

KEY WINES

Cabernet Sauvignon, Merlot, Pinot Noir, Shiraz, Chardonnay, Sauvignon Blanc

Ernst and Gwenda Gouws are now happily ensconced in their ranch-style home, with cellar alongside, slap-bang in the middle of their 22ha spread of premium new vineyard. He found the uncultivated land in 1992 and by the 1993 harvest, home and cellar were complete and the first 10ha of vines were planted.

Of the some 40ha of arable land, just more than half has been cultivated, mostly under reds. Chardonnay is the only white. Gouws believes the Muldersvlei area, low-lying and warm, is red-wine territory and future plantings will reflect this. Hence he chooses to buy in his Sauvignon Blanc, about half of his total production of over 20 000 cases, from cooler sites in Stellenbosch.

Hoopenburg's Pinot Noir is one of the best, showing, like regional compatriot Glen Carlou, that warm areas can make the grade with what is often described as an 'eskimo' variety. It is soft, juicy, mouthfilling, with lots of sweet fruit, mocha coffee and charred wood character, though it can be a bit green in its youth. Gouws' generous use of oak, though always well balanced by fruit, also comes through on the Cabernet Sauvignon, a smoky, spicy wine with rounded fruit flavours and a solid structure. His Merlot is softer, fleshier and more immediately accessible. And a new string to his finely tuned bow is a characterful Shiraz.

Of the whites, his Chardonnay is one of the few that stands the test of time, a lovely drink after bottle-age; it's still lemony fresh, but beautifully smooth with integrated wooding.

ABOVE: Hoopenberg's wines are marked by deft use of new oak by vintner Ernst Gouws (**TOP**), with his wife Gwenda, daughters Inke and Ezanne and son Ernst, vintner in the making.

NEDERBURG

OWNER

Stellenbosch Farmers' Winery

KEY WINES

Nederburg Auction Private Bin wines: R161 Cabernet, R163 Cabernet, R109 Cabernet/Merlot, R103 Cabernet/Shiraz, R121 Shiraz, R115 Shiraz/Cabernet, R172 Pinotage, R121 Shiraz, D270 Chardonnay, D234 Sauvignon Blanc, D288 Sémillon, D218 Chardonnay/Sauvignon Blanc, D250 Pinot Blanc, S354 Gewürztraminer/Rhine Riesling, S306 and S333 Special Late Harvests, Bin S316 Weisser Riesling Noble Late Harvest, Edelkeur, Eminence, Bin C92 Cap Classique; Nederburg standard range: Reserve Cabernet, Baronne, Edelrood, Paarl Cabernet, Duet, Reserve Chardonnay, Chardonnay, Reserve Sauvignon Blanc, Sauvignon Blanc, Paarl Chenin Blanc, Paarl Riesling, Prelude, Premier Grand Cru, Elegance, Lyric, Rhine Riesling, Stein, Rosé, Special Late Harvest, Paarl Noble Late Harvest, Blanquette Cap Classique, Kap Sekt, Premiere Cuvée Brut, Premiere Cuvée Doux

Nederburg is, without a doubt, the best-known South African wine label. What makes this SFW-owned but autonomously run 12 000-ton winery extraordinary is that, while achieving a rare consistency of quality and style among every-day quaffers, Nederburg turns out some of the

Cape's finest noble varietal wines, in no small amounts, under its famous Nederburg Auction label. Its historic 1800 Cape Flemish manor house remains a symbol of constancy in wine quality and character.

The Nederburg image has much to do with the strong German influence of 20th-century owner Johann Graue and Günter Brozel, cellarmaster until 1989. The leaning may still be traditional rather than New World, but the style is distinctly more Gallic. Cellarmaster Newald Marais is a calm, quietly confident, enormously capable vintner. Changes during his tenure of over a decade include riper, richer fruit and the benefits of small oak, always subtly applied.

Nederburg's Cabernet will be among the few in the Cape to benefit from the addition of new Bordeaux classic variety Petit Verdot, with ongoing experiments with Malbec. His Sauvignon Blancs and Chardonnays are uniformly good varietal examples with classic character, and Sémillon is receiving attention. And Nederburg keeps the local flag flying with the world-renowned Edelkeur Noble Late Harvest and the Eminence Natural Sweet. Marais can rely on constant upgrades to the extensive cellar facilities, amounting to millions, and a team of winemakers dedicated to specific categories. This devolution of tasks allows for hands-on involvement by each winemaker, from tasting the berries for ripeness to guiding the pickers on which blocks to pick and when, right through to innovating techniques such as whole-bunch pressing. And a recent cellar redesign has given the winemakers scope to handle small parcels from selected vineyards separately, integral to improving quality.

But the emphasis is on vineyard development and management, under the eye of hugely experienced viticulturist Ernst le Roux,

who draws on SFW's world-class nursery Ernita. The nearly 700ha of existing vineyards, both Nederburg's own and that of its contracted growers, are being rejuvenated, with premium reds in the ascendancy. In the pipeline are plantings of largely unexplored varieties such as Sangiovese, Nebbiolo, Viognier and even the little-known Portuguese white, Verdelho.

ABOVE: Nederburg's 19th-century manor house hosts music and other cultural events, while the modern cellar complex behind is the domain of cellarmaster Newald Marais (**TOP**) and assistants Hennie Huskisson and Wilhelm Arnold.

OWNER
Deon van der Walt

KEY WINES
Veenwouden Classic, Merlot, Vivat Bacchus

With just three red wines, this tiny Tuscan-style cellar on the back-roads of Paarl has established itself among the top echelon of Cape wine producers. Internationally renowned South African operatic tenor Deon van der Walt's love of wine, travels to the finest wine-growing regions of the world and friendship with Bordeaux fanatic Billy Hofmeyr of Welgemeend encouraged him to buy the 18ha table-grape farm Ebenaezer in 1988.

Renamed Veenwouden after the Dutch home town of the first Van der Walt to arrive on Cape soil in the early 1700s, the farm is dedicated to the classic red varieties of the Medoc: Merlot, Cabernet Sauvignon, Cabernet Franc and Malbec. The cool, clay-rich subsoil and cool Mediterranean-style breezes washing the sloping, north-east-facing 15ha of newly planted vineyards proved ideal for especially Merlot and Cabernet Franc.

Meerlust's Giorgio Dalla Cia consulted initially, but by 1995 Deon's brother Marcel, a professional golfer who in 1993 swapped the tee for wine and had worked a vintage under top oenologist Michel Rolland at Château Le Bon Pasteur in Pomerol, was ready to take over winemaking duties. Production is tiny, just 80 to 100 tons, with the demands of size and quality determining limited yields of seldom over five tons a hectare. Grapes are handpicked in 10kg crates. Bunches are inspected before being fed into a small crusher, fermented in stainless-steel tanks and then matured in 225-litre French Nevers oak barrels, racked every three months. Fewer than 6 000 cases are produced.

The dark, inky Merlot combines a smoked meat and fresh berry opulence with dry tannins and a sturdy structure that begs time in the bottle. The Classic blend of Cabernet Sauvignon, Merlot, Cabernet Franc and Malbec is as dense and complex, but slightly softer, more elegant and with gorgeous cassis, cedar and soft berry fruit flavours. While both wines, though made to last, are accessible in youth, the third wine, the Vivat Bacchus blend of the same four varieties in different quantities, is made for earlier consumption.

ABOVE: The small Tuscan-style cellar of Veenwouden, owned by international tenor Deon van der Walt (**TOP**), backed up by winemaker brother Marcel and parents Charles and Sheila, who manage the farm.

VILLIERA

OWNER
Grier family

KEY WINES
Monro Brut, Tradition Brut, Tradition Brut Rosé; Cru Monro, CIWG Auction Reserve, Merlot, Cabernet Sauvignon, Shiraz, Pinotage, Traditional Bush Vine Sauvignon Blanc, Sauvignon Blanc, Blanc Fumé, Chardonnay, Rhine Riesling, Gewürztraminer, Sonnet, LBV Port; Blue Ridge Rouge, Cabernet Sauvignon, Blue Ridge Blanc

The flatland around Villiera, which the Grier clan has turned into champion sparkling-wine territory.

It was from chickens to wine in one fell swoop, when the late Robin Grier sold his chicken business in 1983 to buy a 170ha wine farm between Stellenbosch and Paarl. But his young dynasty is in the safe hands of winemaker son Jeff and daughter Cathy, in charge of exports; their cousin Simon tends the vineyards.

The Grier clan has built the farm into one of the Cape's top all-rounders, despite moderately fertile, exposed low-lying vineyards and soils that vary from chalky, pebbly loam to almost dune-like sand that does not endear itself to the usual premium varieties. 'In fact, it was with our lighter, sandier soils that we decided to go the bubbly route,' admits Jeff.

Entering into a joint venture with experienced Champenoise Jean-Louis Denois, the Griers degorged their first Tradition de Charles de Fère in 1984. Having bottled up to four styles of top Cap Classiques by 1998, they have streamlined the range, now consisting of the Tradition Brut NV, Tradition Brut Rosé NV and the vintage flagship Villiera Monro Brut.

The Griers' close attention to the various sites on the farm has led to some award-winning and pocket-pleasing quality white wines, from the pungent Traditional Bush Vine Sauvignon Blanc to the partly oaked Chenin Blanc that shines with bottle-age. The varietal Merlot remains solid and fruit-rich, while its Cabernet counterpart is a lighter-styled wine. Together, they make up the consistently fine Cru Monro, a concentrated, creamy, soft, sweet and spicy blend. A recent achievement is a delicious Pinotage, creamy, with sweet, ripe flavours and a distinctive bacon, smoked meat, savoury character.

Pinotage crops up in the bubblies, is combined with Cabernet in a Reserve bottling and included in the LBV-style port. A varietal Shiraz is new, adding to Villiera's extensive offerings, which include quaffers under the Blue Ridge label, supplemented with fruit from nearby vineyards which give Villiera some 300ha to draw on.

The Grier cousins: vineyardist Simon, marketer Cathy and winemaker Jeff.

WELGEMEEND

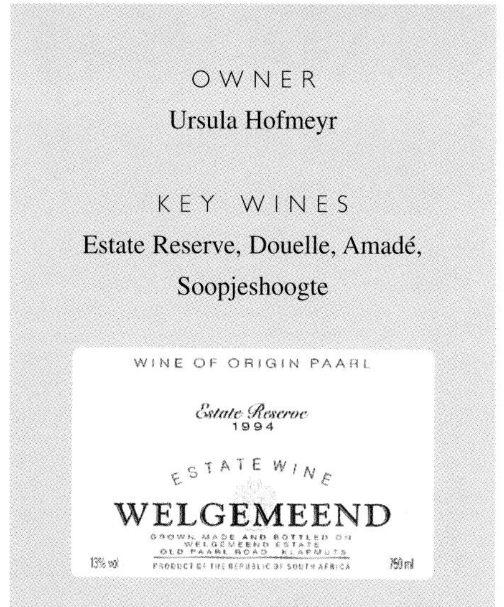

OWNER
Ursula Hofmeyr

KEY WINES
Estate Reserve, Douelle, Amadé, Soopjeshoogte

Founder Billy Hofmeyr was a land surveyor with a passion for wine and especially Bordeaux reds; he realised a dream in 1974 upon buying Welgemeend in Paarl. Despite warnings from winelands' old hands that the very clayey soil was unsuitable for quality wine grapes, Billy and wife Ursula set about replacing the ubiquitous old Muscat d'Alexandrie, Chenin Blanc and Cinsaut with the Mèdoc greats: Cabernet Sauvignon, Cabernet Franc, Merlot, Petit Verdot and Malbec. In this, Hofmeyr was a pioneer, as some of these were unheard of in South Africa. His maiden 1979 Estate Reserve blend of Cabernet Sauvignon, Merlot and Cabernet Franc was the first Bordeaux-style red in the country.

Pinotage, Shiraz and Grenache followed, though most of the Pinotage has since been replaced by Merlot. But it gave rise to his other maiden 1979 blend, a Rhône-style combination called Amadé. By the 1992 vintage, Hofmeyr's health was failing fast and daughter Louise, a fine arts graduate, stepped into the breach. With Ursula's farm-management experience, she successfully bottled the '90 vintage, blended the '91 still in barrel and vinified the incoming '92 in one hectic season.

Her Estate Reserve remains a classic, understated and beautifully balanced in very French vein. The Amadé is easy-drinking, with typical spicy, smoky, leathery characteristics. The Douelle, a later introduction, is less dense than the Estate Reserve, though still very fine; it's a quite earthy, almost rustic melange of Malbec, Cabernet Sauvignon, Petit Verdot, Merlot and Cabernet Franc.

Louise introduced Soopjeshoogte, a lighter, early-drinking, lower-priced version of the Estate Reserve. And, while supporting her father's philosophy that balance and elegance are the key, she is working towards greater fruit ripeness and density in her wines. Yields remain low at five to six tons a hectare. The winemaking is as traditional and natural as ever, from using basket presses to fining with egg white, though more new barrels and some American oak have been introduced. Fewer than 4 000 cases are produced each year from the roughly 13ha of vines.

ASHANTI

Former Belgian maritime lawyer Michel Thuysbaert and California-trained French winemaker Jean-Vincent Ridon are behind Ashanti, formerly Nederburg's farm Languedoc, now sporting a hi-tech, 500-ton, Tuscan-style cellar. Some 95ha of mature vineyards on deep, red clay-based soils include new-clone reds such as Cabernet, Pinotage and Malbec, to be

ABOVE: Welgemeend was inspired by Billy Hofmeyr's passion for the world's finest reds.
TOP: Wife Ursula and daughter Louise have continued Welgemeend's tradition of classically styled wines.

expanded by Cabernet Franc, Petit Verdot, Shiraz, Mouvèdre, Zinfandel and Sangiovese from their own nursery. The Chardonnay and Cabernet Sauvignon are solid, the Pinotage boasts classic banana aromas and unusual meaty, savoury, spicy flavours, and a rare Cape varietal Malbec is dense, wild, herbaceous and savoury. Among Ridon's experiments is a Vin de Paille 'straw wine' and he still finds time for his small Signal Hill range from the 85ha Ashanti Hill on the Paarl slopes of the Simonsberg, where he grows Merlot, Pinot Noir and Sauvignon Blanc.

BERNHEIM

Former Gauteng pharmacist George Schwulst and wife Bernice were persuaded by daughter Gisela, an oenology graduate, to invest in a small 12ha peach and wine-grape farm a few years ago. Equipment in the 100-ton cellar is rudimentary: plastic fermentation tanks to supplement the old *kuipe*, a Heath-Robinson cooling system, a bathroom scale to weigh the baskets of grapes. Soft reds from new plantings of Cabernet, Merlot and Pinotage are made, while Chenin Blanc and Colombard are fruity.

BODEGA

Self-taught winemaker Julianne Barlow is again bottling her fine new-clone Cabernet and Merlot after an hiatus following her well-received maiden '91 and '93 vintages. Brother Jeremy Squier, an Essex farmer, has bought into the 12ha Bodega, enabling an investment of new French-oak barrels for her 'tractor shed' winery.

BOLAND

Co-op turned company Boland handles some 18 000 tons of grapes from vineyards stretching from Durbanville to Malmesbury. The cellar has also linked up with its Wellington counterparts to export under the Cape Wine Cellars banner. Progressive vineyard practices have upped quality, a new red-wine cellar has been built and the barrel-ageing capabilities increased to deal with new Cabernet, Merlot and Pinotage.

BRENTHURST

Home to Cape Town advocate José Jordaan, Brenthurst has just 5ha under Cabernet Sauvignon, Merlot and Cabernet Franc. The vines were planted in '91, in consultation with ace viticulturist Johan Wiese, for a Bordeaux-style blend; it now includes Petit Verdot. Made in a stylish, compact little thatch-roofed cellar by Jordaan, the wine has ripe blackcurrant fruit in an elegant, firm package, made for keeping. A similarly sophisticated varietal Cabernet Sauvignon Reserve makes up the less than 5 000 cases, most of which are exported.

DE LEUWEN JAGT (SEIDELBERG)

One of Paarl's oldest farms, dating back to the 1690s, the former De Leuwen Jagt has been renamed Seidelberg Estate by German businessman Roland Seidel, after restoring homestead and winery during the 1990s. Reds are gaining precedence, with replanting and the introduction of new varieties such as Pinotage increasing vineyards to 120ha. The new premium Seidelberg range includes a soft, velvety Cabernet Merlot blend and a smooth, concentrated Merlot. The farm's always good Cabernet Franc will be used in blends and the second-tier De Leuwen Jagt range. The winemaker is Nicolaas Rust.

DE MEYE

Jan and Philip Myburgh's 60ha mainly red-wine farm, an SFW supplier, has a new 200-ton winery, which has produced a barrel-fermented, fruity Cabernet, smoky Shiraz and Pinotage. Marcus Milner makes around 10 000 cases.

DE VILLIERS

The De Villiers family farm Nantes started bottling its own wine in 1996. About 25 000 cases are made by Dominique Waso. The reds (Merlot, Cabernet, Pinotage) are light and fruity, with the Merlot being the richest. Chardonnay, Sauvignon Blanc and Chenin make up the 180ha.

DE ZOETE INVAL

Eccentric best describes this Berg River farm and its owners since the late 19th century, the Frater family. Patriarch Adrian and son Gerard make mainly rustic reds, assisted by brothers John, Robert and Dan and sister Yogi. Cabernet Sauvignon is the main variety on 65ha. The novelty is the availability of some older vintages, such as Cabernets from the '70s and early '80s.

DIAMANT

Diamant's 45ha of mostly bush vines produce some 350 tons of grapes for owner Niel Malan, who bottles a few hundred cases of red, footstomped by the family and bottled without filtering. The dry red is a variable blend of Cabernet Sauvignon, Merlot and Cabernet Franc or plain Pinotage. The wines, all small French oak-matured, are well fruited. Here's a place to look for a bargain.

EAGLEVLEI

A dream come true for computer and business management boffins Steve and Jean Weir, who 'after a five-year search' finally bought the 50ha property in 1996. It encompasses a 4ha wetland area, home to an African fish eagle. About 12ha of Cabernet Sauvignon and Pinotage have been planted. The planned cellar will handle just 20 000 cases. Consultant winemaker Etienne le Riche has produced a stunning, classic Cabernet, from new-clone, Bottelary fruit and a Pinotage called Eaglet.

KLEIN SIMONSVLEI

This late 18th-century wine farm has been put back on the map by Neil Joubert and son Daan, who tends the 250ha of vineyards. Wines are sold in bulk or exported, but small bottlings of premium reds and whites under the Neil Joubert label have impressed. The dense, juicy, supple Cabernet Sauvignon stands out in the classic Oak-Aged range which includes a Merlot and Pinotage.

KWV

After long legal wrangles with South Africa's new democratic government in the mid '90s, the Cape wine industry's controlling body since 1918 has become a company and relinquished its statutory powers. While continuing to provide logistical and financial support to grape growers, it is forging ahead with major vineyard and cellar developments of its own. The sprawling production complex in Paarl now has four wineries dedicated respectively to the premium Cathedral Cellar selection, the standard KWV wines, a new selection called Robert's Rock, and a general value-for-money range. The state-of-the-art new red-wine cellar completed in 1996 has been followed by a new white-wine winery. Some 15 000 small, new-oak barrels have been bought for its top-notch wines, particularly the international award-winning Cathedral Cellar range, which includes one of the country's finest red blends (Triptych) and premium varietal reds, made by cellarmaster Kosie Müller. Only KWV's fine ports and fortified dessert wines are available locally.

LABORIE

Bought and restored by the KWV in 1972, Laborie's Cape Dutch homestead and cellar is a private KWV function venue. The manor house is a National Monument. A smart new winery and tasting room offer some fine fruit-driven, ripe wines made by Gideon Theron from 50ha of mainly noble varieties Cabernet Sauvignon, Merlot, Pinot Noir, Chardonnay and Sauvignon Blanc, as well as Pinotage. The bottle-aged Cap Classique is a gem.

LANDSKROON

Winemaker Paul de Villiers and brother Hugo are the fifth generation farming Landskroon. The property has a fine reputation for its Vintage port, a plummy, savoury, spicy combination of sweetness and firm alcoholic grip, made from a mix of traditional Portuguese varieties. Landskroon's reds, from a very tasty Pinotage, a smooth Shiraz and elegant Cabernet to various red blends including Cinsaut, Merlot and Cabernet Franc, are distinctively herbaceous. The 275ha are being replanted to mostly premium reds.

MONT DESTIN

German-born and Provence-bred Ernest Bürgin and wife Samantha have added vines to their lemon and clementine orchards on their small farm on the Paarl tip of the Simonsberg. Encouraged by their successful red blend called Passione, made by Laibach's Stefan Dörst, they've added reds to their mix and are planning a cellar.

NELSON

Cape Town advocate Alan Nelson bought his 40ha of vineyard land, plus another 100-odd ha of farmland, in 1988 and has restored, rebuilt and rejuvenated an old homestead, a modern cellar and a conference centre-cum-lunch venue. Winemaker Carl Allen makes pretty good noble reds, particularly a rich, plummy, well-oaked Cabernet, and an elegant, barrel-fermented Chardonnay. Cinsaut is used in an easy-drinking, unwooded Albenet blend. Among new plantings of Cabernet, Merlot, Shiraz, Pinotage, Chardonnay and Sauvignon Blanc is also some Sémillon. The wines appear under the Nelson's Creek label. Farmworkers produce their own wines under the New Beginnings label.

PERDEBERG

This 50-member co-op is best known for its Chenin Blanc, a full, guava-rich, grassy wine. Winemaker Kobus de Kock is also coming up with some rich and fruity reds from Cabernet, Merlot and Pinotage. The co-op handles about 15 000 tons from over 2 000ha of vineyard.

KWV's internationally renowned and acclaimed Cathedral Cellar range of wines is named after the company's imposing large vat-storage facility.

PLAISIR DE MERLE

A showpiece cellar, designed to show the world the modern, new-wave, quality-driven face of owner, wine producer/wholesaler SFW. Says general manager and long-time SFW farm manager Hannes van Rensburg: 'Plaisir de Merle offered the once-in-a-lifetime opportunity of planning from the ground up.'

The 400ha property up against the Simonsberg has been in SFW hands since 1964 – the original owner was a 17th-century French Huguenot. The cellar is an architectural masterpiece, blending in with the renovated historic core of the property. An altitude range of 140m along the riverbed to 500m of granitic mountainside soils allowed for careful vineyard site selection. Four varieties predominate: Sauvignon Blanc, Chardonnay, Cabernet Sauvignon and Merlot, with some Petit Verdot and Malbec for blending. About 80% of the grapes go to SFW, with cellarmaster Neil Bester producing a varietal Cabernet Sauvignon and Merlot with typical French refinement and a dryness of tannin to balance the full-ripe fruit. Château Margaux's Paul Pontallier has consulted. Early Sauvignon Blancs, fully oaked, have been replaced by a fresher, fruitier, livelier unwooded wine. The partially wooded Chardonnays have gained in richness, while maintaining a fresh elegance.

R & DE R FREDERICKSBURG

This is a joint venture between Cape magnate Anton Rupert and the late Baron Edmond de Rothschild, scion of the famous Bordeaux Château Mouton-Rothschild family. (The Baron died shortly before the opening of this classic new French/Cape Dutch winery.)

The 840-ton R & de R Fredericksburg winery on the historic, meticulously restored farm Fredericksburg, dating back to the 1700s, is now run by their sons, Benjamin de Rothschild and Antonij Rupert (owner of L'Ormarins).

Although inaugural 1997 white wines were withdrawn from the market, deemed not to be of

Plaisir de Merle, long a supplier of quality grapes to producer/wholesaler SFW, now sports its own cellar and label, reserved for the pick of the crop from prime viticultural land on the Paarl side of the craggy Simonsberg.

sufficiently high standard, the '97 Cabernet and Merlot in small French oak show potential for greatness. The first tier will carry the R & de R label, the second Fredericksburg. Some 70ha on the prime Simonsberg slopes have been replanted to premium red varieties and Chardonnay. Winemaker Schalk-Willem Joubert is guided by veteran Jacques Borman of La Motte, Antonij Rupert's other wine farm.

RHEBOKSKLOOF

The vineyards on this 17th-century, 450ha Cape Dutch export table grape and olive farm have been replanted by industrialist Keith Jenkins since he purchased it in 1994. Daughter Tracey and her business consultant husband Adrian Thornycroft run the estate, which has just launched its first extra-virgin olive oil.

The 83ha of cool, east- and west-facing hillside vines produce fine Chardonnay: a full-bodied, heavily oaked Grande Reserve and a more citrussy, honeyed Sur Lie. Winemaker Daniel Langenhoven is excited by the newly planted Cabernet, Shiraz and Merlot.

RUITERSVLEI

Managed by John Fauré's three young daughters, Ruitersvlei and adjoining Vrymansfontein farm have 300ha of vineyard. Wine has been made here for more than three centuries and the annual 1 000-ton production was sold in bulk to SFW until 1995. Now Dominique Waso produces about 44 000 cases of Ruitersvlei wines in the labyrinthine old cellar. White vines are being replaced by Cabernet Sauvignon and Merlot, with an eventual 60:40 red to white ratio in mind. A Cabernet Reserve and Merlot Reserve show great density of flavour, ripe fruit and tannins.

SAVANHA (BERG & BROOK)

The old, defunct Drakenstein co-op in Simondium was jump-started by former ad-man Graham Knox in 1996, linking up his Savanha Wines wholesale business with former co-op growers to form Berg & Brook Vineyards, now handling about 4 000 tons of grapes. Savanha is now part of Trylogy Wine Corporation, a joint venture with Longridge and Dick Enthoven's Spier in Stellenbosch. Berg & Brook cellarmaster Nico Vermeulen's reds are solid, particularly the Savanha Reserves such as the dense, plummy Pinotage and a gutsy Shiraz. The Berg & Brook label is kept mostly for blends. Resident French winemaker Stephan de St Salvy also makes special wines for Knox and Bordeaux vintner Alain Mouiex of famous Château Petrus from grapes from their 400ha on five properties in Durbanville, Wellington and Somerset West. The new, limited-release Naledi Cabernet and Sejana Merlot are intended to convince international markets of the Cape's potential for 'First Growth' wines.

SIMONSVLEI

After converting from a co-op to a company in 1997, this winery has become a source of modern, consistently well-made, reasonably priced wines, with a booming export business. Some 2 000ha are under vine and production touches on 300 000 cases. The winery, with its arched facade, now boasts a new fermentation and barrel-maturation cellar. Old concrete tanks have been transformed into a dimly lit vinoteque with stained-glass windows and a visitors' display of the barrel-making process.

Philip Louw, cellarmaster for more than a decade, can now tier his wines according to quality, 'boutique-style'. He is backed up by the winery's dedicated viticulturist Andrew Teubes.

Cape wine fundi, writer and importer Michael Fridjhon (chair of the industry's new Wine Trust) consults on the premium Hercules Paragon range, which offers some gems from selected vineyards in Durbanville: a deeply flavoured, berried, minty, chocolatey Cabernet; a complex, firm Merlot; a rich, creamy, melony Chardonnay; and an oak-fermented Sémillon. The Shiraz is soft, with typically smoky, peppery character. Even the Simonsvlei label is sub-divided into a Reserve and standard range.

WINDMEUL

Most of the wine made at this co-op, recently converted to a company, is sold to wholesalers locally and overseas. But winemaker Hein Koegelenberg bottles a small amount of varietal wines. The choice bottlings have been the fresh and fruity Chenin Blanc, an old-fashioned juicy, stewed-fruit Pinotage from old, low yielding vines, and an American oak-fermented Cinsaut that shows off this stalwart variety's inherent fruity charm.

Windmeul co-op is encouraging its 50-odd members to start upgrading to the major varieties, especially reds.

ZANDDRIFT

Zanddrift is known for its rustic stone buildings, including a chapel, built by Italian World War II prisoners. Now run by winemaker Riaan Marais – Mark Carmichael-Green, formerly with SFW and Stonewall, consults – this 30ha vineyard bottles wines under the Chapel Cellar label (named after the romantic Italianate bell-towered stone chapel on the farm). The Capella Reserve wooded Chenin is the most characterful. New to the range is a sweetish, unwooded Pinotage and a Cabernet, and there's a Chenin-based Cap Classique bubbly in the pipeline.

ZANDWIJK

This historic wine farm is a novelty, dedicated to the production of kosher wines. Gauteng industrialist Mendel Kaplan bought the derelict 17th-century farm in 1983, restored the mid-18th-century Cape Dutch manor house and farmhouse and signed up Leon Mostert as manager/winemaker. Some 14ha of vineyards were established and a hi-tech cellar was built. Elsenberg-trained Mostert, who learned how to make kosher wine in Israel, produces nearly 10 000 cases of wine from mainly Cabernet, Merlot, Cabernet Franc, Malbec, Chardonnay, Sauvignon Blanc and Rhine Riesling. There is a demand from all over the world for these wines, which are pasteurised at high temperatures and sweetened with sugar.

F R A N S C H H O E K

Set about by mountains – the snowcapped Wemmershoek peaks, the Franschhoek range and the cliffs of Groot Drakenstein – the Franschhoek Valley was settled from the 1680s by refugee French Protestants, the Huguenots. This pretty little town has capitalised on its French heritage, with fine restaurants, delis, antique and craft shops and pavement cafés. On the outskirts lies a patchwork of vines, dotted with restored Cape Dutch homesteads on either side of the Franschhoek River.

Classical mouldings on the French Huguenot Monument testify to viticulture's role in Franschhoek's heritage.

The individualistic bunch of wine farmers call themselves the Vignerons de Franschhoek, and form a tightly knit group when it comes to promoting the valley and its wines. This ward of the Paarl district long languished under the reputation as a producer of not very characterful white wines, having traditionally cultivated the flat, sandy, valley floor. But with development and expertise, the decomposed granite on the mountain slopes is being exploited, producing some very fine reds. And the south-easter wind provides suitably cool-climate conditions for whites such as Sauvignon Blanc, Chardonnay and the valley trademark, Sémillon – even the tricky red, Pinot Noir – in an otherwise warm basin.

Pockets of land are now being identified and planted to suitable varieties based on scientific soil analyses, particularly along the Dasberg slopes, up the south-eastern kloof and on the south-east-facing foothills of the Franschhoek mountains. And serious winemakers and dedicated amateurs alike are applying sophisticated cellar equipment and intelligent winemaking techniques to making the most of what the valley has to offer. Their success continues to attract newcomers.

These are small enterprises – anything from 8h to 15ha producing from 4 000 to 15 000 cases. Many vineyards still share space with fruit orchards: pears, peaches, apricots and plums, with the wine grapes traditionally going to the Franschhoek Vineyards co-op. But with a booming wine market in the '90s, canny businessmen-turned-gentlemen farmers have invested in their own little cellars, resulting in a proliferation of new labels joining the old stalwarts.

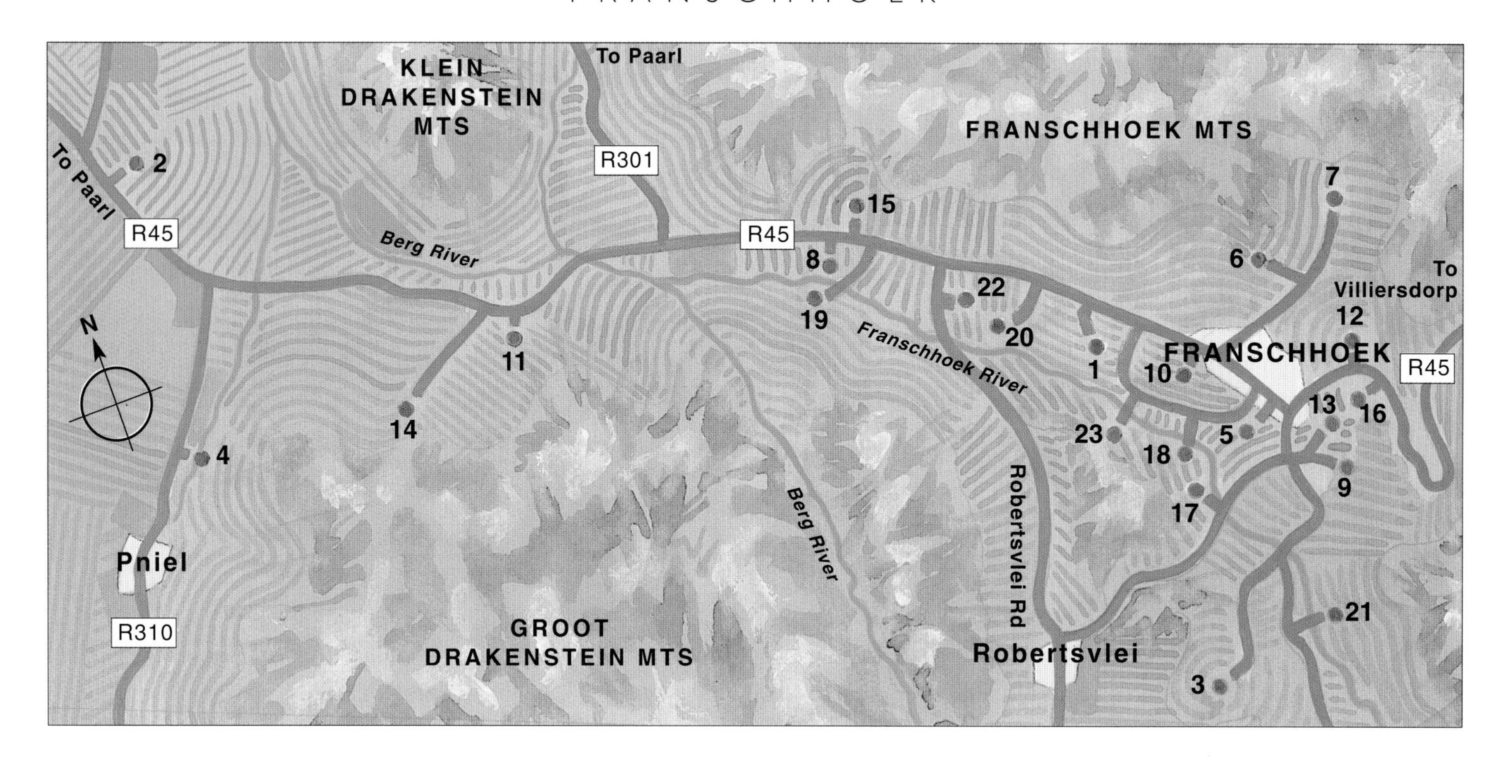

1. Agusta
2. Ashwood
3. Boekenhoutskloof
4. Boschendal
5. Cabrière
6. Chamonix
7. Dieu Donné
8. Eikehof
9. Elephant Pass
10. Franschhoek Vineyards
11. Graham Beck Coastal
12. Haute Cabrière
13. Jean Daneel Wines
14. L'Ormarins
15. La Motte
16. La Petite Ferme
17. Landau du Val
18. Mont Rochelle
19. Môreson
20. Rickety Bridge
21. Stony Brook
22. TenFiftySix
23. Von Ortloff

OPENING PAGE: Vines on Dieu Donné are carefully contoured to derive the full benefit of the sun and cool breezes on the flanks of the Franschhoek Mountain.

GRAHAM BECK COASTAL

OWNER
Graham Beck

KEY WINES
Cabernet Sauvignon, Pinotage, Sauvignon Blanc (new selected varietal and blended labels to be decided)

1998
GRAHAM BECK
PINOTAGE
COASTAL WINERY

'Reds are our future,' says heart-throb, moustachioed young winemaker Charles Hopkins. A sign of a different side to the Franschhoek image and a new direction for this much-loved wine farm known as Bellingham up against the slopes of the Groot Drakenstein mountain. Although first granted in 1693, the farm's winemaking history is more modern: it was in the 1940s that East European immigrant Bernard Podlashuk pioneered South Africa's first Rosé, the crisp, dry white known as Premier Grand Cru, and the semi-sweet Johannisberger in its dumpy flask the shape of a grape bunch.

Bellingham continued its fame as a popular wine brand of consistent – if unexciting – quality through the '70s and '80s under ownership of wine producer/wholesalers such as Union Wine and, later, Douglas Green. The promise of a quality renaissance came in 1990, when coal magnate, horse-breeder and Robertson winery owner Graham Beck acquired the farm through shares in the new Douglas Green Bellingham (DGB) producer/wholesaler. Beck is now sole proprietor of the farm, vineyards and new cellar, but the wines will be sold under the Graham Beck Coastal label, with *négociant* DGB retaining the rights to the Bellingham brand name to be made from out-sourced grapes. The contents of DGB's portfolio, which recently included the premium 'Spitz' label as well as a standard range of good, solid, varietal and blended reds and whites, is still being finalised following the latest settlement.

The farm's new red-wine fermentation and barrel facility, with design elements reminiscent of the old Burgundian Hospice de Beaune and capable of handling 1 500 tons, has just been completed. The old white cellar, now also a 1 500-tonner, has been enlarged and re-equipped. This reflects the ultimate aim in the next couple of years – to divide the 130ha farm equally between noble red and white varieties. Recent uprootings, for example, include 25ha of old Bukettraube on the Bellingham hill behind the farm to make way for classic reds.

Hopkins is up to the challenge, and will be even further extended by recent acquisitions by Beck of two farms in the Firgrove-Helderberg area, renowned for great reds. Grapes are also sourced from red-wine-rich Devon Valley, with whites from Darling, Somerset West and elsewhere. Hopkins has proved his talent with the recent range of premium reds, until recently referred to as the Bellingham 'Spitz' wines.

Of all the single-varietal, single-vineyard and separately vinified wines, the Pinotage is considered one of the Cape's best. The recent '98, under the new Graham Beck Coastal label, continued the track record of its 'Spitz' forerunners, again being voted among the Pinotage Producers' annual 'Top Ten'. From old Bellingham vines, it is nevertheless very New World, with rich, sweet fruit and spicy oak (French and American new wood). The dense Cabernet also draws on mature home-vines, while the Shiraz is a real smoothie, with sweetness and spice from mostly American oak. And then there's Hopkins' 'babe': a leafy, minty, deep-flavoured Cabernet Franc, inspired by a visit to St-Emilion in '92. Cabernet Franc is a rarity as a varietal wine in the Cape, though it does create great excitement in isolated instances (at Cordoba and Warwick, for example).

Charles Hopkins (**TOP**), winemaker for Graham Beck Coastal, is revelling in the ultra-modern facilities of the new cellar on historic Bellingham (**ABOVE**), at the foot of the imposing Groot Drakenstein peaks.

BOEKENHOUTS-KLOOF

OWNER

Newcom Investments

KEY WINES

Boekenhoutskloof Shiraz, Cabernet Sauvignon, Sémillon; Porcupine Ridge Cabernet Sauvignon, Merlot, Sauvignon Blanc, Chenin Blanc

'Precocious' best describes this newcomer to the Franschhoek Valley – in keeping, one might say, with the character and professions of its owners: maverick wine distributor Tim Rands of Vinimark and his mates, which include top ad-men Reg Lascaris and John Hunt. And they leave their equally precocious winemaker Marc Kent up to his own devices on this former fruit farm up a steep kloof of the Franschhoek Valley.

Boekenhoutskloof now provides its owners with a weekend getaway in the restored 18th-century Cape cottage and its winemaker with a small, simple but efficient 160-ton cellar, extended out from a 19th-century stone-walled cellar. Here Kent, in his first winemaking position after training at Elsenburg and a stint under Jacques Borman at La Motte, has turned out a Shiraz (or Syrah) that is one of the closest yet to achieving that elusive Rhône combination of dense fruit and dry tannin, sweetness and peppery spiciness, smoothness and wildness.

His Cabernet is pure ripe fruit, full of wonderful varietal expression, unfiltered and matured in small French oak. And, in an area that has laid claim to Sémillon as its 'own' variety, the Boekenhoutskloof stands out as an elegant, smooth wine – Kent presses whole bunches, encourages malolactic fermentation and ferments and matures in new Burgundian oak barrels in a special cold-room.

The Boekenhoutskloof name – *boekenhout* is Afrikaans for the Cape beech tree that grows here and is apparently the wood used in the range of seven Cape chairs depicted on the unusual label – is reserved for the premium range. Kent's luscious Merlot should soon join the first team, but currently keeps company with a Cabernet Sauvignon, Sauvignon Blanc and lightly wooded Chenin Blanc under the second label, Porcupine Ridge (named for the shy nocturnal animal that inhabits the high ridge behind the farm).

It is over this ridge that the summer south-easterly wind comes sailing to cool the slopes, partly made up of good decomposed granite soils. New and virus-free clones of Cabernet Sauvignon, Cabernet Franc, Shiraz, Merlot, Sauvignon Blanc and Sémillon have been planted on just over 10ha, to be expanded to 20-odd hectares in time. While these young vines mature, grapes are out-sourced: Shiraz from Somerset West; Merlot from the burgeoning new red-wine area around Malmesbury; and Cabernet and Sémillon from Franschhoek.

Boekenhoutskloof winemaker Marc Kent (**TOP**) bottles great Shiraz, Merlot and Sémillon on this secluded property, with its charming, restored 18th-century farm dwelling (**RIGHT**).

1812

BOSCHENDAL

OWNER
Amwines (Anglo American)

KEY WINES
Shiraz, Merlot, Lanoy, Chardonnay, Sauvignon Blanc, Chenin Blanc, Riesling, Premier Cuvée Brut, Blanc de Noir, Blanc de Blanc, Grand Vin Blanc, Le Bouquet, Boschendal Brut, Vin d'Or; Pavillon Rouge, Pavillon Blanc, Le Grand Pavillon Blanc de Blanc; Jean le Long varietal wines (range varies)

Boschendal is one of the picture-book perfect Cape Dutch wine farms in the winelands. The thatched, whitewashed homestead lies in a sea of vines against the dramatic backdrop of the Groot Drakenstein mountain peak. Granted in 1685 to French Huguenot Jean le Long – his name is immortalised in an ever-changing range of experimental premium wines sold exclusively on auction and in the Boschendal restaurant – the farm was developed viticulturally by the De Villiers family (whose descendants farm Landskroon in Paarl).

In the early 1900s, Boschendal, whose vines had been decimated by the phylloxera epidemic, was among several farms in the area bought by Rhodes Fruit Farms, a Cecil John Rhodes project to turn hard-hit wine growers into successful fruit farmers. In the 1960s it was taken over by diversifying mining corporation Anglo American. Boschendal has now come full circle, with Amfarms recently divesting itself of its fruit, dairy and other agricultural interests in both Boschendal and sister farm Vergelegen, to concentrate solely on wine as Amwines.

A 15-year replanting programme, started in 1989 to replace the 500ha of arbitrary white varieties and virus-infected reds, has been given fresh impetus under GM Gerrie Wagenaar and head viticulturist Spekkies van Breda. Dubbed 'Boschendal 2000', the emphasis will be on top-quality reds to act as standard-bearers in the farm's push into world wine markets, although the cellar will remain predominantly white. Plantings of Chardonnay are extensive and the new vine mix includes more Sauvignon Blanc on the cool, high, virgin reaches of the Groot Drakenstein and Simonsberg mountains.

But Shiraz, Cabernet and Merlot are the focus of the farm's viticultural renewal, with Cabernet Franc and Pinot Noir also in there. About 60ha of old virus-infected plants were uprooted and replanted in '98, 115ha in '99. More Pinot Noir and some Cabernet Franc are also planned. 'The idea is to look at the two farms [Boschendal and Vergelegen] as a whole,' explains new Boschendal cellarmaster JC Bekker. 'So we're specialising in Sauvignon Blanc at Vergelegen, for example, while the Shiraz is particularly good here.' So is the Merlot – it's big and complex.

Current annual production of 200 000 cases is a result of a four-fold increase in as many years. 'And we've still got space,' says the cellarmaster, referring to the R22-million dedicated red-wine cellar completed in time for the '97 vintage and now able to take in bought-in grapes, after Boschendal recently deregistered as an estate. Carefully designed for minimum impact on the historic core heritage area, the cellar is a Cape Victorian-style green-and-white building sunk 1,5m into the ground with a wrap-around, roofed, stone-columned colonnade to break the height. It houses 44 conical stainless-steel tanks, with individual capacities of up to 32 000 litres, suspended from the ceiling – it's an engineering feat considered a world first in cellar design. Each tank has its own control system for fermentation at varying temperatures, depending on the variety. Despite its apparent size, Boschendal is nevertheless geared to handling premium wines in small batches. Only about 500 cases of Shiraz and 1 000 of Merlot are made at the moment, from one and two vineyard blocks respectively. All blocks are vinified separately, 'picked on taste as each one reaches optimum ripeness,' explains Bekker.

Raymond Greyling, in charge of red wines, explains that gentle handling is a prerequisite. The Shiraz and Pinot Noir are fermented in open vats and the cap is punched down manually. Boschendal's new varietal reds, which may include a Cabernet soon, have always been elegant, but they now display a new, soft fruitiness. A flagship red blend, unnamed, but made up from Merlot and Cabernet Franc – maybe Cabernet – promises to be an exceptional wine. Among the whites, the fresh, herby Sauvignon Blanc develops nicely in bottle, while the new Chardonnays are less full-bodied, more delicately wooded, for fresher, easier appeal. Both bottle-fermented bubblies are consistently fine.

OPPOSITE: Boschendal's Cape Dutch manor house, now a museum, sports a gable with Baroque and Neo-Classical elements. By contrast, winemakers JC Bekker and Raymond Greyling (RIGHT) make particularly tasty reds with the help of push-button technology.

02

CABRIÈRE/HAUTE CABRIÈRE

OWNER

Achim von Arnim

KEY WINES

Pierre Jourdan Blanc de Blancs, Brut Sauvage, Cuvée Brut, Cuvée Reserve, Cuvée Belle Rose, Petit Pierre Ratafia, Fine de Jourdan; Haute Cabrière Pinot Noir, Chardonnay-Pinot Noir

The tall, always dishevelled, exuberant Achim von Arnim – he's now officially Baron von Arnim – is of Prussian descent and Geisenheim-trained, making him somewhat of an oddity in the strongly French-flavoured valley. Von Arnim has been single-minded in his quest to produce classic Champagne on his domaine, purchased in 1984 and now, with the addition of the Haute Cabrière site, totalling some 25ha producing about 25 000 cases. The Cabrière cellar in town is dedicated to *methode champenoise* production, complete with its own well-chilled 'salmanazar room', where he is the first after the Champagne House of Pommery to bottle-ferment in these massive nine-litre flagons.

The Pierre Jourdan label (named after the French Huguenot who founded Cabrière in 1694) encompasses a whole range of *methode champenoise* bubblies in varying styles, from the 'oyster-dry' Brut Sauvage (with no dosage) and the broader Blanc de Blancs (most highly rated) to the richer though still elegant Cuvée Brut (most popular) to the pink, pure Pinot Noir Belle Rose (a delicate, fruity drink).

These wines are singular among Cap Classiques: they do not generally perform well in 'blind' tastings, with many 'wine fundis' finding them too dry, slightly harsh and lacking in character and development. Yet the wines sell out quickly and one suspects they are often drunk (and tasted) far too soon, needing bottle-age to come into their own – they are all about finesse and elegance and subtlety. The Cuvée Brut, sold off the farm only and left on the lees for at least four years before degorgement, shows the benefits of maturity, giving a more fulsome, yeasty, less racy mouthful.

Von Arnim again followed the Champagne tradition when using excess wines for his Ratafia, a sweet Chardonnay, fortified with pot-still Chardonnay; similarly the Fine, which is distilled from Chardonnay and aged in Limousin oak – a potent *digestif*. It was the

Cape's first 'estate' pot-still brandy in years, following the repeal in the early '90s of legislation prohibiting private 'home' distilleries.

This individualistic wine grower also led the way when it came to Cape Pinot Noir. First released in 1994, the Haute Cabrière style of pure, strawberry fruit in a dense, chocolatey mouthful elicited rave reviews from critics and wine lovers alike. New Burgundian clones, closely planted à la Burgundy on a 10ha site below the Franschhoek Pass, provided a fresh take on the leafy, vegetal, mushroomy character of other Cape Pinots, made mostly from the Swiss Champagne clone BK5. Subsequent vintages have vacillated between rather simple, quaffable, 'strawberry cooldrink' wines and that early promise of pure fruit density and sweet, lip-smacking savouriness. This latter character came back in the '98 with the promise of more regular appearances as the young Haute Cabrière vines mature.

For all his rarified image, Von Arnim has proved himself capable of the common touch, with his best-selling Chardonnay Pinot blend, a still wine, just off-dry, with Pinot raspberry fruit weight and Chardonnay citric crispness.

OPPOSITE: A three-storey cellar languishes behind the flower-bedecked façade of the hilltop Haute Cabrière winery, where vintner Achim von Arnim (**ABOVE**) makes elegant Pinot Noir to match his Pierre Jourdan Cap Classique range.

LA MOTTE

OWNER
Hanneli Rupert

KEY WINES
Millennium, Shiraz, Cabernet, Chardonnay, Blanc Fumé, Sauvignon Blanc

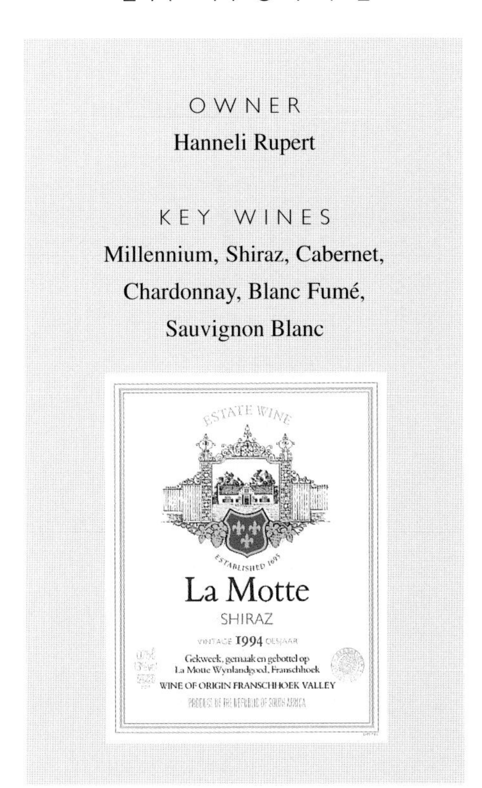

One of several Rupert-renovated Cape wine farms, La Motte is now home to patriarch Dr Anton Rupert's daughter Hanneli, a mezzo-soprano of international acclaim. Granted to a 17th-century German settler, the farm was named La Motte by later French Huguenot owner Pierre Joubert, but only planted to vines late in the 1700s. One of the largest Franschhoek farms, it was incorporated into Rhodes Fruit Farms in the 1900s, falling into conservation-conscious Rupert hands in 1970.

The old Cape Dutch homestead, original cellar and working watermill were meticulously restored, and supplemented with a modern pressing cellar when winemaker Jacques Borman came on board in 1984. Borman is a bit of a Francophile and definitely a red-wine man. Together with viticulturist Pietie le Roux, he spearheaded the planting of classic red varieties on what was once a mainly white-wine farm: Cabernet Sauvignon, Merlot, Cabernet Franc and Shiraz. Shiraz is his métier, although there is just one-and-a-half hectares under this Rhône classic. The wine is invariably rich in fruit, with great density and concentration, yet

always elegant; it has that typical spicy pepperiness that many get on the Rhône reds. Borman uses a combination of French and American oak – he is a classicist without being a traditionalist – and prefers a combination of new and used barrels.

His second love is blending, specifically the estate's great Millennium, a Bordeaux-style combination of Cabernet, Merlot and a touch of Cabernet Franc. Again, an elegant wine, though firmly fruited. 'We [the name was selected by Dr Rupert] wanted to make a Bordeaux-style classic, but in the South African tradition. We were looking for a smooth, world-class red, drinkable at an early stage, but with ageing potential that we hoped would take it well into the next century.'

The straight Cabernet is a firmer, more structured wine, which benefits from several years' bottle-ageing. A new string to this Francophile's bow is a Chardonnay, a heavy-weight, made in small quantities with only selected barrels bottled under the La Motte label. And while his Sauvignon Blanc is fairly ordinary, the more full-bodied Blanc Fumé benefits from time on the lees and in the barrel.

Borman's French connection comes from first-hand experience: working harvests at Châteaux Lafite, Latour and Margaux; visits overseas with international business tycoon, gentleman and wine lover, old-man Rupert; a co-consultancy with renowned French vintner Michel Roland at a joint Rupert-De Rothschild winery, R & de R Fredericksburg, just down the road; and now a reciprocal arrangement with the Coursodon family in St Joseph, a rising star in the Northern Rhône, where Borman's assistant Lukas Wentzel recently boned up on Shiraz production.

The farm boasts over 100ha of vines, spanning the main road that cuts the valley in half, and creeping up the slopes of the Franschhoek mountain. Only La Motte's best wines appear under its own label: about 15 000 cases. The rest is sold, as grapes or wine.

AGUSTA WINES

Italian count and international racing car driver Riccardo Agusta has reunited, after a 150-year division, the two historic Franschhoek wine properties of La Provence and Haute Provence. The home of the premium Count Agusta and second-label La Provence ranges is a swish new cellar behind the cosy old Haute Provence tasting room and rustic 'Angels' Tears' winery. Annual production is up from 250 to 600 tons, from about 25ha of own vineyards as well as top-quality grapes bought in, mostly, from Stellenbosch. Filling the rather large shoes of the late John Goschen (the young winemaker responsible for an award-winning, simply gorgeous Cabernet and a powerful, buttery Chardonnay under the former Haute Provence label) is Jean-Luc Sweerts. There may be a swing to more elegant wines from the above two varieties. The best-selling, slightly sweet Angels' Tears blend of Chenin and Muscat d'Alexandrie is still there, and a Chardonnay sparkling wine has joined the band.

PREVIOUS PAGE, TOP: La Motte winemaker Jacques Borman is a Shiraz specialist.
RIGHT: A modern cellar has replaced the historic old cellar and a restored Cape Dutch cottage is now home to owner, international opera singer Hanneli Rupert.

ASHWOOD

This is a budding new wholesale wine producer that moves some 200 000 cases each year, bottling wine for local producers and retailers such as Woolworths, as well as for its own ranges. These are made by New Zealand 'flying winemaker' Clive Hartnell at Ashwood's new winery in Simondium, as well as at several cellars in Worcester from where much of the fruit is sourced. Cape Colours is middle-of-the-road stuff, including varietal wines such as Pinotage, Chenin, Sauvignon and Chardonnay. Wines labelled Michael Paul include a Chenin and a Merlot from France, and the Le Parfait range comprises quaffing blends. Ashwood is run by Rob Meihuizen for a host of partners.

CHAMONIX

The high-lying 40ha of Chamonix vineyards is owned by West Africa resort developer Chris Hellinger. Here Geisenheim-trained winemaker Peter Arnold has made a name for himself with a solid Cabernet and highly toasted, powerful, bottle-aged Chardonnays since his maiden 1992 vintage. His wood-matured Sauvignon Blanc is one of the Cape's more successful versions. But the scales will soon be tipped to the side of red varieties, including Cabernet, Pinotage and Pinot Noir.

DIEU DONNÉ

Even higher up the Franschhoek mountain than Chamonix lies Dieu Donné, another traditionally white-wine farm turning to reds. This change comes with input from the horse-racing Maingard family's new plantings of Cabernet, Merlot, Pinotage and Shiraz on the farms Normandie and La Cotte elsewhere in the valley. Current annual production will go up from 10 000 cases to about 40 000, and the new cellar being planned may even be stretched to 60 000 cases in the next few years. Winemaker is Stefan du Toit, a well-travelled, newly graduated Cape Wine Master. Dieu Donné's young reds are medium-bodied and quite tannic, with the farm's own Cabernet the best of the bunch.

The mountainside vines of Dieu Donné catch the cooling south-easter breezes that temper the summer heat in the Franschhoek Valley basin.

EIKEHOF

The Malherbe family farm Eikehof grew grapes for sale to other wineries until son Francois decided to bottle some of their own Sémillon from ancient bush vines. The vines date back to 1903, the year the farm was bought by these descendants of one of the first French Huguenots to arrive in the valley. Malherbe's Sémillon, both the regular and the special Bush Vine bottling, remains seminal. The latter is full of ripe, tropical and citrus fruit, a weighty wine with plenty of ageing potential. The former is lighter, fresher and for earlier drinking, and includes fruit from new trellised vines. From 35ha of vines also come a fruity, buttery Chardonnay and a gorgeous Cabernet redolent of cassis, blackberry, chocolate and new-clone mintiness. A young Merlot is new and Shiraz was recently added to the vine mix.

ELEPHANT PASS

Retired businessman Peter Wrighton has acquired the services of champion winemaker Jean Daneel, formerly of Morgenhof and now based in Franschhoek, to make wine from his restored Oude Kelder property, which boasts newly planted Cabernet Sauvignon, Merlot, Chardonnay, Sauvignon Blanc and Chenin Blanc on just 8ha, looked after by vineyardist Krige Siebrits. The Sauvignon Blanc is a delicious, rounded, soft wine, the Chardonnay is given serious barrel treatment, while the Chenin is still in an 'experimental' phase. The two oak-matured reds promise good things.

FRANSCHHOEK VINEYARDS

Despite more and more wine growers building their own cellars over the past 10 or so years, the neo-classical, creeper-covered Franschhoek Vineyards' co-operative winery, founded in 1945, still has nearly 100 members and produces around 100 000 cases. Resident winemakers Deon Truter and Driaan van der Merwe recently introduced some serious, barrel-fermented whites under the Franschhoek Vineyards label. Then there's the longstanding La Cotte range, liberally peppered with the noble varieties everyone in the valley is planting. Plus they make wines for local and overseas buyers, including UK supermarket chain Tesco.

JEAN DANEEL WINES

Jean Daneel, who helped put Buitenverwachting and then Morgenhof on the map, has re-united with former Morgenhof proprietor Gert Probe on the farm Guldenheuvel next door to Oude Kelder. Brand new, unused horse stables have been converted into cellar space, where Daneel has produced small quantities of a Sauvignon Blanc, Chenin Blanc and Cabernet Merlot blend, simply called JD.

LANDAU DU VAL

Former Toyota and Gencor Industries boss Basil Landau, at home in the restored historic homestead of La Brie, has some 14ha of vines, including Sauvignon Blanc and 80-year-old Sémillon. The former is full of grassy, gooseberry freshness, the latter a wonderfully rich, fruity wine with butterscotch creaminess, quite toasty oak and a slight sweetness. About 500 cases are made by Jean-Luc Sweerts at the nearby Agusta cellar.

LA PETITE FERME

Here Mark Dendy-Young moves mash with buckets instead of pipes and pumps; small steel tanks boast adjustable lids tailor-made by his father John, who is vineyard manager, fruit farmer and master iron craftsman; and some 2 000 cases of very fine wine are made from just 8ha of mountainside vineyards on this fruit and wine farm, which also boasts a fine, family-run restaurant. Dendy-Young's award-winning Sauvignon Blancs hail from a three-ton-a-hectare vineyard. The Chardonnay is rich, yet fresh, barrel-fermented and lees-stirred à la Burgundy. The Merlot is full of rich, concentrated, plummy fruit. An 'experimental' new Shiraz shows a lovely combination of fruitiness, pepperiness and sweet, spicy oak, with a bit of a tannic bite.

L'ORMARINS

Another Rupert investment, L'Ormarins is owned and managed by son Antonij, who lives in what is one of the winelands' most beautiful Cape Dutch homesteads with its text-book, neo-classical gable dated 1811. L'Ormarins reds can be very fine, especially the Cabernet and Shiraz named Maison du Roi after first 18th-century owner, French Huguenot Jean Roi. The farm's flagship, the Optima Merlot/Cabernet blend, is usually a wonderfully rich, smooth, drinkable wine, benefiting from a few years' bottle-age before release. Among the classic varietal whites, the Rhine Riesling, delicately off-dry, can be a star. One of the Cape's few Late Bottled Vintage ports is made from traditional Portuguese varieties Souzão and Touriga Naçional among the 200-odd ha spread on the foothills of the Groot Drakenstein mountain. Wrensch Roux is the winemaker.

MONT ROCHELLE

Proprietor, former ad-man Graham de Villiers, recently lost his very able young winemaker, Anne-Marée Mostert, to Warwick in Stellenbosch. New winemaker Justin Hoy is now making himself at home in the 150-year-old Victorian packing shed, transformed into a compact 12 000-case winery. 'And with Rod Easthope [who rejuvenated Rustenberg] consulting, we're going to reinvent ourselves; there'll be a total overhaul of winemaking techniques,' says De Villiers, a descendant of one of the original French Huguenots – a Jac de Villiers was the farm's original owner. The 10ha of new terraced vineyards planted up the Dasberg slopes produce some lovely, ripe, fruity, richly oaked Chardonnays and a big, tasty Cabernet Sauvignon. A hand-pressed and unfiltered Merlot has impressed.

MÔRESON

Owned by Richard Friedman, the farm was a spur-of-the-moment auction buy by his Johannesburg-based parents in 1986. Citrus trees and Chenin Blanc were soon joined by Sauvignon Blanc, Chardonnay, Weisser Riesling and Sémillon. Early wines under the Matin Soleil label (a suitably French translation of Môreson or 'morning sun') were made at the local co-op until 1994, when Richard tried his hand at it in their new cellar. He met with such success with a Chenin and Chardonnay – the Premium is still a goodie – that a full-time winemaker, Pierre Wahl, was employed. But the recent reds have really put the winery on the map, especially the Cabernet and Merlot. The Pinotage is good too, and the Shiraz is worth keeping an eye on.

RICKETY BRIDGE

This 18th-century farm, originally named Paulina's Dal by then-owner, the widow Paulina de Villiers, has been given a hi-tech makeover by new proprietors Alan and Celia Tonkin, at home in the restored historic Cape Dutch house since 1997. The cellar is now a smart 300-ton facility, complete with push-button technology, hi-tech equipment and a 400-barrel underground maturation cellar. Winemaker Boela Gerber has turned the 25ha of two-thirds red and one-third white grapes into some classy wines. All are from noble varieties, planted around the cellar at the foot of the Dasberg. The Classic Selection comprises easy-drinking whites, as well as a new varietal Malbec, a Cape rarity. The Premium Selection encompasses a range of unwooded and wooded white and reds, including a very good

Merlot, an award-winning, spicy Shiraz and a Cabernet. The Reserve Collection label is set aside for special parcels of the farm's finest. One such is the Paulinas Reserve, a Cabernet of wonderful depth and concentration.

STONY BROOK

This is the new domain of determined, self-taught winemaker and now 'retired' Grahamstown GP Nigel McNaught and his teacher wife Joy, who first set up home in the valley at historic Rickety Bridge in 1988. He caused quite a stir with his maiden Cabernets, made in a makeshift cellar, until financial demands required him to seek something more humble. Undeterred, the couple simply moved up-valley.

McNaught's wines are truly individualistic and powerful, with high alcohols. The barrel-fermented Sémillon from 70-year-old vines is a winner, as is the Chardonnay, a lovely lemony wine, also barrel-fermented. The reds – Cabernet, Shiraz and Pinotage – are equally full-bodied and somewhat rustic.

TENFIFTYSIX

This quirky name was taken from the numbered portion (1056) of the farm Watervliet, bought by Cape Town property developer and fruit farmer Michael Falkson in 1989. Four years after planting a small Cabernet vineyard, he decided to bottle his own wine. Now he has a compact, one-man cellar behind his home where he handcrafts and personally bottles about 3 000 cases of Sauvignon Blanc, Blanc Fumé, Chardonnay and a Cabernet, which has very ripe fruit and firm tannins, calling for time in the bottle.

VON ORTLOFF

Dassenberg farm, home of Von Ortloff Wines, is a study in German aptitude and precision. Over the past five years, former BMW human resources manager Georg Schlichtmann and architect wife Evi have established their 15ha of Sauvignon Blanc, Chardonnay, Cabernet Sauvignon and Merlot vineyards, carefully planted after extensive analysis of the fairly rich soils on the foothills of the Dasberg. They've just completed a simple, stylish, efficient 200-ton cellar behind their restored 300-year-old Cape cottage, taking production up from 3 000 to 5 000 cases. Most of it, made in consultation with La Motte winemaker Jacques Borman, is exported, mainly to Germany and the UK. The wines are elegant and drinkable, with the Cabernet Merlot blend and Chardonnay usually the best.

Vine cultivation in Franschhoek is moving up from the sandy valley floor to the slopes of the surrounding mountains, making for a step up in wine quality.

W E L L I N G T O N

Here, as elsewhere in the Cape winelands, winemakers are seeing red, with premium varieties Cabernet Sauvignon, Merlot and Shiraz, as well as Pinotage, being planted. It is a direct result of the shortage and demand for red wine, and here, too, co-operatives long dedicated to mass production of marginal whites are responding to market demands.

Wellington is one of the early 17th-century Cape settlements, drawing from Dutch as well as French Huguenot cultural, architectural and agricultural influence.

The area is dominated by well-drained Glenrosa shale above decomposed granite on the steeper slopes of the Groenberg outcrop and foothills of the Hawequa and Limiet ranges, where slopes are cool south-, south-east and south-west-facing. With greater viticultural know-how, these cool areas in a warm valley are now being exploited.

While fairly new, small independent cellars such as Claridge, Napier and Oude Wellington are turning out some fine wines, the general viticultural reputation of this Paarl ward has been given a substantial boost by the Linton Park development of Slangrivier. The Cape Wine Cellars joint venture between the Wellington-based South African Dried Fruit Company (SAD) and three local co-ops (Wellington, Wamakersvallei and Bovlei) in conjunction with nearby Boland co-op in Paarl is also doing well on the export market. Forged in 1994, this alliance has 'flying winemaker' Kym Milne, the New Zealander who heads International Wine Services, consulting with local blender Jeff Wedgwood and the co-op winemakers to produce what buyers in Europe and Asia want. Production more than tripled from 1996 to 1999. The ultimate figure being touted is 600 000 cases.

Wine-grape growers still deliver to longstanding private wholesaler Huguenot Wine Farmers, which produces lower-priced wines, dessert wines, port, Muscadels and such. And amid the premiums and stalwarts such as Cinsaut and Chenin comes a novelty like a crop of Carignan from Welgegund, a 50ha wine farm supplying Bovlei. Owned by Gauteng businessman Alex Camerer and MP wife Sheila, Welgegund has 2ha of 20-year-old Carignan bush-vines that produce an interesting, peppery, spicy Beaujolais-style wine, the Cape's only bottled example.

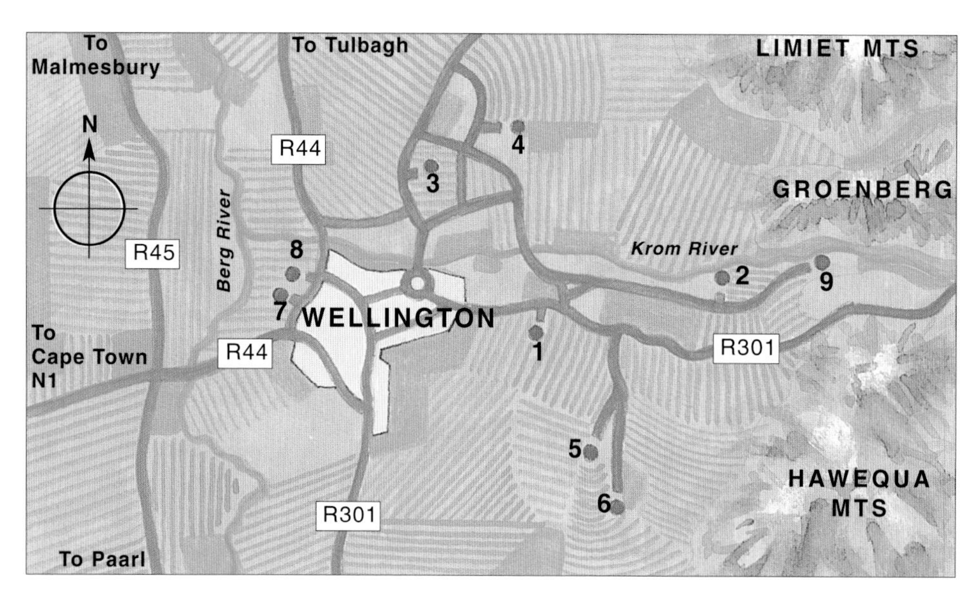

1. Bovlei
2. Claridge
3. Jacaranda
4. Linton Park
5. Napier
6. Oude Wellington
7. Wamakersvallei
8. Wellington
9. Welvanpas

OPENING PAGE: Wellington, with the Limiet mountains in the background and Groenberg sloping up to the right, is the focus of renewed interest in premium wine-grape growing by aristocratic French vintners like JP Moueix of Pomerol fame, multinationals and local entrepreneurs.

CLARIDGE

OWNERS

Roger and Maria Jorgensen

KEY WINES

Red Wellington, Claridge Chardonnay, Klein Optenhorst Pinot Noir, The Pinotage Company Pinotage

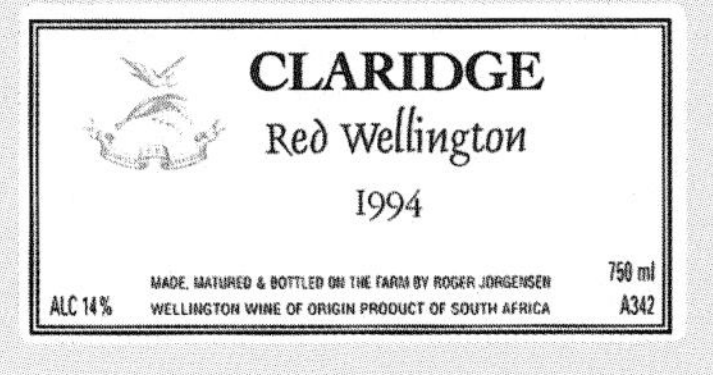

A strawberry farmer from Kent and his South African Greek wife lead an individualistic life on their rambling Cape Dutch farm Rustenburg, nestled beneath the vertigo-inducing historic Bains Kloof Pass. When Roger Jorgensen is not diamond prospecting in Namibia and the tiny Maria is not cooking up a storm in the kitchen, they're making and bottling some very distinctive wines in their homespun cellar.

Production is small, boutique-stuff, only about 3 000 cases from some 15ha of vines. Jorgensen spends a lot of time in his vineyards; he ruthlessly prunes his vines, halving yields to a quality-driven five tons per hectare. He weighs his yeasts on a kitchen scale. Wine-making is kept as simple and unrefined as the cellar itself: small stainless-steel tanks, no filtering, natural fining agents such as egg white and minimal sulphur. He allows time for malolactic fermentation in his barrel-fermented Chardonnay, giving his reds up to 18 months in barrel and another year in bottle before release.

His two signature wines are gutsy, as intended. 'I don't like pussycat wines,' says Jorgensen. He has modified his style lately, looking for 'more finesse, restraint, maybe wines that drink a little earlier'. The Red Wellington is a a rich, complex, tough, high-octane combination of Cabernet Sauvignon and Merlot, with a dash of Cabernet Franc. The Claridge Chardonnay is a powerful, toasty wine, smothered in vanilla and freshened by zesty lemon. These are wines for the long haul: the '91 Chardonnay (his maiden vintage) was a drinking delight nearly eight years later, as was the '93 Red Wellington.

A Pinot Noir from neighbour Naas Ferreira's Klein Optenhorst farm is made by Jorgensen from a vineyard he manages. Again, not your standard Pinot: sweetness combines with an earthy character, and despite its light colour the wine has tannins that require softening in the bottle. He also vinifies grapes from cousin Julian Johnson's farm across the way, bottling some Merlot, rich in blackberries and toasty oak, and a blend of Shiraz and Merlot. As with his wines, for which Burgundy and Bordeaux are benchmarks, his pet project, an 'estate', copper-pot-distilled brandy, still maturing, seeks to emulate the finest Cognac.

ABOVE: Rogerand Maria Jorgenson and their young family all chip in to turn out wonderful Burgundian-style wines on their hillside property overlooking the Hawequa peaks (**LEFT**).

LINTON PARK

OWNER
Linton Park Plc

KEY WINES
Linton Park Cabernet Sauvignon, Chardonnay; Capell's Court Cabernet Sauvignon, Shiraz, Chardonnay, Sauvignon Blanc

1998
LINTON PARK
CLAIRE DIVISION, SLANGRIVIER
CHARDONNAY
SOUTH AFRICA

This is a major investment in fruit and wine-grape farming in Wellington by rather swish London-based, agricultural multi-national Linton Park, which farms tea, coffee, citrus, nuts, avocados and table grapes from California to Chile, Australia to Africa. This is its first venture into wine (Australia may be next) and the company is geared to producing some excellent wines headed for the international market. Winemaker Ian Naudé can scarcely contain himself for excitement.

The 285ha property, on the south-facing slopes of the Groenberg, is considered prime viticultural land: limey soils on well-drained Malmesbury shale. The microclimate is a whole 5°C cooler than the warm Wellington valley. Some 120ha include established Cabernet, Shiraz and Chardonnay, as well as Sauvignon Blanc. These are being expanded by a further 30ha of the same, plus Merlot and Pinotage. Recently planted Ruby Cabernet is proving particularly successful and some mature Chenin vines have been retained.

After buying the farm in 1995, Linton Park MD Malcolm Perkins renovated the 1809 manor house and built a new 1 000-ton cellar. He then poached Naudé from Berg & Brook in Paarl, where he'd been working with the Slangrivier grapes, particularly a much-talked-about Shiraz, for the Savanha range.

Heading the Linton Park portfolio is the Linton Park Cabernet, a modern melange of delicious, smooth, supple drinkability under-pinned by some serious blackcurrant, mint and new, small French-oak structure. It is from the farm's best block and is vinified separately. The Chardonnay is equally delicious, again sourced from a selected vineyard and new-oak matured. It is lemony fresh, with a creamy, butterscotch layer beneath.

A single-vineyard Shiraz will join these two soon – fermentation problems have relegated it to the second-label Capell's Court range for now. The wine is almost off-dry at 6g/litre sugar. But lots of fruit and varietal pepperiness and big alcohol provide quite a mouthful. Most of the wines, even the reds, are marked by a touch of residual sugar, which enhances earlier drinkability, but takes nothing away from their basic quality and potential to last a good few years. Big, bold wines, 'for international palates', reckons Naude.

TOP: Ian Naudé is upbeat about his new Linton Park range, backed by a London-based multi-national whose MD Malcolm Perkins is a part-time resident of the restored Slang River Cape Dutch homestead (**RIGHT**).

New, healthy vineyards show up with golden foliage in autumn rather than the russet colour indicative of the virus-infected material that used to cloak the Cape winelands.

BOVLEI

This roadside co-op at the foot of the Bains Kloof Pass has spectacular views of the towering Hawequa mountains from the tasting room's picture windows. Cellarmaster Tinus Broodryk and winemaker Henk Wentzel are overseeing the replacement on their 70-odd member growers' farms of the ubiquitous Chenin with premium red varieties. Sites and soils are being carefully identified, with the Groenberg foothills undoubtedly the prime spot. Cabernet Sauvignon has the most impressive track record: a regular Veritas gold medal winner, it has typical blackcurrant and cedary flavours, while remaining an easy, value-for-money drink. A host of marginal white wines keep co-op traditionalists happy.

JACARANDA

Those who know the farm call it 'Jan se Dam' (Jan's Dam). When the affable Jan Tromp – a retired accountant – and his wife Trish bought Jacaranda farm in 1988 and decided to make their own wine, this rangy, jeans-clad antithesis of the stereotype accountant installed the necessary equipment along a narrow walkway formed between an original old concrete water reservoir and a slightly smaller dam built within. With the help of a 2 000-litre water tank and chiller, this cellar-in-the-round maintains an ideally cool ambient temperature of below 15°C.

Jacaranda has produced some fairly off-beat, earthy and full-bodied Chenins, dry and off-dry. Tromp has now diversified into reds with a Cabernet Merlot blend called Debutante, an uncommonly low-alcohol (10%), light-coloured and delicately fruity and spicy wine. A Dry Red offers a similar combination, with a varietal Cabernet and a Chenin-based fortified dessert wine completing this idiosyncratic range.

NAPIER

A former member of heart surgeon Dr Chris Barnard's team, Chris Kühn has approached his new winemaking career with pure professionalism and surgical precision. He has around 20ha under mainly Cabernet Sauvignon, Merlot, Cabernet Franc, Chardonnay and old Chenin. His carefully designed hillside cellar sports a gravity-fed production line, custom-made stainless-steel tanks and an ingenious nitrogen-fed system to prevent wastage when barrels need topping up. He waited more than three years before releasing his maiden Bordeaux-style red called Red Medallion, a big wine. His Chardonnays have become fruitier and his Loire-like Chenin is bone dry and high in acid. There's also a varietal Cabernet. Most of his wine, including a second label Lion Creek, is exported to the US and Europe.

OUDE WELLINGTON

This 30ha estate was bought by German dental surgeon Rolf Schumacher in 1995. Together with self-taught winemaker Vanessa Simkiss, formerly in the hotel trade but always harbouring a dream to make wine, handyman Schumacher renovated the 200-year-old manor house and converted an old barn into a small winery. The 18ha of sad-looking Ruby Cabernet (now bottled as a rich, rare varietal wine first labelled as Rubignon), Cabernet Sauvignon, Chenin and Muscat d'Alexandrie (Hanepoot) were nursed back to health. Cabernet and Chardonnay have been added and Merlot and Pinotage are in the pipeline.

Schumacher has produced his first Grappa and is working on a copper-pot-still brandy. The funky wine labels juxtapose papal purple and gold with a wacky Wellington boot.

WAMAKERSVALLEI

This co-op, founded in 1940, carries the name by which Wellington was originally known: the 'valley of the wagon makers', a thriving industry at the time when Wamakersvallei (or *Val du Charron*, as the French Huguenot settlers called it) was a remote border of the Cape Colony.

Some 69 member growers of this co-op, founded in 1940, bring in about 12 000 tons of grapes, handled by 28-year veteran cellar-master Chris Roux and long-time winemaker Pieter Rossouw. That Cape stalwart Cinsaut is the star of the show here, though a soft, succulent Merlot is challenging for the crown. An off-dry Chenin, gentle and fruity, can be pleasant. There is also a limited-edition Cabernet-based Port and a fortified Muscat d'Alexandrie dessert wine.

WELLINGTON

Adjoining Wamakersvallei is Wellington co-op – founded in 1906, it is one of the country's first. Producing about 20 000 cases from more than 1 500ha of vineyards, Wellington handles mostly white wines, though new plantings of Cabernet, Merlot, Shiraz and Pinotage will eventually account for at least 40% of production. It's the place for well-priced Pinotage of the cherry-sweet, lightly wooded style and other similarly quaffable single-varietal bottlings of Cabernet, Shiraz and Merlot. A fresh, guava-like Chenin is new to the range. Chardonnay and Sauvignon Blanc make up the balance.

WELVANPAS

True-blue Afrikaner *volks* territory, this farm is the rustic seat of the family that spawned 19th-century Voortrekker Piet Retief. While Piet was conquering the hinterland, brother Daniel was making wine at the foot of the Bains Kloof Pass.

Welvanpas, then known as 'De Krakeel Hoek' (Corner of Storms/Battles), had once belonged to his great-grandmother, who had married French Huguenot Francois Retief in 1688. The thatched 180-year-old gabled farmhouse with its highly polished Cape antiques is now home to Dan Snr. With his son, Stellenbosch University-trained winemaker 'Young Dan', the Retiefs supply nearby Bovlei co-op from their 45ha of grapes. They also bottle minute quantities of a Cabernet, Chenin/ Chardonnay blend and Bukettraube, made in a large, ramshackle cellar dating back to 1887.

The 1817 mud-brick stable is being spruced up for wine tastings.

S W A R T L A N D

Cool hilly pockets in the Swartland produce stunning Sauvignon Blanc among the white wines grown here.

The Swartland district, which falls within the Coastal region, is marked by rolling wheatfields. But among the golden chaff lie pockets of hilly, very good viticultural land. These pockets are being increasingly exploited by visionary vintners looking for the edge in quality.

Closest to the sea is Darling, in which lies the Groenekloof ward, encompassing perhaps Swartland's best vineyard ventures. Further inland is the Riebeekberg ward, centred on the twin towns of Riebeek West and Riebeek Kasteel at the foot of the Kasteelberg. Further south-east is Malmesbury, where fine, modern red wines are emerging.

The Atlantic Ocean on the West Coast is between 8 and 15km away from the western parts of this generally warm region, placing the Darling enclave within reach of the cooling mists and breezes so sought-after for fine-wine production. The average summer temperature ranges between 19°C here to 21°C elsewhere. Rainfall is fair (between 450 and 60mm) but Malmesbury is dry (the average is around 240mm). Malmesbury shale is the most common soil type, with patches of granite (red and yellow clay) and gravelly sandstone on the hills. The plains are mostly sandy.

Though traditionally a white wine area, the farmers are now rooting for reds. Shiraz is the new star, with prolific Pinotage and classy Cabernet hotfooting it behind. Grenache, Mouvèdre and Carignan are also being explored.

New investments are set to help the Swartland become the future source of some of the Cape's most modern wines – a commercially exciting combination of quality and quantity. Besides the Spice Route, Groote Post and Groene Cloof, former SFW marketing executive Koos Jordaan has shares in a 12ha vineyard on Kasteelberg and plans to build a cellar here for his Stormsberg wines. Stellenbosch Farmers' Winery's Papkuilsfontein venture is another example. The Cape's Rupert family and the De Rothschild dynasty of Bordeaux, already cohorts in the promising R & de R Fredericksburg cellar in Paarl, have plans to develop a large farm called Januarieskraal.

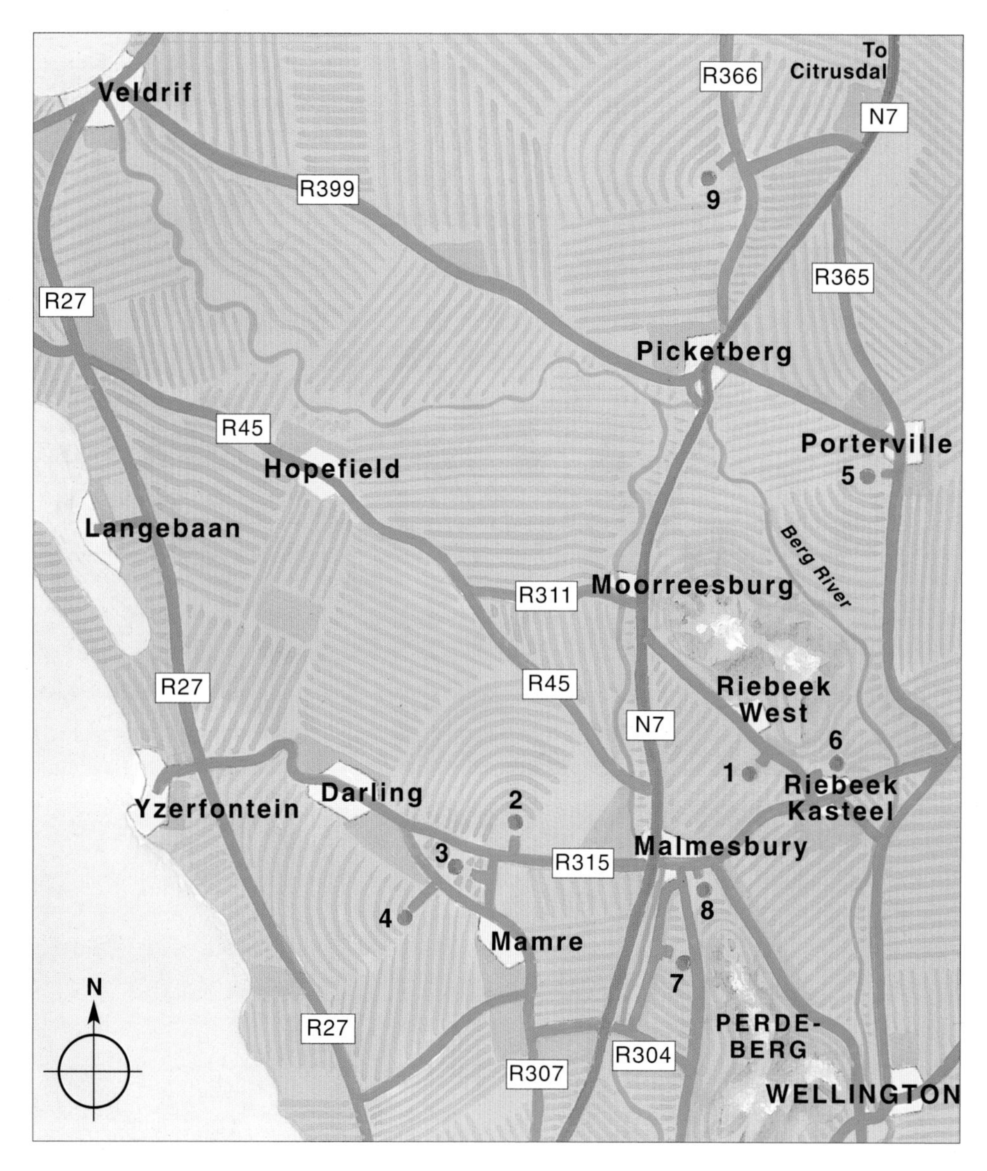

1. Allesverloren
2. Darling Cellars
3. Groene Cloof
4. Groote Post
5. Porterville
6. Riebeek
7. Spice Route
8. Swartland
9. Winkelshoek

OPENING PAGE: Riebeek Kasteel is one of the sections of good viticultural land being developed in the Swartland, traditionally a wheat-growing area now emerging as a source of solid reds such as Shiraz.

ALLESVERLOREN

OWNER
Danie Malan

KEY WINES
Shiraz, Cabernet, Tinta Barocca, Port

For a long time the Swartland's only wine estate known to wine lovers, Allesverloren was first granted in 1704. The first Malan arrived here in 1870. His elder son, DF Malan, became the country's first nationalist, 'apartheid' prime minister in 1948, while the second son Stephanus continued the family dynasty, establishing commercial vineyards in the 1950s.

Son Fanie bottled the first wine in 1974. The 160ha of vines are now managed by his son, Danie, who has continued making the best of the farm's fine port and robust, somewhat old-fashioned reds. The wines – a Shiraz, a Cabernet, one of the Cape's few varietal Tinta Baroccas and a port – make no claims to be chasing the modern blockbusters. Yet the '96 Shiraz won Danie the 1998 Diners Club Winemaker of the Year award, boasting structure, subtle wooding and smooth drinkability. This, despite that, as Malan maintains: 'You can't make a delicate wine in the Swartland'.

The Cabernet is invariably good, often underrated, and marvellously mature when released. The '96 is as palatable as its Shiraz stablemate – medium-bodied, balanced and soft, with great fragrance and sweet fruit and spicy oak on the palate. While retaining open concrete fermentation tanks and the Burgundian style of cooling the mash before fermentation, Malan is experimenting with a 'decent, dry red blend' that's expressive of the Swartland. It could be Shiraz and Cabernet, perhaps with a port variety thrown in.

He's also added Touriga Naçional to his classic port varietal mix of Tinta Barocca, Souzão, Malvasia Rei, Pontac, Tinta Roriz and Tinta Francisca. While currently available vintages are Tawny-like, usually released well bottle-aged, the style is likely to become more authentically Late Bottled Vintage.

Port, Shiraz and Cabernet are the mètier of the Malans, Fanie and father Danie (**TOP**), whose family has farmed Allesverloren at the foot of the Kasteelberg (**ABOVE**) since the late 19th century.

OWNERS
27 growers

KEY WINES
Groenekloof Cabernet, Pinotage, Shiraz, Chardonnay, Sauvignon Blanc; DC Cabernet Sauvignon, Merlot, Pinotage, Shiraz, Chardonnay, Sauvignon Blanc; Mamreweg range of reds and dry, semi-sweet and sweet whites

Not so long ago, lowly Mamreweg co-op, founded in 1949, was home to several rather ordinary, cheap West Coast wines. Yet, with its cool climate due to the close proximity of most of its vineyards to the cold Atlantic West Coast, and the deep, red Hutton clay-based soils up against the Darling hillsides, its terroir belongs more firmly in the Coastal Wine of Origin region than the rest of the drier Swartland district. And its potential for fine wine is finally being realised.

The change came in the '90s, with the planting of mainly premium varieties. In 1995, some R15-million was spent on the cellar, including investment in new, small French-oak barrels, a quality controller/analyst and a new bottling line. Next came the conversion into a company. This was followed by the appointment of one of the Cape's eminent winemakers, Abé Beukes, formerly with Lievland, whose passion for reds is being fully indulged here.

The DC Merlot shines with tannins that are soft yet dry, and a smooth texture. The DC Cabernet offers a generous mouthful great for bottle-ageing. The Groenekloof Pinotage is distinctive and individual: a big, rich, herbaceous, slightly tarry, wild wine. The Groenekloof Cabernet is equally unusual and even more herbaceous, but ripe and chunky in the mouth.

Says Beukes: 'My greatest challenge is to prove that you don't need a small winery to produce quality. By knowing the vineyards and rigorously selecting the best, we too can offer flagship wines.' He's got it cut out for him, with just under 2 000ha of vineyards and an annual production of around 300 000 cases to deal with. But the top tier under the Groenekloof label consists of small quantities from hand-picked vineyards and barrels. The second, DC tier captures the modern, New World style of fruit-driven wines. The pocket-friendly Mamreweg has always been pleasant but is also earmarked for a quality revamp.

Beukes rates the Cabernet – 'no aggressive tannins, typical yet refined flavours' – and the Shiraz as the most exciting red varieties. He also praises the Sauvignon Blanc, with its fresh, figgy fruit from the southern, sea-facing slopes of the Darling Hills. Most of Darling Cellars' vineyards are divided between the gravel soils at the foot of these hills and the yellow and red clay higher up. 'Lower night temperatures ensure that flavour is locked into the grapes, while the depth of soils here is incredible.'

TOP: Abé Beukes oversees Darling Cellars' fine-wine production, assisted by Johan Nesenberend and Conrad Vlok.
RIGHT: Elevated sites with views of Table Mountain and the Atlantic Ocean offer good clay soils and cool temperatures.

Allesverloren's vineyards, which include Cabernet, Shiraz and classic port varieties, cloak the foothills of the Kasteelberg.

GROENE CLOOF

Cape Town advocate Johan van den Berg launched his maiden '97 Pinotage and Cabernet (made by Kevin Arnold in the Rust en Vrede cellar) quietly at his home in Newlands, Cape Town. But, besides the confusion surrounding the name (with both Darling Cellars and Neil Ellis marketing wine using the ward name, Groenekloof), it was the scale of developments on the farm that had people agog.

The 1 500ha spread, bought in 1994, boasts an ultra-modern, 1 000-ton cellar designed by architect Gilbert Colyn (former owner of Zevenwacht). About 175ha is already under vine: ongoing plantings will add Merlot, Shiraz, Sauvignon Blanc and Chardonnay to the existing Cabernet, Pinotage, Cinsaut, Chenin Blanc and Bukettraube. Though the area is renowned for some fine Sauvignon Blanc – and Groene Cloof has established its own high on the south-facing slopes of nearby Dassenberg hill – the focus will be on reds; bush vines and unirrigated. Winemaker Frikkie Botes finds a distinctively spicy character on his reds. The fruitful Cloof Pinotage has an edge on the slightly lean Cabernet.

GROOTE POST

Father and son Peter and Nick Pentz have been raising dairy cattle on this 6 000ha spread since 1974. The farm served as a trading post for the Dutch East India Company in the 18th century, and it still has Cape Dutch gables and old slave bells; several buildings, declared National Monuments, date back to 1706.

More than 50ha of vines have been planted since 1993 against the south, sea-facing slopes of the Darling Hills and a modern, 300-ton cellar in a renovated old barn produced the first wines in 1999. These include a supple

Sauvignon Blanc, full of asparagus aromas and figgy flavours, Chenin Blanc, Chardonnay, Pinot Noir and Merlot. Merlot and Cabernet are earmarked for a Bordeaux-style blend. New name Francois van Zyl is the winemaker.

PAPKUILSFONTEIN

This is a progressive new joint venture between Stellenbosch Farmers' Winery and Gauteng-based retail and property consortium Leopont Properties. It makes provision for a minority shareholding by a local community trust, allowing staff and farm workers a stake.

Some R30-million has been spent on 250ha of vineyard on the 975ha farm below the Dassenberg in the Groenekloof ward near Darling. Grapes from the existing 113ha of Chenin Blanc, Pinotage and other lesser varieties are being used to generate income for the project until the new plantings of Shiraz, Cabernet, Pinotage and Chardonnay come on-stream. An ultimate crop of some 2 500 tons of noble varieties is envisaged to supply Nederburg and SFW. About 20% of the fruit will be reserved for an own range, the first member of which is a Tukulu Chenin Blanc (named for the rich, red, clay-based soils on the farm), to be joined by a Pinotage.

Young SFW winemaker Carmen Stevens will vinify the wines in the SFW cellars until a winery is built.

PORTERVILLE

Even the lesser co-ops are getting into reds, increasingly aware of market demand amid recent shortages of good wines from recognised varieties.

For years mostly whites were taken in from the more than 100 member growers: Chenin Blanc, Colombard and Sauvignon Blanc. But, with a new pressing cellar and an influx of fruit from recently planted noble red varieties in cooler, hilly areas, new cellarmaster Andre Oberholzer has just introduced a blend of Merlot, Shiraz and Cabernet, called Enigma. There's also a Pinotage and Pinotage Reserve, small-oak matured, ripe and plummy. Oberholzer (formerly with Vlottenburg, renowned for the excellent price-quality ratio of its red) is also playing around with special vineyard selections of classics such as Chardonnay.

RIEBEEK

Reds have been *de rigueur* since the arrival of former Zevenwacht cellarmaster Eric Saayman at this 60-member co-op in 1997.

A new red-wine fermentation cellar, temperature-controlled maturation facilities, a tank storage area and the replanting of mainly recognised reds have taken place. Cabernet, Pinotage, Shiraz and Merlot are top of the list, some of which, together with Chardonnay and Sémillon, are headed for a 'reserve' range for sale from the cellar door. The winery handles nearly 20 000 tons from over 2 000ha, exporting the prime crop in conjunction with the KWV.

SPICE ROUTE

Fairview's Charles Back is now the sole proprietor of what was an equal-partnership business launched in 1997 by him and Gyles Webb of Thelema, wine writer John Platter and winelands black-empowerment facilitator Jabulani Ntshangase.

The investment comprises the 390ha Klein Amoskuil farm just outside Malmesbury with established, unirrigated, mostly bush-vine Shiraz, Pinotage, Merlot, Cabernet, Sauvignon Blanc and Chardonnay. New plantings include the Rhône varieties Mouvèdre and Viognier, as well as more Shiraz. From these and neighbouring vineyards, young vintner Eben Sadie makes about 30 000 cases of wine in a hi-tech, converted tobacco shed. Richness of fruit on the reds has impressed. A Spice Route Cabernet/Merlot blend is a thick, chewy, spicy wine. The Shiraz is loaded with fruit and spicy oak. Premium varietal reds under the Flagship label show great richness. Easy-drinking, new-wave alternatives include Andrew's Hope Cab/Merlot and a Shiraz containing dashes of uncommon Grenache and Carignan.

SWARTLAND

Founded in 1948, this 100-plus-member, 25 000-ton winery has been one of the most progressive co-ops in the country.

Growers have long been paid, not for quantity but according to the sugar/acid ratio of their fruit. Since the early '90s, before the export boom, Swartland Colombard, Chenin Blanc and Sauvignon Blanc were finding their way into UK supermarkets. At home, these value-for-money wines were repeated winners in the then leading commercial Wine-of-the-Month Club tastings.

Now production head Olla Olivier and his three winemakers are preparing for a future in red wines. Shiraz, Pinotage and Cabernet Sauvignon plantings will see a 50/50 balance of white and red by 2005. A brand-new red-wine cellar and barrel-maturation cellar will come up in support. Special vineyard selections have been made since '96, now finding fruition in an upmarket Reserve range. 'Boutique wines,' says marketing dynamo Charlto Opperman.

Red winemaker Andries Blake turns out a fine unirrigated, bush-vine Shiraz and a barrel-matured Cabernet/Merlot; a plump Pinotage has earned a place among the country's Top Ten, selected annually by the Pinotage Producers' Association.

Kas Huisamen and Abrie Beeselaar nurture Sauvignon Blanc and a barrel-fermented Chenin. Olivier reserves the right to vinify the rich, fully flavoured, citrussy, toasty Chardonnay. The vast range also contains a good Vintage-style port.

WINKELSHOEK

The producer behind the large, thatch-roofed new Winkelshoek wine shop and restaurant on the main N7 West Coast road just opposite Piketberg is a small private cellar, owned by winemaker Hennie Hanekom and his partner, Jurgens Brand. Here Hanekom bottles the colourfully labelled Weskus range of quaffing whites and reds. The Winkelshoek name is reserved for sweet and fortified dessert wines, sherries and brandies.

T U L B A G H

There are things a-ferment in the Tulbagh Valley, a basin of fruit and wine grape farms formed by the Groot Winterhoek mountains in the north, the Witzenberg along its eastern side and the Obiqua range along its western boundary.

An ideal viticultural climate – hot, dry summers and generous rainfall in winter – keep Tulbagh vines healthy.

Vergelegen's Willem Adriaan van der Stel, 18th-century Cape governor, settled the valley in 1700 with farmers, including a few French Huguenots. Wine grapes have always been grown here. Tulbagh is still a Cape Dutch gem, the poignancy of its restored past enhanced by the remarkable rebuilding that took place after an earthquake in 1969.

It is the intellectual Nicky Krone who places the valley's viticultural complexity in perspective when explaining its confusing mish-mash of soils, a result of the basin being a geological 'wash': an area in which water action over the millennia has deposited layers of shale, then ferocrete, topped by granite and sandstone. It makes for 'bloody hard work' establishing a vineyard, says Krone, but the effort is well worthwhile.

This band of viticultural gold stretches from the foot of the Winterhoek down the western side of the valley. Though perceived as hot and dry (which it is, though prime viticultural areas like Paarl can get hotter), the valley's vines benefit from cool nights and a relatively high average annual rainfall ranging from 450mm on the harsher, south-east-windswept eastern side to at least 750mm in the rain-shadow of the north-western mountains. The Little Berg provides a permanent source of water for dams and irrigation, and the clay substructure of many of the soils retains moisture during the stressful summer-ripening months.

Recognition of the potential – or in some cases, the opportunity to exploit it – seems to have dawned, with a more scientific approach. And the name of the game is red wine in a traditionally white-wine valley: Cabernet and Pinotage, while Merlot and Shiraz seem to be particularly promising. Small-scale experiments with new varieties, such as Petit Verdot, Malbec and Italian varieties Nebbiolo and Barbera, are taking place behind the scenes.

TULBAGH

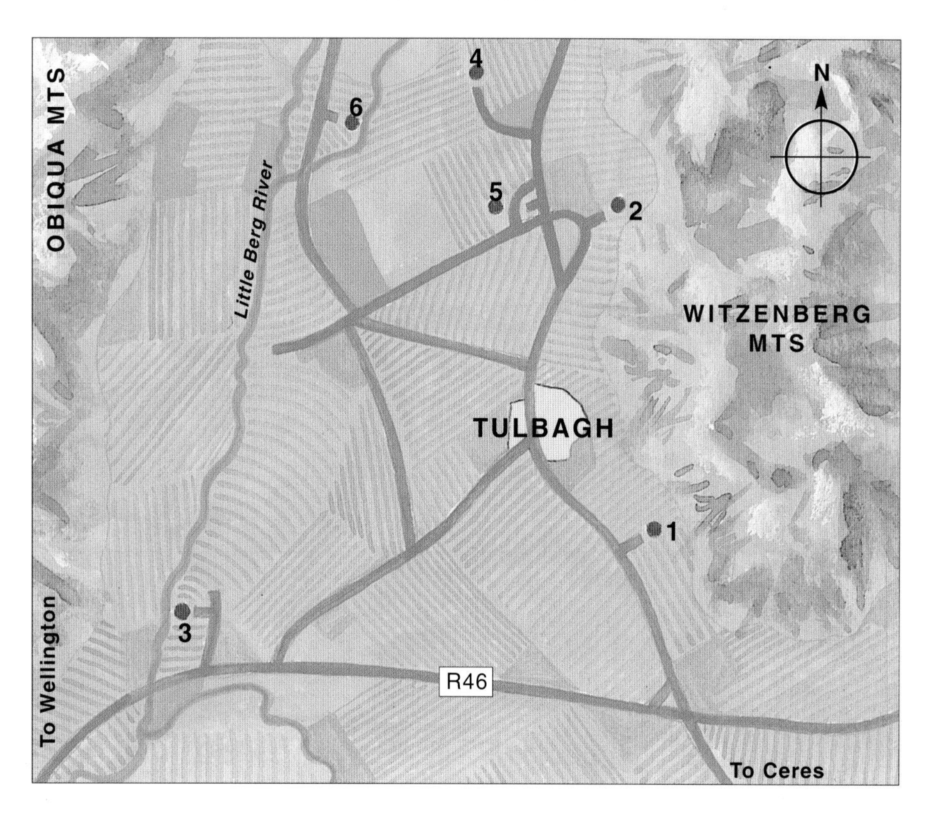

1. Bianco
2. Drostdy
3. Lemberg
4. Theuniskraal
5. Tulbagh
6. Twee Jonge Gezellen

OPENING PAGE: At the heart of Tulbagh wine country lies the hamlet of Tulbagh – its historic Church Street is a microcosm of 17th and 18th century Cape Dutch architecture.

TWEE JONGE GEZELLEN

OWNER
Nicky Krone

KEY WINES
Krone Borealis Cuvée Brut; Twee Jonge Gezellen Rosé NV; TJ 39, TJ Light; Schanderl, Night Nectar, Engeltjiepipi, Pinot Noir

First granted in 1710 to two Dutch farmers – the 'two bachelor companions' of the name – Twee Jonge Gezellen is the oldest grape-growing family farm in the valley, with an unbroken line of inheritance since 1745. The current Krone clan has been in residence since 1916 and seems set to carry on the tradition with owner and winemaker Nicky Krone's son, NC, a star viticultural and oenological student in Stellenbosch.

Krone has spent 20 years battling against the rocky, complex soils of this 270ha estate and an inheritance of a multitude of mostly lesser white varieties, from Gewürztraminer and Furmint to Pinot Blanc and Muscat de Frontignan. He has a lot of Chenin and some good Weisser and has been slowly tipping the scales towards other classic whites such as Chardonnay (for his bubbly), Sauvignon Blanc and Sémillon.

Now the Geisenheim-trained Krone feels he is on the cusp of turning the farm into a leading, quality-driven, internationally competitive wine producer. Having carved a name with his Krone Borealis Brut Cap Classique as one of the Cape's finest bottle-fermented sparkling wine producers since 1987, the future seems to lie in reds. The Twee Jonge Gezellen name has long been associated with a consistent range of easy-drinking white blends, from the popular 'TJ39', a melange of white varieties, and a best-selling, low-alcohol 'light' wine to others of varying degrees of sweetness. These will continue – production has doubled to 24 000 cases – and have just been joined by a carbonated bubbly, a delightful dry rosé made of Chardonnay and Pinot Noir.

But much as he would love to be *the* 'Champagne' house in South Africa, Krone has decided that specialisation is a marketing risk, especially as a New World estate. 'Popular taste is a fickle thing,' says Nicky. 'The wine consumer is not very brand loyal.' Champagne, though, has never really gone out of fashion. Hence the Krone Borealis remains his *raison d'être* and a star in the Cape firmament of Cap Classiques. A classic combination of Chardonnay and Pinot Noir, fermented together, with two to three years on the lees before degorging, it is a beautifully biscuitty, complex, delicately flavoured wine with excellent bottle-ageing capabilities. It's the result of in-depth study of and experiments with Champagne yeasts and a precise selection of specific clones chosen for their varying characteristics. He prefers to make up his blends 'in the vineyard, rather than in the cellar'. Malolactic fermentation is a must, he maintains, as it softens and adds complexity; it also stabilises the wine, obviating the need for anything but the minutest amount of sulphur.

Krone has had to fight against nature to establish his first extensive planting of reds, some 30ha of mostly Shiraz, a bit of Merlot and some more Pinot Noir. An expanse of pure rock took its toll on workers' backs, bulldozers and drilling bits before he discovered a way in which a machine-driven steel tooth is able to dig a hole and drop in each vine. But the greatest excitement came in the spring of 1999, when this newly planted tract of Shiraz grew green and verdant, vindication of an earlier investment in his own nursery.

He is also looking at Bordeaux classics such as Petit Verdot and Malbec, as well as Rhône favourite Mouvèdre (commonly called Mataro) and leading Italian varieties such as Barbera. He may also plant some Viognier.

Mary and Nicky Krone with their son NC, who is set to take over the reins at Twee Jonge Gezellen. The farm is renowned for its classic bubbly Krone Borealis and old favourite 'TJ39'.

1719

BIANCO WINES

The Bianco family, originally from Piedmont in Italy, has settled on De Heuvel Farm between Tulbagh and Wolseley and is producing some magnificent new reds in this traditionally white-wine enclave.

Antonio Bianco, a former Gauteng business-man, bought the 60ha property, first registered in 1714 and with a viticultural history dating back to the early 1900s, in 1991. He established a Bonsmara cattle stud, a 30ha olive grove and about 13ha of vines: Cabernet, Shiraz and Pinotage. Early crops were sold to Tulbagh co-op before the first bottling of Bianco Cabernet in 1997 in the simple, Italian-styled cellar. The wine is outstanding, with subsequent vintages showing ever fruitier, richer and beautifully wooded wines promising a future star in the Cape winelands. Viticulturist Paul Wallace and consultant winemaker Mark Carmichael-Green are helping out until two of the four Bianco sons, agriculturist Craig and winemaker Toni, join what will be a family business. Craig will see to vineyards and olive orchards, while Toni will look to the winemaking and marketing. The Piedmontese variety Nebbiolo is being grafted by Bianco himself to make a Barolo-style wine.

DROSTDY

The home of Distillers' Drostdy-Hof brand, Drostdy is not a crushing cellar but buys in wines, mostly from local growers, for its consistently good, value-for-money range of whites and reds. Long-time cellarmaster Frans du Toit has produced a jolly fine, good-value Chardonnay and Merlot and also bottles the Two Oceans range including a varietal Sauvignon Blanc, Cabernet and Merlot. There's a nice Claret Select, comprising Pinotage, Shiraz and Ruby Cabernet, in the extensive Drostdy-Hof range, which also includes sweet wines and sherries, bag-in-the-box and dinky-sized bottles.

LEMBERG

This tiny wine farm, with just 4ha under Sauvignon Blanc and locally uncommon Hungarian variety Hárslevelü, was bought by German forestry scientist Klaus Schindler in 1994. The new-look Lemberg wines are solid and good drinking, and the herby, pear-flavoured Hárslevelü is particularly pleasant with slightly spicy food. Schindler has also made a Pinot Noir – he's replaced some Hárslevelü with a little of this and Pinotage. And he's produced a Cabernet Merlot blend from grapes bought from equally tiny Kloofzicht Estate next door (which no longer bottles its own wines).

Twee Jonge Gezellen (**OPPOSITE**) has been in the Krone family since 1745; even the underground sparkling wine *cave* (**ABOVE**), though a modern addition built by Nicky Krone and his staff, seems timeless.

THEUNISKRAAL

Named for French Huguenot Theunis Bevernage to whom it was granted in 1714, Theuniskraal has a reputation for meticulous vineyard tending by the Jordaan family, originally table-grape growers from the Hex River Valley who have farmed wine grapes here since 1927. Brothers Kobus and Rennie, now joined by winemaker son Andries and Rennie's young son Wagner, who oversees the vines, have introduced scientific farming methods, including weather stations and soil moisture monitors for controlled, computerised irrigation.

Most of the 10 different white varieties on the 130ha goes towards value-for-money Distillers ranges such as JC Le Roux, Grünberger and Drostdy-Hof. The whites have recently been joined by about 15ha of Cabernet, Ruby Cabernet, Shiraz and Roobernet.

TULBAGH

Founded in 1906, Tulbagh is arguably the oldest co-op in the Cape – the claim to this title is disputed by Helderberg, formed in Stellenbosch in the same year.

A major investment from 1995 in new cellar equipment, including crushers and cooling machines, left the 75-member co-op in financial difficulties. But new brooms in management and marketing, supporting new winemaker Michael Krone (brother of Twee Jonge Gezellen's Nicky), are turning this 'wine tanker' around. Producing around 10 000 tons, the cellar sells bag-in-the-box wines and wine in bulk, bottling only about six per cent under the Tulbagh label. Out are the Blanc de Blancs and Premier Grand Crus, the grape juices and bubblies; in are blends of Sauvignon Blanc, Chardonnay and Sémillon, and Cabernet and Merlot, as well as the odd, premium varietal wine.

O V E R B E R G

ABOVE AND OPPOSITE: The open vistas of Caledon's wheatfields ringed by blue mountains separate the wine wards of high-lying Elgin and coastal Walker Bay in the Overberg.

The Overberg district effectively begins south-east of the Hottentots Holland mountain range traversed by Sir Lowry's Pass. It stretches from the high-lying, mountainous timber belt and apple-farming area of Elgin, across the wheatfields between Bot River and Caledon and into the Hemel-en-Aarde Valley, which opens out onto Walker Bay in Hermanus. It also encompasses the new viticultural area east of Caledon towards Bredasdorp. From Elgin it creeps north towards Villiersdorp.

The Overberg demarcation is one of the anomalies in the Cape winelands Wine of Origin classification system. The wine district is not ascribed to any region, though the Hemel-en-Aarde area in one of its two wards, Walker Bay, clearly falls within the Coastal region with its maritime position. The other ward, Elgin, though inland, boasts similar cool-climate influences on its wine styles. Just to confuse the issue, the viticultural area around Bot River is warmer, producing wines of a different character. But for the purposes of conformity, the simple sub-division of the Overberg into its two official wards, Walker Bay and Elgin, has been retained here.

WALKER BAY

The Walker Bay ward in the Overberg district was pioneered only in recent decades, but has fast become a site for prime-quality wines, mainly because of long-overdue recognition of the benefits of a cool, maritime climate in fine-wine production.

The prime mover and shaker here has been former ad-man Tim Hamilton-Russell. After an intensive 10-year search of the Cape winelands for the 'perfect' terroir for cool-climate wines, he settled on the then-unexploited Hemel-en-Aarde Valley. Buying some 175ha in 1975, he proceeded to do battle with wine industry authorities to get the area designated an official viticultural region, thereby enabling certification of his wines.

His pioneering work has since been vindicated, not only in the quality of HRV wines, but also in the spate of new wineries here and further inland. As a result, Walker Bay has become synonymous with some of the Cape's most aristocratic wines. Other Hemel-en-Aarde wine farms are still being developed, such as winemaker Bartho Eksteen's venture with a grower.

Tim Hamilton-Russell's concentration on Burgundian classics in the Hemel-en-Aarde Valley – Chardonnay and Pinot Noir – has found resonance with several other leading winemakers in the area. Sauvignon Blanc is another Walker Bay speciality, planted by most of the wineries and sometimes supplemented by fruit from similarly cool-climate vineyards in Elgin. These wines typically exhibit a racy, steely herbaceousness, often gentled by tropical fruit. Pinotage is also proving right at home here, while warmer pockets hold promise for Cabernet and Merlot.

WALKER BAY

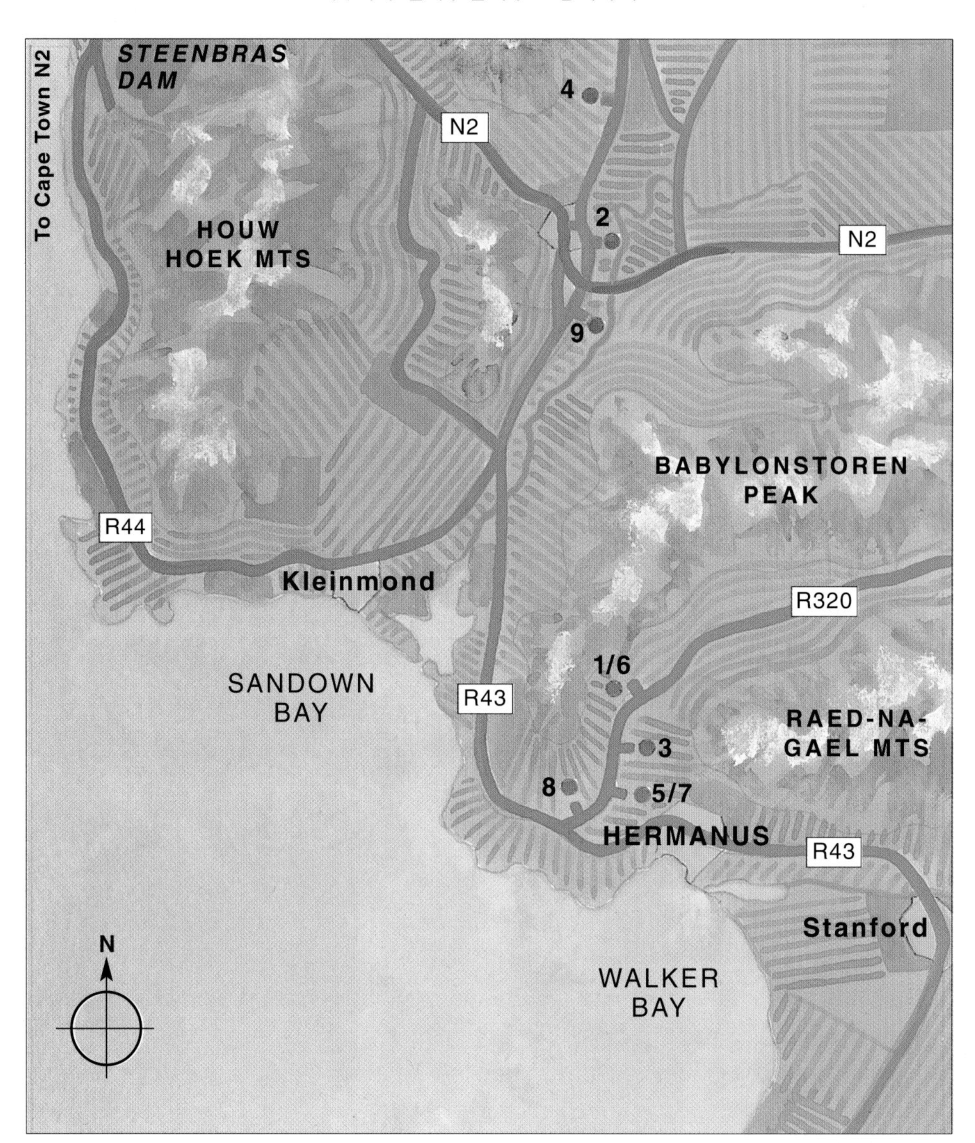

1. Bartho Eksteen
2. Beaumont/ Compagnes Drift
3. Bouchard Finlayson
4. Goedvertrouw
5. Hamilton Russell
6. Newton Johnson
7. Southern Right
8. WhaleHaven
9. Wildekrans

Most Hemel-en-Aarde Valley vineyards have been established on virgin territory along the northerly and north-easterly slopes of the 260m-high rolling Raed-na-Gael range. This range separates the valley from Hermanus, a popular coastal town on Walker Bay, some 120km along the south-east coast from Cape Town. South-facing aspects below the Babylonstoren peak are also being cultivated. Soils are predominantly lean and stony shale-derived types, containing enough clay to ensure good water retention. Lower slopes are made up of Table Mountain sandstone.

But the district's vinous history goes back much further across the mountain in Bot River, where grapes were grown on Compagnes Drift, a Dutch East Indian Company outpost dating back to 1750. Some rich, spicy Shiraz is coming out of this area, while vintners are also looking into other Rhône varieties such as Grenache and Mouvèdre.

Wine growers are also casting their eyes further along the coast south-east of Hermanus towards Stanford and on to Bredasdorp. Hamilton Russell, Villiera and Rustenberg are among the big names from across the Cape winelands with designs on this area.

OWNERS
Raoul and Jayne Beaumont

KEY WINES
Pinotage, Shiraz, Ariane red blend, Raoul's Tinta Barocca, Chenin Blanc (Beaumont, Hope Marguerite Barrel Reserve), Chardonnay, Sauvignon Blanc, Port, Goutte d'Or Natural Sweet

ABOVE: This old basket press reflects the belief in traditional winemaking methods, held by Jayne and Raoul Beaumont (**BELOW**), with their winemaker Niels Verburg and son Sebastian, a student of oenology and viticulture.

Ex-sailor Raoul Beaumont and artist wife Jayne farmed fruit and wine grapes on historic Compagnes Drift – an 18th-century Dutch East Indian Company outpost depicted on an original painting on the label – for nigh on 20 years before launching their own commercial bottling in 1994. The big, ripe, tannic Pinotage, from 20-year-old vines that had been making award-winning wines for Villiersdorp co-op for years, established this rustic property as a cellar of note.

Following the success of the maiden '94 and '95 vintages and the appointment of winemaker Niels Verburg in '96, subsequent vintages have enjoyed the treatment of a new press and new French-oak barrels. But the massive old concrete tanks, still lined with beeswax, are simply being re-conditioned and the Pinotage is still fermented in open *kuipe*.

Verburg turns out strong Pinotages and new-wave barrel-treated Chenins as well as a full, toasty Chardonnay. But he's also keen on the Rhône varieties. A densely coloured and textured, spicy Shiraz – the first varietal version from Walker Bay – may soon see the added fillip of Mouvèdre and Grenache from the latest plantings on the farm's nearly 50ha of vineyards. Meanwhile, the soft, drinkable Ariane Bordeaux-style blend shows the potential of newly established Cabernet Sauvignon, Merlot and Cabernet Franc.

Verburg's philosophy of minimum handling in the cellar suits the rustic winemaking style of the farm, though he shares a readiness to take risks with the determined Jayne who, with the help of Beyers Truter and Jeremy Walker, made those first few vintages herself. (There's another winemaker lurking in the family: older son Sebastian, a viticulture student.) And there's always something in the pipeline to appeal to wine buyers, from an elegant Natural Sweet to a pretty authentic Port, made from Pinotage and Tinta Barocca. The Tinta has also been bottled recently as a quaffing red.

The idea is not to go much beyond 10 000 cases – the rest of the crop, which also includes some Sémillon, is sold to Villiersdorp co-op and other buyers.

BOUCHARD FINLAYSON

OWNER

Klein Hemel-en-Aarde (Pty) Ltd

KEY WINES

Tête de Cuvée Pinot Noir, Galpin Peak Pinot Noir, Missionvale Chardonnay, Overberg Pinot Noir, Kaaimansgat Chardonnay, Oak Valley Chardonnay, Chardonnay Sans Barrique, Walker Bay Sauvignon Blanc, Blanc de Mer

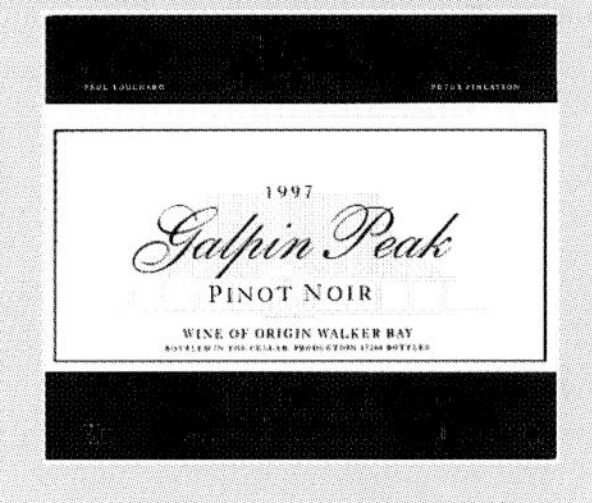

New World in winery style, Old World in viticultural practice, Bouchard Finlayson truly reflects its origins: a venture into the Cape winelands by a Frenchman, 10th-generation Burgundian *négociant* Paul Bouchard, spurred on by Hemel-en-Aarde Valley winemaker Peter Finlayson. Finlayson bought Klein Hemel-en-Aarde farm next to Hamilton Russell while still winemaker at the latter, started planting on the fynbos-covered land and crushed his bought-in grapes in 1991, which is when Bouchard joined him and his manager Mike Clark.

Finlayson makes no bones about following Burgundian tradition, from his closely planted, five-row blocks (leaving the sixth row open to accommodate the tractor for spraying) to his sourcing of barrels from Burgundian cooper Francois Freres only. 'I'm dealing with Burgundian varieties – only a Burgundian

The Bouchard Finlayson winery is newly established below the Raed-na-Gael ridge, but already it is a Cape benchmark with its Chardonnay and Pinot Noir.

Avuncular Peter Finlayson is a man of the soil, whose wines reflect a closeness to nature.

cooper understands their special needs,' he maintains. He also opts for a mixture of new and used barrels, ferments in wood and gives his wines long lees contact. This and his belief in careful vineyard management, from dense planting to contain yields to canopy care and selective picking, results in wines marked by a fullness of fruit, always in harmony with natural acidity and elegant tannins.

A big, burly, bearded man, Finlayson is the outdoor type, quiet and introspective, with a love of nature perfectly encapsulated by the rustic nature of the unobtrusive, low-lying thatched winery he built on the north-east-facing slopes of the Raed-na-Gael mountains.

Finlayson started planting pre-1990, producing his first vintages under the Bouchard-Finlayson label from grapes carefully selected from similar cool-climate areas in the Overberg district such as Elgin and Villiersdorp. He retains these relationships with growers for his vineyard-specific wines, invariably indicated on the label. Examples are the barrel-fermented, leesy and lemony, rich and buttery Kaaimansgat Chardonnay from Villiersdorp, and Sauvignon Blancs from Elgin (sometimes labelled as Oak Valley), Walker Bay or a composite of sources under the Overberg label.

His first 'domaine' (home-grown) wines made from his own 14ha of vineyards came with the 1996 Galpin Peak Pinot Noir (named for the hillock behind the winery) and the 1997 Missionvale Chardonnay (the farm was part of a Moravian mission station in the 1800s). The former is a gorgeous wine, crimson-coloured, full of raspberry fruit and spice, underpinned by firm tannins and hints of coffee. The latter is elegant, marked by melony, tropical fruit.

Of Bouchard Finlayson's total production of around 13 000 cases, these two wines comprise not even a couple of 1 000 cases and command high prices.

Yet Finlayson's other offerings can sometimes outstrip these two stars, especially the barrel-fermented, leesy and lemony, rich and buttery Kaaimansgat. Like Hamilton Russell, these wines earn top ratings abroad, too. Each of his other labels shows distinctive differences, a measure of this winemaker's talent and recognition of individual terroirs. For example, the Sauvignon Blanc from his own Walker Bay vineyards is typically tight and lean, while the Elgin Oak Valley is more fruitful; the Old Lands is almost creamy. Yet interestingly, his belief in terroir as a deciding factor in quality wine production plays second fiddle to clones, to which he attributes far greater influence in deciding fruit concentration and ripeness.

The Burgundian style of vinifying and bottling small batches of selected wines has found fruition in his latest star turn: the Tête de Cuvée Pinot Noir, representing his finest barrels in only the best vintages. From 20 cases of an experimental '96 to about 120 cases and a few hundred magnums of the '97, this wine has shown extraordinary flavour and complexity. In total, Bouchard Finlayson bottles just 13 000 cases.

He is also trying out two new-to-the-Cape Italian varieties: Nebbiolo and Sangiovese. Experimental vinifications show great promise for the cool-climate Nebbiolo (at home in high-lying, mist-shrouded Italian terroirs). The Sangiovese has been less inspiring, mostly because of the inferior clones available to South African winemakers.

Hamilton Russell Vineyards' squire Anthony Hamilton-Russell and winemaker Kevin Grant discourse on terroir.

HAMILTON RUSSELL VINEYARDS

OWNER

Anthony Hamilton-Russell

KEY WINES

Ashbourne Pinot Noir and Chardonnay; Hamilton Russell Vineyards Pinot Noir, Chardonnay, Sauvignon Blanc

One of the Cape's 'great growths', Hamilton Russell Vineyards recently applied for 'estate' status, to the surprise of many, with founder Tim Hamilton-Russell having fought long and hard to have his early vintages made from bought-in grapes certified. Yet this new move signifies the culmination of two decades of working with specific soils, climates, varieties and clones, to reach a point where the HRV team feels secure in offering what has long been a holy grail: 'wines that reflect the character of a unique terroir; the ultimate expression of origin,' as the erudite Oxford-educated Anthony Hamilton-Russell pronounces. Even so, HRV is taking it one step further, experimenting with seasoning the estate's own wooden staves for its Allier barrels. 'The effect of the local climate on the raw wood must also add to the uniqueness of terroir,' says Anthony.

His father Tim settled on this 175ha farm in 1975 after a 10-year search of the Cape winelands for a cool climate in which to grow fine Burgundian wines. Yet it has never been the aim to produce Burgundian look-alikes; the idea was always to strive towards a distinctive identity – produce the best the farm was capable of. Each harvest was treated as a trial run to identify the right site for the right variety, and clone. Even after Hamilton-Russell Snr's initial planting, vineyards have subsequently been moved, especially after son Anthony came on-board in 1991. Top New Zealand viticulturist Steve Smith was called in to consult. Thus the Chardonnays and Pinot Noirs have been settled on 30ha and 22ha respectively of shale-derived, clay-rich soils. Sauvignon Blanc, including the old South African 'Weerstasie' clone and a new Loire clone, is on sandier, gravel, well-drained ground.

A major move has been the gradual phasing out of the old BK5 Pinot Noir clone, on which HRV's early worldwide reputation for those wonderful, truffley, Burgundian-style wines was built. What is in fact a Swiss sparkling wine clone has been replaced by a selection of Burgundian clones, with the '97 vintage being the first made up entirely of the new material. Vinification remains an ongoing experiment. Natural yeasts are used for the Pinot Noir, and it is not filtered.

In winemaker Kevin Grant, who joined him in '94, Hamilton-Russell found a like-minded individual, passionate enough to laboriously vinify

The tiny tasting room, production cellar and barrel-maturation cellar at Hamilton Russell – the simple construction belies the complexity of this estate's wines.

numerous individual parcels of wine in order to 'map out' the vineyards. Finally, in '95 and '96 they found what they were looking for: two vineyard blocks, a Chardonnay and a Pinot Noir, deemed too distinctive to blend away in the standard HRV wines. Thus was the flagship Ashbourne label born, showing 'more length, texture and complexity' than the two standard-bearers.

Hamilton Russell's slant is towards Burgundian elegance and refinement. The Pinot is silky, smooth and full of raspberry fruit, yet taut. The Chardonnay often shows vintage variation, from rich and toasty wines to something gentler, fresher, more citrussy, but always has remarkable length of flavour. The Sauvignon is invariably steely, minerally, Loire-like, fleshed out with tropical fruit.

At Hamilton Russell you'll not only find a rare elegance and finely tuned balance but a truth of varietal expression that forces you to admit that, yes, this is really good stuff.

NEWTON JOHNSON

A long-held dream by *négociant* and Cape Wine Master Dave Johnson and wife Felicity (nee Newton) was realised with this 4ha hillside vineyard and hands-on, 70-ton cellar, perched on the south-facing hills across the Hemel-en-Aarde Valley from Bouchard Finlayson.

Johnson had already established a successful export venture with his Cape Bay wines (made, bought or blended to his specifications by various estates and co-ops) before he planted his own vines in 1997: Sauvignon Blanc next to the winery and Pinot Noir on a property just down the valley. Both Johnson sons, Bevan and Gordon, are Stellenbosch University-trained winemakers with working experience at Médoc châteaux d'Angludet and Palmer, and the Napa Valley. Former Wildekrans winemaker Bartho Eksteen consults.

Bought-in grapes from Walker Bay and Stellenbosch have produced a flavoursome Sauvignon, a lemony Chardonnay, with leesy fullness and an elegant, quite dry Cabernet Merlot blend. 'I want to make elegant, easy-drinking wines,' maintains Johnson.

BARTHO EKSTEEN WINES

Having parted ways with another Walker Bay vineyard, Wildekrans, after making his mark with some excellent Sauvignon Blanc and Pinotage, Bartho Eksteen refused to leave a region 'to which my heart belongs'.

Wife Suné opened an exclusive little wine shop in Hermanus, while her strong-minded husband found a consulting job with fledgling Newton Johnson, where he now also happily vinifies his own wines.

His maiden own-label wine had to be a Sauvignon Blanc, his passion. A gooseberry-fresh class act, it comes from local grapes bought in but grown under his supervision. There's a Shiraz in the offing, too, the first from Walker Bay.

WILDEKRANS

This is a farm with great potential. But wine competes with fruit in EK Green's Houw Hoek Farms business and increased exports have seen a quieter presence on the local market. New winemaker Jacques Fourie can rely on solid groundwork in the 42ha of vineyard and produces some 10 000 cases. The flagship Pinotage is a modern mix of plummy fruit and dense tannins. New clones of Cabernet, Merlot and Cabernet Franc vines show solid fruit and structure that augur well for the future. The Sauvignon Blanc is a good example of cool-climate raciness and the wood-fermented Chardonnay has all the right ingredients. Chenin is treated to French and American oak and some Sauvignon and Sémillon for a fairly heavy-weight Reserve wine.

SOUTHERN RIGHT

Flowing out of Hamilton Russell Vineyards' commitment to wines expressing origin comes Southern Right, under joint ownership of HRV's Anthony Hamilton-Russell and winemaker Kevin Grant. Having established HRV as the reserve for their classic Chardonnay and Pinot Noir and a site-specific Sauvignon Blanc, another label was sought for exploring the Cape's traditional grape Pinotage, as well as Chenin Blanc and Sauvignon Blanc.

Plantings on different sites in the Walker Bay area and bought-in grapes from similar cool-climate vineyards in the Elandskloof and Stettyn near Villiersdorp go towards a full, plummy, eminently drinkable Pinotage. There is also a gentle, tropical Sauvignon Blanc and a substantial Chenin, fruitful and wood-enhanced. A dedicated 30 000-case 'home' cellar is planned on a 113ha property recently bought next to HRV.

GOEDVERTROUW

A retired engineer who maintains an interest in restoring vintage BMWs, octogenarian Arthur Pillmanm bought the old Goedvertrouw farm-house and 250ha in 1984, where he produces some fine Pinot Noir and Chardonnay. The former has great depth of fruit and tannin balance, the latter is powerful, toasty and citrussy, often ageing remarkably well. A steely yet fruity Sauvignon Blanc, a raspberry-like Pinotage and a deeply flavoured Cabernet make up the range. Production, all *au naturel*, is usually around 1 000 cases off 8ha in a cool, dry climate and low-vigour stony soils.

WHALEHAVEN

A brave new venture by former Hamilton Russell Vineyards' winemaker Storm Kreusch-Dau, who went out and built her own winery just down the road in 1994. WhaleHaven produces some 4 000 cases.

Internationally trained and experienced Kreusch-Dau sources grapes from vineyards in the Hemel-en-Aarde Valley, nearby Stanford and Elgin. Her skill with that difficult grape Pinot Noir, honed at Hamilton Russel Vine-yards, remains undiminished, and she still includes some old BK5 in her mix of mostly new Burgundian clones for a sweet, supple and slightly spicy wine. Both the Merlot and the Cabernet are marked by solid fruit and the Baleine Noir blend of Shiraz and Merlot gives great drinkability.

ELGIN

Like Walker Bay, Elgin is a ward of the Overberg district. Set in the rugged Hottentots Holland range, which divides the Cape Peninsula from the rolling wheatfields of Caledon, Elgin's cool climate augured well for wine grapes, reasoned top viticulturist Ernst le Roux of Nederburg, former Nederburg cellarmaster Günter Brôzel and the late Ronnie Melck of Stellenbosch Farmers' Winery. Neurosurgeon and local fruit grower Paul Cluver was game, and cleared virgin land at 400–500m altitude on his apple farm De Rust. Elgin was proclaimed a Wine of Origin ward in the early '90s.

Paul Cluver remains the only cellar in the ward, but Le Roux reckons there's potential to cultivate at least another 200ha of premium-quality wine grapes in the region. A joint community project between De Rust, the SA Forestry Company and local Safcol workers on the deproclaimed Lebanon forestry station is seeing the development of some 100ha of former forestry land for fruit and wine grapes (mainly Sauvignon Blanc, Cabernet and Merlot). A maiden 1998 Chardonnay and Pinot Noir under the Thandi label (Xhosa for 'nurturing and trust') are solid, well-made wines. They're available from the Cluver farm.

The intention is to make the most of the enormous potential of this cool-climate ward, with its altitude, variety of aspects and micro-climates, and low-vigour Bokkeveld shale-derived and granitic soils. Other leading winemakers such as Peter Finlayson and Neil Ellis have also earmarked farms in the area as suppliers of fruit.

Those in search of cool-climate terroirs also draw on pockets of land around Villiersdorp along an extension of the Hottentots Holland range. Here, 'snowline' vineyards between the Aasvoël and Riviersonderend mountains provide grapes for excellent wines such as Bouchard Finlayson's 'Kaaimansgat' Chardonnay.

E L G I N

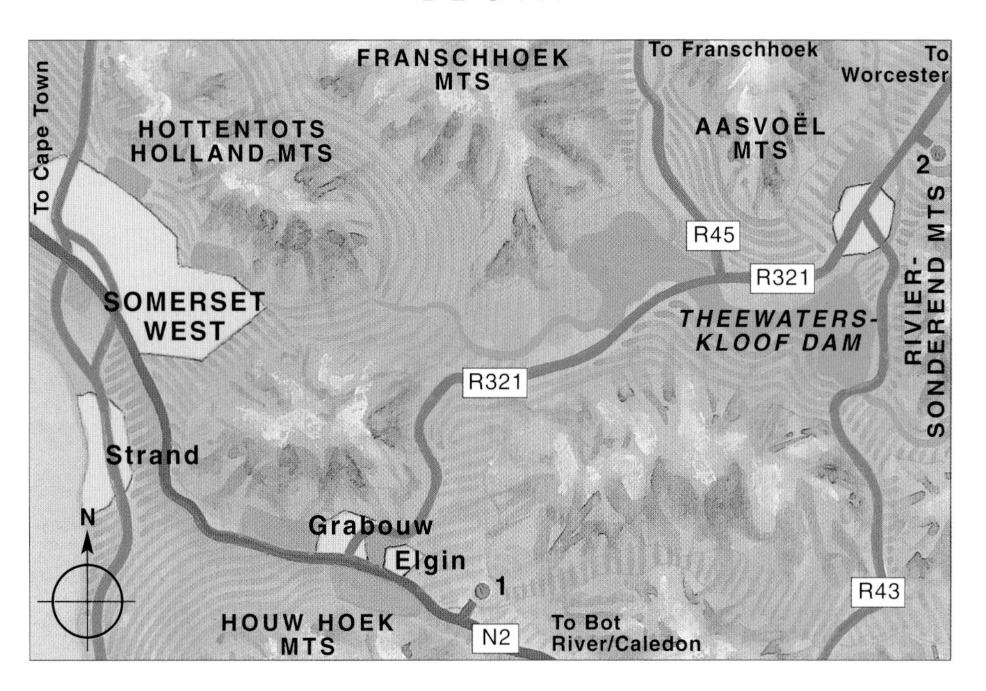

1. Paul Cluver
2. Villiersdorp

PAUL CLUVER

OWNER
Dr Paul Cluver

KEY WINES
Pinot Noir, Cabernet Sauvignon, Sauvignon Blanc, Chardonnay, Weisser Riesling, Gewürztraminer

Paul Cluver Estate is a family affair. A tall, blonde aesthete, Dr Paul Cluver juggles his profession as a top neurosurgeon with an executive position at export fruit co-operative Kromco and his latest role in a joint-venture community farming development. Yet, with the help of wife Songvei and three of his four equally tall and blonde daughters – the fourth, a nurse, has provided him with a son-in-law to oversee the winemaking – Cluver still manages to produce some fine wines from his 54ha of premium varieties. (Son Paul may soon join the fray after completion of his oenological studies.)

Meanwhile, son-in-law Andries Burger has been in charge of the Cluver cellar since 1997, lately with back-up from local trainee winemaker Patrick Kraukamp. Before then, grapes went to Nederburg, whose former cellarmaster Günter Brözel came out of retirement to help the Cluvers transform a fruit-packing shed into a cellar that now produces nearly 9 000 cases a year.

The cellar is small, but modern and practical. Treatment of grapes, juice and oaking is meticulous and always hands-on. The various vineyard blocks are vinified separately to isolate site-specific characteristics. 'A lot is expected of this area. I have to prove its potential,' says Cluver. Father- and son-in-law both emphasise their aim to produce wines that are distinctive of this very specific terroir.

Sites for more Sauvignon Blanc, Pinot Noir and the first Merlot have been identified, while Sauvignon is being grafted onto old Gewürztraminer stock. While Cabernet has been settled on the warmer slopes, Burger is convinced that this variety does best in cooler regions.

The coolth comes through on all the wines. A newcomer to the range, the Cabernet is typically tight, restrained and minerally, but promises luscious fruit as the vines mature. The unwooded Sauvignon is racy and flinty; some barrel fermentation provides a buttery version. The first Pinot Noirs came up with wonderful sweet cherry, then went through a dip, but now seem to be back on track. The off-dry Weisser has changed from an elegant wine to something fuller, fatter and usually filled out with some botrytis, which promises longevity.

VILLIERSDORP

A co-op founded in the 1920s, Villiersdorp draws fruit from a swathe of about 500ha of vineyards from as far afield as warm Worcester to the cool Overberg wards – wines are now usually designated 'Western Cape' or 'Overberg'.

Manager/cellarmaster JP Steenekamp comes up with excellent value for money whites and reds. A well-fruited, oak-enhanced Pinotage can charm, and an authentic port is promising.

TOP: The Cluver clan, including protegé Patrick Kraukamp and son-in-law and winemaker Andries Burger, produces stylish cool-climate wines on De Rust farm (**RIGHT**) in the lush Elgin apple district.

R O B E R T S O N

Robertson, like Worcester, is a ward of the Breede River Valley region. Though dry (the average rainfall can be as low as 300mm) and arid-looking, and once thought too hot for quality wine production, Robertson draws succour from the south-east wind funnelling cool, moisture-laden air up the valley from the coast less than 100km away.

Robertson wineries like Rooiberg are priding themselves on modern, fruity reds, marketed with a new-found sense of style.

The Brandvlei dam provides a permanent water source via a canal system flanking the wide Breede River, which is lined with lush green trees and vineyards. Vines grow prolifically in the sandy, alluvial, often excessively organic fertile soils. In seeking naturally lower yields, conducive to better-quality, more concentrated fruit, wine growers have been moving onto slightly higher ground with its friable clay content combined with limestone. Similarly, they're exploring the cool-climate, rockier foothills of the Langeberg range to the north.

The result is a revolution in quality, and proof that Robertson can produce fine wine from the classic varieties, both white and red. Though traditionally a white-wine area – predominantly Chenin Blanc and Colombard – with particularly Chardonnay and, on the right sites, Sauvignon Blanc now coming into their own, the move is towards reds: Shiraz is the emerging star, while Cabernet Sauvignon is also proving successful, as are Merlot and Pinotage. Ruby Cabernet is another favourite, lending colour and fruitiness to blends when picked really ripe.

Wine farmers have organised themselves into the Robertson Valley Association, the first to introduce a regional certification system, whereby palates familiar with the area's conditions and style of wines act as arbiters. The process is still monitored by the industry's Wine & Spirit Board, but it is a significant step towards introducing the concept of regionality to Cape wine styles.

But the main project has been establishing reds and selected whites in a viticulturally scientific way by matching the right varieties (and preferably the premiums) to the most suitable sites.

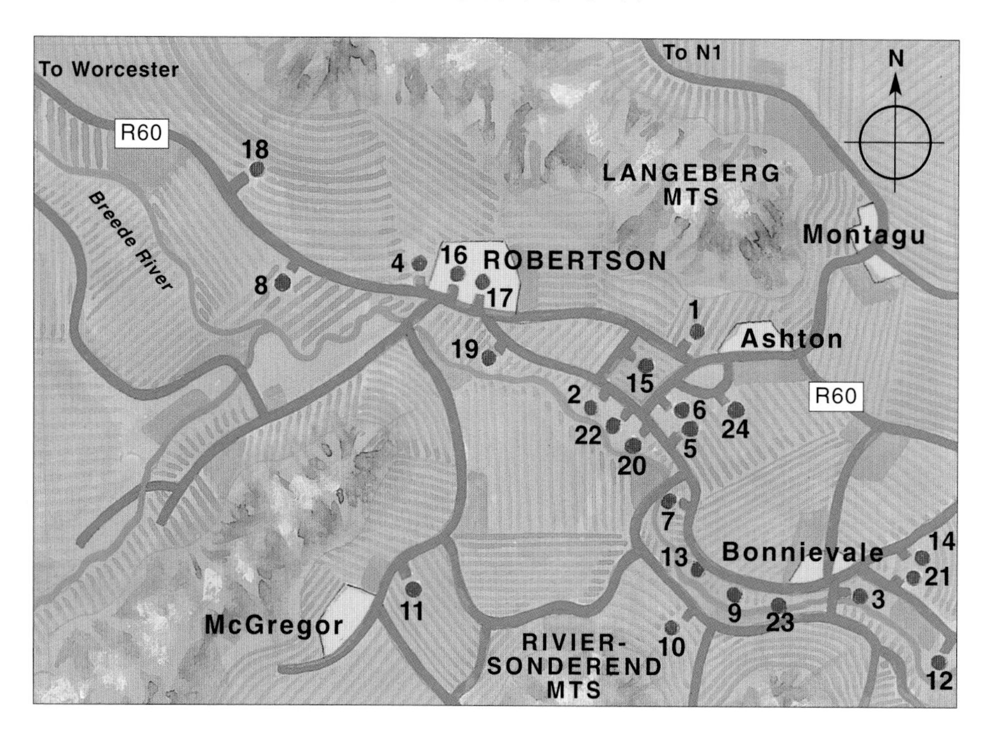

1. Ashton
2. Bon Courage
3. Bonnievale
4. Clairvaux
5. De Wetshof
6. Excelsior
7. Goedverwacht
8. Graham Beck
9. Jonkheer
10. Langverwacht
11. McGregor
12. Merwespont
13. Mooiuitsig
14. Nordale
15. Rietvallei
16. Robertson
17. Roodezandt
18. Rooiberg
19. Springfield
20. Van Loveren
21. Van Zylshof
22. Viljoensdrift
23. Weltevrede
24. Zandvliet

OPENING PAGE: Not as dry and arid as some think, Robertson is often cloaked in mist and moisture-laden clouds, providing necessary coolth for quality wine-grape production.

GRAHAM BECK CELLARS

OWNER
Graham Beck

KEY WINES
Cap Classique Brut Blanc de Blancs, Brut NV, Ridge Shiraz, Railroad Red, Lone Hill Chardonnay, Sauvignon Blanc, Waterside White, Rhona Muscadel

Happiness is a perfect bubble. 'In my mind I'm always in the centre of that bubble, examining it for flaws. It must have no edges.' Intense stuff from Graham Beck's sparkling-wine specialist Pieter Ferreira who, much like the nature of the elixir he makes, matches it with a naughty sense of fun, aptly expressed in a strong experimental streak, be it revolutionary new yeasts or a Pinotage Cap Classique.

Ferreira moved from picturesque Franschhoek, where he worked under Cabrière's *champenoise* fanatic Achim von Arnim, to dry and arid Robertson at the bidding of Graham Beck. This powerful, publicity-shy coal magnate and horse breeder – Robertson is also renowned for its ideal stud conditions – bought his first wine farm in 1983 (he now also owns Bellingham and two Helderberg properties).

The Robertson wine farm was systematically replanted, with grapes going to nearby Rooiberg co-op before being incorporated into the first wines produced by Ferreira in 1991: a barrel-fermented Chardonnay and a Cap Classique combining equal amounts of Chardonnay and Pinot Noir.

Ferreira has the privilege of working in an unorthodox-looking but highly efficient dedicated sparkling-wine cellar and applies classic Champagne practices. Whole-bunch pressing, the use of free-run juice, wood-fermentation, years on the bottle-fermentation lees before degorging. Also, a cache of base wines has already been built up over the vintages, adding a rare complexity and maturity to the finished product and ensuring consistency of style in the best tradition of the top Champagne houses.

The Chardonnay/Pinot Noir Brut NV, with its slightly higher dosage than the 100% Chardonnay Blanc de Blancs, is made for earlier drinking with just two years instead of nearly four on the lees. But Ferreira and assistant Manie Arendse are extending their horizons and have premium reds in their sights, having mastered a very creamy, fruity, fat Chardonnay from a vineyard block called Lone Hill, and fine-tuned large-scale production of their excellent value-for-money blends, Waterside White and Railroad Red.

Total production at Graham Beck Cellars, boosted by a successful export business, is a massive 150 000 cases from what is a nearly 180ha spread.

The Railroad Red is from Cabernet and Shiraz, of which plantings have recently been increased by 22ha. Ferreira, who confesses to a soft spot for Shiraz, bottled just over 1 000 cases of his first varietal wine in 1997, from 6ha planted in 1994 on new sites earmarked for premium reds on the nearby Langeberg slopes. He opted for American oak on his modern, succulent, full-fruited Ridge Shiraz. He also bottled a varietal Merlot and Cabernet, which occupy about 6ha and 2ha respectively on the same slopes as the Shiraz.

Pieter Ferreira (**TOP**), a dab hand at bottle-fermented bubbly, is now producing some fine Shiraz at the colourful, ultra-modern Graham Beck Cellars (**ABOVE**).

SPRINGFIELD

OWNER
Abrie Bruwer

KEY WINES
Méthode Ancienne Cabernet Sauvignon, Cabernet Sauvignon, Life from Stone Sauvignon Blanc, Special Cuvée Sauvignon Blanc, Sauvignon Blanc, Méthode Ancienne Chardonnay, Wild Yeast Chardonnay, Colombard/Chardonnay

Not so long ago, Abrie Bruwer, fourth-generation wine farmer, avid game fisherman, pilot of his own small plane, conservationist and (very low-key) saxophonist, was content to grow grapes and supply wine for Stellenbosch Farmers' Winery. Then, one day in 1995, after being rebuffed when asking for an increase in price, he decided to go it alone. 'And we're doing far better than we did then,' says this genial, erudite winemaker.

The Bruwer family settled on Klipdrif farm in 1902. 'Winemaking is all I've ever wanted to do,' admits Bruwer. He has helped in the vineyards by father Piet. Of his 160ha on the banks of the Breede River, the best sites are stony, needing a steel rod to be hammered into the ground to make holes for trellising poles and vines alike. Abrie has picked up pruning tips on trips to France, encouraging vigorous growth from new shoots which are left to protect the ripening berries against Robertson's scorching sun. He relieves grape stress with drip irrigation. Yields are kept down to between 5 and 6 tons per hectare. Picking is done in the cool of the night.

He follows a policy of minimum interference in the cellar: no filtration, no stabilisation. The inspiration is traditional French methodology. It's evident in his use of wood, too, which is invariably delicate and entirely complementary to the fruit. Yet most of his wines are for the long haul.

His first elegant, flinty, figgy Sauvignon Blancs and dense, fruitful Cabernets were a revelation in Robertson, never considered suitable for these varieties. And after a year or so in bottle, the true class of his Special Cuvée Sauvignon Blanc comes through.

With his new Chardonnay Méthode Ancienne in 1997, Bruwer was again attracting attention, this time with the use of wild yeasts that exist naturally on the skin of freshly picked, ripe grapes. Again, it is an ancient Burgundian method, involving a nearly three-month fermentation, about a year on the lees in French oak and straight into a heavy-weight Burgundian bottle, with no fining, filtering or stabilising. The beautifully bottle-ageing '97 and lovely, lemony '99 are a significant step up from the still very fine standard Wild Yeast Chardonnay, which is more lightly wooded, but also now fermented with natural yeasts.

Which simply egged him on to try it on a 3ha block of prime Cabernet, whole-berry pressed (like all his Cabernets) and barrel-matured for 18 months. Due for release only after plenty of bottle-ageing, this wine is simply stunning, with the typically minerally, spicy character underpinned by solid fruit.

From being simply a supplier of wine to wholesalers, Abrie Bruwer (**ABOVE**) has established Springfield (**LEFT**) as synonymous with parcels of top-quality Sauvignon Blanc and Cabernet.

ZANDVLIET

OWNERS

Paul and Dan de Wet

KEY WINES

Zandvliet Kalkveld Shiraz, Shiraz, Chardonnay, Cabernet, Merlot, Cabernet/Merlot; Astonvale Shiraz, Chardonnay, Sauvignon Blanc, Colombard

A year ago Zandvliet estate introduced a new phase in its development, under the catch phrase 'new directions'. The nub of the whole thing is Shiraz, long the focus of the viticultural endeavours of this extensive 1 000ha racing stud, fruit and wine farm. The first Shiraz bottled was a 1976. After nearly three decades it is to become the sole variety to carry the Zandvliet label. And wine is increasingly supplanting its agricultural bedfellows in the hearts and minds of owners Paul and Dan de Wet.

The two brothers are the fourth generation to farm Zandvliet. It was their father 'Paulie' who, in 1947, re-established winemaking after the collapse of the ostrich industry (following the boom in the international feather trade early in the 20th century that saw many properties pull up their vines in favour of these great birds). Now the stud, too, is being substantially downsized as the lime-rich soils so favourable for grazing are being planted to vine.

They're moving away from the dark, fertile, alluvial soils along the banks of the Cogmans River and exploiting the cooler, low-lying hills opposite, where well over 100ha of mostly virgin territory may see the farm's 150ha of vineyards doubled in time. The areas earmarked are red, gravelly Karoo soils, an excellent friable clay combination containing bands of limestone.

Consulting is international viticulturist Phil Freese of Sonoma, California, who advises several other Cape cellars (nearby De Wetshof and Thelema). Shiraz, Cabernet and Merlot will all do well on these hills, but it is the Shiraz that's already showing a change of style. The first wines vinified from these *kalkveld* (chalkland) vines were from the '96 vintage, launched at the end of the millennium as Zandvliet Kalkveld Shiraz. They, and subsequent vintages tasted, show a depth of colour and fruit concentration on an all-new-oak base that charts a fresh course for Zandvliet. The De Wets are playing around with French and American oak, varying times on the skins and the use of free-run and pressed juice. Fruit from different vineyard blocks are being vinified separately to track the quality and development of each.

Zandvliet has built a successful export market with its Astonvale label. The range of whites and reds, now also available in South Africa, is designed to be immediately accessible – to both pocket and palate. With the Zandvliet name to be associated solely with Shiraz in future, another label is being planned to brand the Cabernet, Merlot and wooded Chardonnay that are to date sold as Zandvliet. The farm's final mix will be predominantly red – Pinot Noir may also be planted – with the rest comprising mostly Chardonnay.

ASHTON

Red-wine production is on the increase among members of this once primarily Chenin Blanc and Colombard producing co-op. Hence the decision to invest in a dedicated new red-wine cellar. Cabernet Sauvignon, Cabernet Franc, Merlot, Shiraz and Pinotage are being planted, with the Shiraz showing the most promise. But this remains sweet-wine country, with the fortified Muscadel Jerepigos, especially the white, offering a delicious, inexpensive dessert.

BON COURAGE

André Bruwer and son Jacques popped into the public consciousness with a very fine Cap Classique from their family estate a few years back. The Jacques Bruère Brut Reserve, a traditional mix of Chardonnay and Pinot Noir, shows a rare richness and yeastiness, balanced by lovely appley, melony fruit. With a slightly higher dosage – it finishes with around 7g per litre sugar – it appeals to popular tastes. Bruwer senior's trademark Gewürztraminer, a lovely, full, floral, off-dry wine, is still a great buy – as is the botrytised Gewürz Special Late Harvest. Meanwhile, the go-ahead Jacques is working with small batches of Sauvignon Blanc and Chardonnay in wood, producing Prestige Cuvées of some substance. New plantings of Cabernet, Merlot and Shiraz are showing good character as early-drinking wines.

BONNIEVALE

Established in 1964, this co-op, another Chenin Blanc and Colombard mass producer, has added Chardonnay to its member growers' shopping list, as well as the much-in-demand red varieties such as Cabernet Sauvignon, Pinotage and Ruby Cabernet. These premiums are appearing in rather novel blends under the Riggton label.

TOP: The De Wet brothers, Paul (**standing**) and Dan, are investing heavily in the future of red wines on family farm Zandvliet (**OPPOSITE**), famous for its Shiraz.

CLAIRVAUX

The co-op of the novel names. How about Madonna's Kisses (guess who?) for a very ripe, fruity Special Late Harvest and delicious new Noble Late Harvest? For the rest, there's the usual line-up of dry and semi-sweet whites, Muscadels and Jerepigos – the semisweet Rhine Riesling can be nice.

DE WETSHOF

Big, burly owner/winemaker Danie de Wet, Geisenheim-trained, has established his wine estate as a Chardonnay specialist. He uses the full palette of clones and barrels to produce five Chardonnays, from the juicy, unwooded Bon Vallon to the lightly wooded, lemony Finesse, a surprise winner of the Diners Club Winemaker of the Year award in '94, a time when big, toasty brutes were *de rigueur*. Another step up is the fully oaked, toasty d'Honneur, followed by the Bateleur, a special barrel selection, made to his personal taste. Now he's come out with a Chardonnay Sur Lie, barrel-fermented with extended time on the lees for a creamy texture. De Wet is a long-time standard-bearer for Rhine Riesling, making it both dry and full-flavoured, semi-sweet and as a botrytis dessert wine.

EXCELSIOR

The home of Stephen and Freddie de Wet, Excelsior is back in bottle under a new-look label after several years of delivering in bulk to the wholesale trade and building up a successful export business. Winemaker Jaco Marais makes a flavourful, characterful Sauvignon Blanc and some very drinkable Cabernets, all well-priced. Merlot and Shiraz are to follow. With 200ha under vine, this is one of the Cape's largest family-owned estates.

GOEDVERWACHT

Largely a bulk-wine supplier, Jan du Toit's estate has expanded from its maiden bottling of a '93 Colombard to include a Sauvignon Blanc and some serious Chardonnays in its range, the results of experimentation with reductive winemaking and extended periods on the lees. Newly planted reds will soon start delivering, and up to 30% of the crop may be bottled.

JONKHEER

Dirk Jonker, armed with an MBA and assisted by brother Andries and father Nicholas, is establishing some interesting new brands at this winery with its 150ha of rejuvenated vineyards. The Bakenskop label has become synonymous with two fine fortified dessert wines: Red Muscadel and a smooth, bottle-aged White. These have been joined by a tasty Chardonnay, while the new-look Jonkheer label features a range of premium varietal reds and whites.

LANGVERWACHT

Perhaps best known for its fresh, guava-rich Colombard, this Bonnievale co-operative cellar is also taking in increasing quantities of Sauvignon Blanc and Chardonnay, the latter showing some good tropical fruit. The cellar handles about 10 000 tons of grapes, only bottling about 1 000 cases.

MCGREGOR

Co-op winemaker Danie Marais has made some lovely Chardonnay/Chenin Blanc blends, while his straight Chenins and just off-dry Colombards can be deliciously fruity and zesty. The Village Red, a lightly wooded, quite dry but fruity Ruby Cabernet, is not bad.

MERWESPONT

This co-op is concentrating on the 'big six' Cape varieties on its 65 growers' farms: Chardonnay, Sauvignon Blanc, Cabernet Sauvignon, Merlot, Shiraz and Pinotage. Driven by sound viticultural guidelines based on years of record-keeping, and their own nursery, members are also exploring the cooler slopes of the Langeberg mountains. The best of the new varietal bottlings are the Chardonnay and Cabernet.

MOOIUITSIG

This producer/wholesaler is owned by the Jonker and Claassens families, selling Mooi-uitzicht table wines and Oude Rust Muscadels and Hanepoots. It is also the source of rare dessert wines such as Malmsey and Marsala.

NORDALE

New co-op winemaker Tinus Els bottles just 3 000-odd cases of a select few wines – the rest go to wholesalers. The Nordale label includes a fine Chardonnay and typical Robertson blend of Chardonnay and Colombard. A Vin Rouge Ruby Cabernet/Cabernet Sauvignon drinks easily, while the Red Muscadel Jerepigo is a goodie. Mon Don is a small, second-label range.

RIETVALLEI

Johnny Burger is the fifth generation in charge of this family estate. Most of the grapes from its 170ha go to Distillers in Stellenbosch. Rietvallei bottles a Chardonnay and a more famous red Estate Muscadel. It's a fresh, clean and elegant drink, made to an age-old recipe and including grapes from vines more than 70 years old.

ROBERTSON

This is one of the most progressive of the area's co-ops, hence its involvement with Robin Day's Long Mountain wine company. Bowen Botha heads a team of winemakers handling around 23 000 tons from nearly 1 500ha of vineyard. The wines are modern, fruity, easy drinkers. The Wide River label marks new-wave varietal Sauvignon Blancs, reserve Chardonnays and Cabernets from selected sites. The Robertson range offers a modern take on many stalwarts, from a barrel-matured Cabernet to very drinkable Merlots and Pinotages. A delicious new Weisser Riesling Noble Late Harvest appears under the Almond Grove label.

Botha pioneered the packaging of good wine in one-litre and 500ml tetra-packs and won the battle for legislation allowing varietal identi-fication on premium box wines.

ROODEZANDT

While co-op winemaker Christie Steytler's vote goes to Ruby Cabernet and Chardonnay, lovers of *soetes* (sweet wines) clamour for the Red and White Muscadel. Roodezandt also makes one of the area's few ports, in a Ruby style.

ROOIBERG

Source of some of the best value in Robertson. Rooiberg co-op has become synonymous with Shiraz, which cellarmaster Tommy Loftus is encouraging his growers to plant more of. His juicy Pinotage is another winner, as is the Ruby port. Cabernet and Merlot plantings are on the rise, with members consulting Californian viticulturist Phil Freese, advisor to Zandvliet.

VAN LOVEREN

Nature is at the core of the Retief family's winegrowing activities, coming through in the quaffable, fruit-driven wines produced by Nico, his brother Wynand and son Bussell, and the latter's three siblings. Long noted for its unusual whites (Hárslevelü, Fernão Pires, Pinot Gris), Van Loveren has been coming up with drinkable white and red classics. Pinotage is the latest addition, while the River Red and River White blends are great value. Vineyards are being replanted to reds to match the whites 50:50.

VAN ZYLSHOF

The small, 30ha estate has been in the Van Zyl family for three generations. The decision to bottle their own wine comes courtesy of owner Chris van Zyl's son Andri, fresh from Stellenbosch University with an oenology and viticulture degree. Carefully sited Chardonnay and Sauvignon Blanc, some Chenin Blanc, and a 3ha block of newly planted Cabernet Sauvignon make up the mix.

VILJOENSDRIFT

The fifth-generation Viljoen brothers, winemaker Fred and viticulturist Manie, bottled their first wines in '98. Some 70 tons of Chenin Blanc, Colombard, Chardonnay, local rarity Sémillon, Cabernet Sauvignon and Pinotage went into mostly export wines until recently, when the wines became available locally.

WELTEVREDE

Owned by affable KWV chairman Lourens Jonker, Weltevrede was the first estate in the Breede River Valley to bottle its own wine for sale to the public in the mid '70s. Other firsts include the country's first certified Red Muscadel and first fortified wine (the rare Muscat de Hambourg) selected for sale on the Nederburg Auction. Graduation to classic varieties has seen an elegant Chardonnay, flinty Sauvignon Blanc and a wooded blend of the two. The Philip Jonker Brut Cap Classique is named after Jonker's son, now winemaker. Among the 100ha of mostly white vines is some newly planted Merlot and Cabernet on high-lying, shale ground. Limited quantities of top premium varietal wines are now bottled under the Oude Weltevreden label. A red and white Muscadel are winners.

Van Loveren is one of those canny Robertson wineries exploiting hillside slopes and putting the warm climate to good use to vinify fruity, friendly wines.

WORCESTER

Worcester is one of the newer wine districts, falling within the Breede River Valley region. Vineyards in the mid-1800s bore grapes for a flourishing raisin market. These were converted to wine grapes in the mid-1900s, becoming the heart of the brandy distilling industry. Worcester remains the home of the KWV's brandy cellar (the world's largest such production facility under one roof) and accounts for 25% of the country's total wine-grape crop, making it, in terms of volume, the biggest district.

Early morning mists are not unknown in the vast Breede River Valley, more usually associated with extreme heat.

Where Colombard is the most common variety in Robertson, Chenin Blanc remains the backbone of the Worcester wine industry, traditionally for distilling and more recently for the growing grape juice and concentrate markets. But the last decade of the 20th century saw an earnest attempt by some of the more forward-thinking vintners to tap into the quality wine market. Growers started looking at the Cape's classical varieties: mainly Chardonnay, some Sauvignon Blanc; among the reds mostly Cabernet Sauvignon and Shiraz, with some Merlot and Pinotage.

The warm climate is conducive to rich, ripe fruit for red wines that are juicy, upfront and easy-drinking. From about 1995, viticultural consultants started pinpointing areas for specific varieties, advising co-ops accordingly. For example, Shiraz, happy in sandier soils derived from Klein Karoo shale, settled at De Wet, Slanghoek and Du Toitskloof. Merlot, made for more clayey ground, performed at Botha, Bergsig, Romansrivier and Badsberg. Cabernet Franc showed up well at Nuy, with its lime-rich soils.

Cellar upgrades were next on the list, with millions spent on new bag presses and red-wine fermenters. Equipment sorties to manufacturers in Italy and France had a spin-off in stimulating local thinking, already more progressive due to a new generation of young, qualified winemakers running the co-op cellars. 'Whereas the old hands were essentially cellar managers, the new guys are qualified vintners,' says Jaco Potgieter of the rejuvenated Worcester Winelands Association.

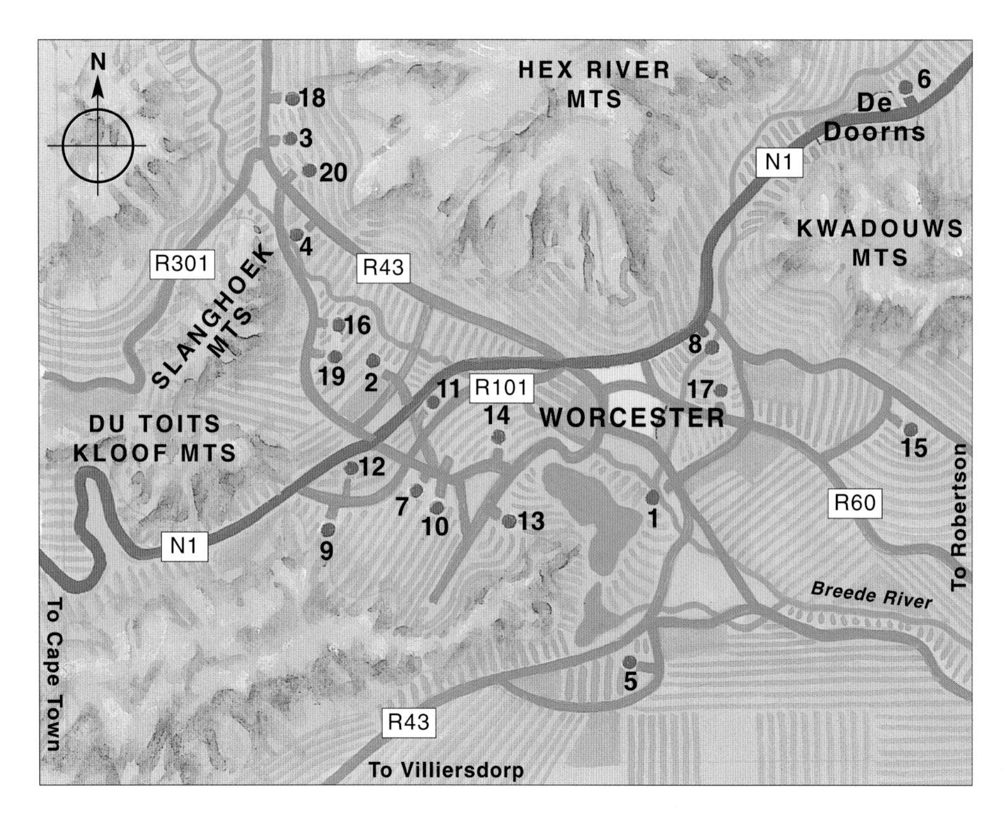

1. Aan-de-Doorns
2. Badsberg
3. Bergsig
4. Botha
5. Brandvlei
6. De Doorns
7. Deetlefs
8. De Wet
9. Du Toitskloof
10. Goudini
11. Groot Eiland
12. HL Du Preez
13. Louwshoek-Voorsorg
14. Merwida
15. Nuy
16. Opstal
17. Overhex
18. Romansrivier
19. Slanghoek
20. Waboomsrivier

OPENING PAGE: The spectacular Du Toitskloof mountains separate the Cape winelands Coastal region from the hinterland, which starts at Worcester. Here the traditionally distilling-wine producers are investing in classic red varieties for fruit-rich wines.

NUY

OWNERS
21 member growers

KEY WINES
Red Muscadel, White Muscadel, Cabernet Sauvignon, Rouge de Nuy, Sauvignon Blanc, Colombard, Riesling (Crouchen Blanc), Chant de Nuit, Fernão Pires, Sauvignon Blanc Sparkling Wine

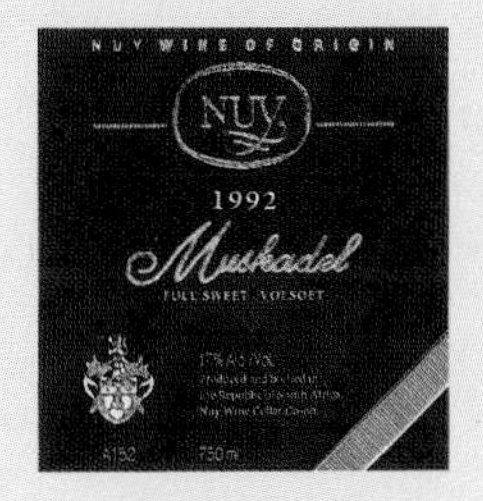

The range may not look that impressive from a premium varietal point of view, but this classy co-op's cellarmaster for the past 30 years, Wilhelm Linde, has single-handedly elevated the Cape's much-maligned Muscadel wine style to great heights.

Linde credits modern technology, such as cold fermentation, for the ability to produce quality wine in not always ideal climatic conditions. He also has a relatively small co-op membership of around 20. This enables him to keep a weather eye on vineyard development and spend time vinifying the just on 10 000 tons of grapes that are brought in, most of which goes to long-time, sole buyer SFW. A work study group he initiated among his growers a few years ago has them 'obsessed with improving viticultural and winemaking techniques, plant material and everything that will help them produce better quality wines'.

Nuy's 500ha of vines, while fanning out across deep, fertile alluvial soils, also occupy sites of heavier, lime-rich sandstone soils on the lower slopes of the Langeberg mountains, often frostbitten and snow-covered in winter. In summer, these foothills catch the cooling

TOP: Wilhelm Linde has established a niche for Nuy co-op (**ABOVE**) as a producer of arguably the Cape's consistently finest Muscadel fortified dessert wines.

summer south-easter. But there's not much more, other than pure oenological skill, that explains why Linde can make more of an ordinary Colombard – it shows rare development in the bottle – or unexciting Crouchen Blanc than most of his compatriots. Or come up with an all-time favourite like Chant de Nuit, a blend of Colombard and Chenin Blanc. Or make Muscadels that are simply streets ahead of others.

While others forge ahead with red-wine plantings, the progress at Nuy has been gradual, but meticulously planned. Premium varieties have been confined to Merlot, Cabernet Sauvignon and Cabernet Franc, and Sauvignon Blanc and Chardonnay among the whites. Nevertheless, new varieties are creeping into the range. A red blend called Rouge de Nuy is gaining in complexity and stature with each vintage, dropping Pinotage as an early ingredient and focusing on Cabernet and Merlot. Lightly wooded, with deep cassis flavours, it is a modern, drinkable wine at a bargain price. Similarly, the Sauvignon Blanc and Chardonnay, with their delicate varietal character, get better each year.

It is this same elegance that makes Nuy Muscadels magic. The White Muscadel probably just nudges the Red off the podium. A 1996 has been one of only a handful of wines considered worthy of a five-star rating by local *WINE* magazine. The wine is concentrated, filled with fragrant, floral, grape flavours, fresh in its youth, honeyed with a bit of bottle-age. The Red Muscadel is heavier, with a massive 225g/litre sugar and a 17% alcohol by volume, yet nevertheless offers a beautifully balanced grape-spirit flavour and silky texture.

AAN-DE-DOORNS

On the road to Villiersdorp, this co-op grows and sells mainly white varieties that can do duty as distilling wine: Clairette Blanche, Colombard and Chenin Blanc.

Some good wine grapes are being planted here, though, such as Chardonnay, Merlot, Pinotage and Ruby Cabernet. Johan Morkel's Tinta Barocca port can be most drinkable.

BADSBERG

Winemaker Willie Burger has been quite busy in recent vintages, substantially extending the range of bottled wines to include several noble varieties. These have been fairly successful, given the vineyards' position in the viticulturally better quality area around Rawsonville. The Chardonnay, with its generous dose of American oak chips, and a fruity, charry Chardonnay Chenin combo should be enjoyed young. The Sauvignon Blanc can show surprising varietal character.

BERGSIG

This wine estate has been in the Lategan family for six generations. It is now run by affable Prop Lategan and his three sons, of whom De Wet is the winemaker. The 370ha under vine include some fine sites on the lower reaches of the twin Mostertshoek peaks. Chenin Blanc and Chardonnay show well here, the latter a lovely melange of toasty, buttery, citrussy flavours. Their Ruby Cabernet is good too, blended with Merlot and accompanied by a Cabernet and Pinotage in the red-wine range. Own-label wines form a minuscule part of total production; the bulk is vinified to spec for local supermarkets Woolworths and Spar and exports through Cape Vineyards and International Wine Services.

BOTHA

This co-operative winery has been converted into a company, and is the place for drink-now reds. It offers rare richness at an unbeatable price since being rejuvenated under the management of long-time Rooiberg cellar-master Dassie Smith. With a new red-wine cellar, Botha is turning out jolly good wines. 'Dassie's Rood' is a ripe, sweet and spicy blend of Cabernet Sauvignon, Ruby Cabernet and Cinsaut and there are some super premium varietal wines such as the Reserve Cabernet, Merlot and Pinotage. A master of Jerepigos, the winery produces a white Hanepoot (Muscat de Alexandrie) and a red Hanepoot from Pinotage, Ruby Cabernet and Shiraz. The Ruby Port is also a winner.

BRANDVLEI

Producing wines mainly for wholesalers and brandy production, this co-op bottles one of the area's nicest Chenin Blancs, bright and fruity. Other noble varieties now appearing in the vineyards (and in bottles) include Sauvignon Blanc, Chardonnay, Merlot and Ruby Cabernet.

DE DOORNS

Grape-juice concentrate is the big thing here, with most of the growers for this Hex River co-op being table-grape farmers or churning out Chenin, Colombard and Clairette Blanche. Winemaker Danie Koen bottles small quantities for members' consumption and cellar door sales, which are beginning to include Chardonnay and Cabernet Sauvignon and ever-popular Pinotage.

DEETLEFS

Formerly known as Lebensraum Estate, renamed Deetlefs Estate is being developed and more actively marketed by sixth-generation wine grower Kobus Deetlefs. Some 100ha of vines produce good wine for wholesale buyers, as well as an exciting small range under the Deetlefs label. The speciality is Sémillon, with fresh, citrussy aromas and lemony, grassy flavours. Added complexity from partial barrel-fermentation and time on the lees makes for a serious wine that needs time. A Reserve bottling from selected barrels is richer and fuller with great ageing potential. A Chenin Blanc delivers similar richness of fruit. The gently wooded Chardonnay is elegant and balanced. New is a Pinotage, the first red from the estate and already one of the best in the area.

DE WET

Zakkie Bester bottles a mere 1% of his crop – the rest is bought up by wholesalers such as SFW, Distillers, KWV and Douglas Green. Reds comprise some 20% of total production. The Worcester Dry Red is a rare local blend of the Bordeaux greats Cabernet, Merlot and Cabernet Franc, drinkable and 'oak-influenced' (using oak staves instead of barrels). These, like the vast array of dry and semisweet whites, do not pretend to be more than easy-drinking wines. Bester's Ruby Port, a Shiraz with a dash of Merlot, surprises with its authentic character.

DU TOITSKLOOF

This is one of the district's quality co-op producers. Winemaker Philip Jordaan's extensive range includes a fairly concentrated Cabernet, a smoky, ripe Shiraz and a good Pinotage. An award-winning Cabernet Shiraz blend shows beautifully soft, ripe fruit. Jordaan's full, fruity Special Late Harvest and rich, raisiny fortified Hanepoot Jerepigo successfully balance sweetness and refreshing acidity.

GOUDINI

Besides bottling good-value wines under the Goudini label, vintner Hennie Hugo also supplies the visionary international Long Mountain winery, an indication of the quality of his members' grapes. Ruby Cabernet shines in a Reserve varietal bottling, a blend with Merlot and a port. His Umfiki Chardonnay/Sémillon blend appeals with its fresh and fruity character.

GROOT EILAND

This Rawsonville co-op has Pieter Carstens at the helm, encouraging members to replant vineyards to premium varieties such as Chardonnay and Cabernet Sauvignon. A charming blend of Sauvignon Blanc, Chenin Blanc and Colombard called Meander and a lemony fresh, long-finishing Chardonnay/Colombard has impressed. Groot Eiland also makes attractive Hanepoot (Muscat de Alexandrie), partnered with Bukettraube in a delicious semisweet and as a fresh, fragrant fortified dessert wine.

HL DU PREEZ

A budding new star on the Worcester wine scene, this family wine farm previously known as Excelsior has successfully re-invented itself as HL Du Preez Estate. Owned by Hennie du Preez and son, also Hennie, the 150ha of vineyards have always supplied fruit to SFW and now has the KWV after its quality red. Young Hennie believes the excellent rocky sandstone soils and cool terroir gives him unlimited potential to produce top-quality wine. Hence the decision in '98 to start bottling. The Sauvignon Blanc is a gorgeous wine. His '98 Pinotage is dense, with very ripe, sweet fruit. Polla's Red is equally full and fruity, an exuberant, partly wood-fermented mix of Shiraz, Pinotage, Ruby Cabernet and rare Petit Verdot.

LOUWSHOEK-VOORSORG

Jaco Potgieter specialises in Sémillon at this co-op, with vineyards that occupy some of the best viticultural land up against the slopes of the Du Toitskloof mountains in the Rawsonville basin. With members pinpointing prime sites for premium varieties, their winemaker has established a new label, Daschbosch, for the fruits of their labour. Look out for the Nectar de Provision, a Colombard fortified with pot-still brandy matured in old brandy vats.

MERWIDA

Merwida is a family-owned co-op in the prime Rawsonville area, like many others also testing the waters with red wines. Besides Ruby Cabernet, winemaker Wollie Wolhuter takes in Cabernet Sauvignon and Merlot, bottling small quantities of a blend. Chardonnay and Sauvignon Blanc have joined the ranks of the white wines.

OPSTAL

The owner of this pretty little estate in the Slanghoek Valley, Stanley Louw, is the sixth generation at Opstal and exports practically all his wine. He recently made an amazingly inky, dense, ripe Cabernet Sauvignon, barrel-matured. Look out for the Carl Everson label which includes a Reserve Chardonnay and a Classic Red mix of Cabernet, Ruby Cabernet and Pinotage.

OVERHEX

The Chardonnay is distinctive and winemaker AB Krige is experimenting with barrel-fermentation. Cabernet Sauvignon, Merlot and Pinotage represent a new direction, and one with great promise, judging by the success of the Shiraz, uncommon in Worcester.

ROMANSRIVIER

One of the first co-ops in Worcester to start exploring mountain vineyards, Romansrivier introduced a Wine of Origin Ceres label for the premium varieties planted on cooler slopes. Winemaker Albie Treurnicht makes a deliciously fruity Chardonnay. New red plantings feature mainly Shiraz and Merlot, the latter a particularly elegant version, with concentrated fruit. Some 30-year-old Pinotage vines produce a fresh, fruity, again slightly herbaceous wine. The Cabernet is good, too. Novelties include a botrytised Chardonnay Noble Late Harvest and an innovative Vin de Paille (straw wine), a Natural Sweet dessert from Muscat de Alexandrie and Colombard.

SLANGHOEK

Co-op cellarmaster Kobus Rossouw is producing some stunning Sauvignon Blanc, currently somewhat lost in the Private Reserve Chardonnay Sauvignon Blanc blend. The Sémillon is also good, adding body to a best-selling blend with Riesling (Crouchen Blanc). The sweet wines sing, particularly a Noble Late Harvest, which is deep gold, full-bodied and complex, yet finishing with a freshness and delicacy. A Natural Sweet is good too, as are the Hanepoots and Jerepigos.

WABOOMSRIVIER

This 50-year-old co-op has recently made Ruby Cabernet its speciality, while the Merlot is good, too. Red wines in general are receiving increasing attention from cellarmaster Chris van der Merwe, to the extent that a new, hi-tech dedicated cellar has been built.

K L E I N K A R O O

At first glance the arid, scrub-covered Klein Karoo is hardly the environment for viticulture – hot in summer, frosty cold in winter and with an average rainfall of less than 300mm. It is far better suited to that hardy bird, the ostrich, with which intrepid farmers made millions at the turn of the last century. But when the international ostrich feather market went bust in the early 1900s, farmers turned to grapes, organising themselves into co-operatives and finding a steady market for distilling wine.

ABOVE AND OPPOSITE: The schist-like soil of the rugged Karoo with its rocky ridges and scrub is reminiscent of the Douro region of Portugal, home of great ports.

Most of the co-ops continue in this vein today, selling in bulk but bottling small quantities of mostly sweet, fortified dessert wines, such as Muscadels and Jerepigos, relying on the adaptability, versatility and high yields of Muscat d'Frontignan, Muscat de Alexandrie (Hanepoot), Chenin Blanc and Colombard. Yet the demand for fine-wine grapes from bulk buyers has led to the appearance of varieties such as Chardonnay, Cabernet Sauvignon, Pinotage and others, though with no great success in the bottle.

Except in specific areas, that is. The wards of Tradouw and Montagu have been identified as having viticultural potential where cool nights and deep, clayish shale on mountain foothills allow for production of better-quality wine from premium varieties: Cabernet Sauvignon, Merlot, Pinotage – it's surprising that Shiraz has not been considered – and Chardonnay.

As for the district of Calitzdorp ... well, some intrepid winemakers, notably the Nel cousins of Boplaas and Die Krans, recognised the suitability of the schist-like shale soils of the area for port varieties. Now some of the Cape's finest ports are coming out of Calitzdorp, dubbed the 'port capital' of the country. Headed by Carel Nel of Boplaas, the SA Port Producers Association provides guidelines on classic port varieties, traditional production methods and authentic Portuguese styles. Sadly, it has lost the fight against the European Community's decision to give Portugal sole claim to the generic use of the term 'port', and has five years in which to find another name.

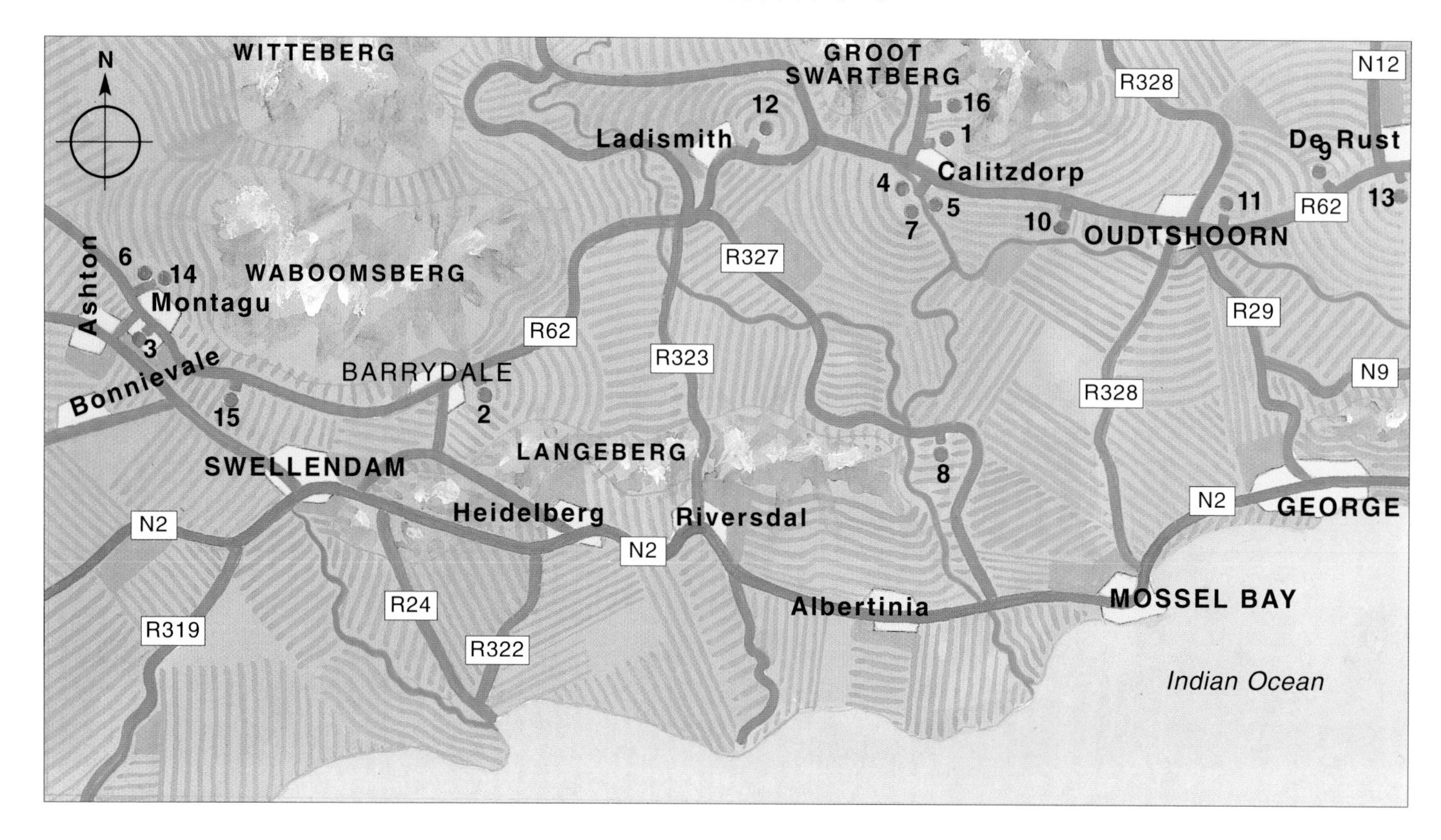

1. Axe Hill
2. Barrydale
3. Bloupunt
4. Boplaas
5. Calitzdorp
6. Cogmans
7. Die Krans
8. Die Poort
9. Domein Doornkraal
10. Grundheim
11. Kango
12. Ladismith
13. Mons Ruber
14. Montagu
15. Rietrivier
16. Withoek

BOPLAAS

OWNER
Carel Nel

KEY WINES
Cape Vintage Reserve Port, Cape Vintage, Cape Ruby, Cape Tawny, Cape White, Cabernet Sauvignon, Merlot, Pinotage, Dry Red, Chardonnay, Sauvignon Blanc, Blanc de Noir, Golden Harvest, Late Harvest, Hanepoot, Red Dessert, Sweet Muscadel, Pinot Noir Brut, Sweet Sparkling

Carel Nel joined his late father Danie at Boplaas in 1980, which is when he decided to gear the 70ha of vineyards to port production. The Nels have been farming grapes here since the mid-1800s – Carel's great-grandfather exported brandy to London.

Nel has been in the vanguard of planting new port varieties, introducing authentic Portuguese styles, encouraging port makers to strive for quality, marketing Cape port overseas and lobbying against international restraints on the use of the generic term for anything other than Portugal's product. While Boplaas has traditionally relied on Tinta Barocca, supplemented by Souzão and Tinta Roriz, Nel was one of the first Cape winemakers to plant an even more highly rated Portuguese port variety, Touriga Naçional, in recent years. All except his White Port now contain this powerfully fruited, classic ingredient, which has been joined by newcomer Touriga Francesa.

'The climate in Calitzdorp is just right for port grapes, and some of the soils here, with their high clay content, are similar to that of the Douro in Portugal.' This ideal stony, shale-like Karoo ground is found mostly on the farm's boundaries, against the lower slopes of the valley floor, which has mainly deep, alluvial, sandy soils.

Nel's Vintage Reserve, made only in exceptional vintages (both '96 and '97 have yielded one so far), is a dark, plummy, powerful wine, with a massive structure designed for long life in the bottle. His multi-award-winning 100% varietal Touriga Naçional from the '95 vintage is in the same mould. The Cape Vintage is more immediate, with elegance rather than power. In fact, all Boplaas' ports are marked by balance and harmony, though the Ruby, Tawny (a newcomer to the range) and LBV do have a fairly spirited grip.

Despite the terroir not being ideal for classic white table-wines, Nel has introduced noble white and red varieties such as Chardonnay, Sauvignon Blanc, Cabernet Sauvignon and Merlot, as well as Pinotage. After deregistering as an estate recently, he buys in grapes from Stellenbosch (his Auction and Reserve Cabernets are pretty good) as well as his cool Ruiterbosch vineyards just inland from Mossel Bay.

ABOVE: Boplaas vineyards on the outskirts of Calitzdorp, the Klein Karoo village that has been put on the wine map by top-quality ports made by progressive vintners such as Carel Nel (**TOP**).

DIE KRANS

OWNERS

Boets and Stroebel Nel

KEY WINES

Cape Vintage Reserve Port, Cape Vintage, Cape Ruby, Cabernet Sauvignon, Pinotage, Tinta Barocca, Chardonnay, Sauvignon Blanc, Chenin Blanc, Golden Harvest, Late Harvest, Spumanté Sparkling, White Muscadel Jerepigo, Heritage Collection White Jerepigo

Die Krans is home to Carel Nel's cousins, winemaker Boets and vineyard specialist Stroebel Nel. The farm was formerly part of a larger property bought by the cousins' grandfather in 1890 and farmed by their fathers. Much like Carel, Boets and Stroebel inherited vineyards full of Chenin Blanc, Muscat d'Alexandrie and Muscat de Frontignan and Pinotage and Tinta Barocca. And, again following in his cousin's footsteps, Boets started concentrating on port production, having since built on a base of Tinta Barocca by adding Souzão, Tinta Roriz and Touriga Naçional.

Die Krans ports perhaps show greater depth of flavour and fleshiness than Boplaas. They're arguably more modern in their richness of fruit, where Boplaas offers elegance underpinned by a marked dryness and quite a tart, spirity character. Die Krans Cape Vintage Reserve has a rich, peppery, spicy character, great depth of flavour and sheer succulence. The recent Die Krans Cape Ruby ports have been deftly capturing the style's typical sweet fruitiness touched with spice.

Demand from overseas has persuaded the brothers to invest in varieties other than port: primarily Cabernet, Merlot and Chardonnay. No longer an estate, they buy in Sauvignon Blanc from Durbanville, using their existing white grapes for sweeter wines that include a fortified White Muscadel Jerepigo. It's sometimes available as a Reserve labelled as the Heritage Collection. Ripe fruit also recommends the Cabernet and an unwooded Tinta Barocca.

ABOVE: Brothers Stroebel and Boets Nel on the ridge that gave their port-wine cellar Die Krans (**RIGHT**) its name, evocative of the arid, Douro-like terroir.

AXE HILL

Well-known wine fundi and Cape Wine Master Tony Mossop, who lectures for the Cape Wine Academy and writes about wine, decided to do what few prolific industry commentators are willing to risk: make his own wine, but specifically port, about which this retired leather industry executive is passionate.

A tiny Cape cottage outside Calitzdorp bought as a weekend getaway now sports one hectare of precious vines, mostly the classic Touriga Naçional with some Tinta Barocca. On this rocky, hillside property, low-yielding vines produce super-concentrated fruit, crushed by foot and matured in traditional 500-litre oak port pipes for one to two years. The result is Axe Hill Vintage port, a dense, complex fusion of plummy, tarry, smoky and peppery ingredients, medium-bodied but intensely flavoured, with a sweetish entry but classical dry finish (20% AV). With fellow Cape Wine Masters Carel and Boets Nel, Mossop produces a Masters Cape Vintage Reserve, 'combining the weight and structure of Die Krans, the plummy fruit of Axe Hill and the harmony of Boplaas'.

BARRYDALE

Originally a distillery, Barrydale co-operative winery just outside the charming little village of Barrydale added bottled table wine to its portfolio in the mid '80s.

It still supplies brandy to Distillers in Stellenbosch. Today, Cabernet Franc as well as noble varieties such as Sauvignon Blanc, Chardonnay, Cabernet Sauvignon and Merlot were planted by its member growers and a new 2 000-barrel maturation cellar, with a capacity for 2 000 barriques, was recently completed.

The best wine goes under the Tradouw label, named after the valley noted for its good soils and surprisingly cool nights, despite its position in the arid klein Karoo. (International vintner Robin Day sources some of his Long Mountain wines from this area.) The Reserve is a classically elegant Bordeaux-style blend, and the Merlot shows good fruit. A Chardonnay Sur Lie from French and California Davis clones and partly barrel-fermented is a rich, lemony wine, while a blend with Chenin Blanc, lightly oaked, is well handled.

Harsh, arid foothills, increasingly planted to port varieties, are juxtaposed with verdant vines on the valley floor at Calitzdorp, in the Klein Karoo.

BLOUPUNT

Former banker Philip Hoffman and wife Dixie turned their country retreat in Montagu into the town's first privately owned family winery, specialising in Chardonnay. Since the maiden '97 of a wooded and unwooded Chardonnay, called Bloupunt after the highest mountain peak overlooking the village, the wines show greater finesse, with more subtle wooding, and are very drinkable.

A Merlot is new. The tiny cellar, right on the main road running through this peaceful hamlet, turns out about 4 000 cases a year. The rest of the 9ha goes to Montagu co-op, where winemaker Sonnie Malan has supported self-taught Philip and son Paul, an economics graduate, in their winemaking venture.

Philip also tends their orchards of apricots grown commercially.

CALITZDORP

The bulk of this co-op's wines, made by Alwyn Burger, is sold to wholesalers.

New plantings include important port varieties such as Touriga Naçional and Tinta Barocca, which is showing up to increasingly good effect in a Cape Vintage and Cape Ruby port. Reds, particularly Merlot, Cabernet Sauvignon and Ruby Cabernet, have also added interest to the list of varietal wines bottled. The White Muscadel can be an unctuous mouthful.

COGMANS

Previously known as Soetwynboere co-op, Cogmans co-op still specialises in Muscadels, though some dry-white table wines are also bottled under the Montagu and Cogmans labels. The bulk of production is sold to wholesalers.

DIE POORT

With its alluvial sandy soils, Jannie Jonker's farm on the banks of the Gouritz River lends itself to grapes for sweet wines, fortified Muscadels and Jerepigos and brandies (also a stylishly packed *eau de vie* made from local apples). The Raisin Jerepigo from Hárslevelü is a novelty, while the Lissa Jonker Hanepoot, named after his teenaged daughter who lent a hand with the making, has lovely Muscat character. The other wines are generally light-bodied and pleasant.

DOMEIN DOORNKRAAL

Another dessert wine specialist, Domein Doornkraal, between Oudtshoorn and De Rust, has been the home of the Le Roux family for three generations. Piet le Roux has taken over the reins from father, 'Oom Swepie', winemaker for nearly 40 years. And he's been exploring red varieties, producing some surprisingly serious, well-fruited though firm-tannined reds from Merlot, Pinotage and Cabernet Sauvignon, having been inspired by a stint at California's cult Mondavi Winery. The rest of the range is a bag of all-sorts.

GRUNDHEIM

Owner and winemaker Danie Grundling confines himself to bottling a very fine Red Muscadel, a White Muscadel and a non-vintage, dessert-wine style of port from 20ha of vines. He is primarily a distilling wine producer.

KANGO

This co-op sells its wines in bulk, though it recently re-introduced a small range of table wines – Chardonnay, Sauvignon Blanc, Merlot and Pinotage – under the Mont Noir label. Fortified dessert wines appear under the Rijkshof label.

LADISMITH

Though churning out mainly distilling wine, this co-op does bottle small quantities of table wines under the Towerkop label. Varieties include Chardonnay, Crouchen Blanc and Ruby Cabernet.

MONS RUBER

The Meyer brothers, Rade and Erhard, combine ostrich farming with about 40ha of wine grapes, primarily for distilling but also for some table wine.

Despite the arid conditions on the farm, whose name was derived from the landmark red hill rising behind the cellar, the brothers are trying Chardonnay and some red varieties such as Cabernet Sauvignon. The latter pops up in the most astonishing guises, including a port and a fortified Jerepigo.

MONTAGU

This co-op comes up with some delightfully inexpensive Muscadels, especially the full-sweet Red Muscadel. Yet one or two quite respectable white and red varieties have crept into member growers' vineyards, giving winemaker Sonnie Malan the opportunity to bottle a Chardonnay and a Merlot Ruby Cabernet blend. The bulk of the whites goes to producer wholesalers.

RIETRIVIER

Rietrivier co-op makes wine for bulk buyers, using some of its Chardonnay, Sauvignon Blanc, Colombard and Muscadel grapes for off-dry whites, sweet sparkling wine and a fortified dessert wine.

WITHOEK

A new little quinta in the port 'capital' of Calitzdorp, Withoek is owned by Free State businessman Koos Geyser. He's revived the farm cellar last used in the 1930s, installed second-hand equipment and planted 1ha of traditional port varieties Tinta Barocca and Touriga Naçional, as well as Pontac. With Tinta Barocca and advice from Carel Nel of Boplaas, he's produced two Ruby ports in progressively more serious style. There's also a sweet Hanepoot and White Muscadel from his own 15ha of Muscat de Alexandrie and Muscat de Frontignan.

O L I F A N T S   R I V E R

The scrub and red sandstone formations of the Cederberg belie the suitability of some sites for vine cultivation.

The history of winemaking in the Olifants River Valley dates back to some time in the early 19th century, when Napoleon Bonaparte, exiled on St Helena far off the west coast of southern Africa, is noted to have enquired after the sweet wines of a Brakfontein Estate along the southern reaches of the river. The cellar on the farm still exists, though grapes now go to the Citrusdal co-op for its Goue Vallei wines.

But, besides sweet dessert and other wine made for own consumption, the emphasis here was always on brandy distillation. Until the 1920s, that is, when the KWV and the government's department of customs and excise took control of issuing permits and closed down many home-grown 'estate' distilleries. Grape farmers subsequently mobilised themselves into co-operatives to handle their crops.

This is rugged, hot and dry country, with citrus trees, vines and other crops such as rooibos tea carving a green band alongside the Olifants River. The waterway is flanked by the craggy Cederberg range running south from Citrusdal and flattening out towards Vredendal in the north-west about 20km from the Atlantic on the West Coast. The northerly part, where it is hotter and drier despite being closer to the West Coast, will never be the ideal terroir for fine wine. Many vines are still planted in overly fertile, organic soils close to the Olifants River water source.

But recent years have seen the introduction of some premium varieties such as Chardonnay, Cabernet and Merlot, with Pinotage also on the upsurge. Newcomer Ruby Cabernet does well in these warmer climes, adding colour and a bit of structure to those reds previously reliant on Cinsaut fruitiness. The Rhône variety Grenache does the same, and Cinsaut remains a stalwart. There is also the odd bottled Sémillon.

Fuelled by international demand for reasonably priced, New World wines, co-ops have been encouraging their members to seek out more suitable pockets of land for quality grape growing.

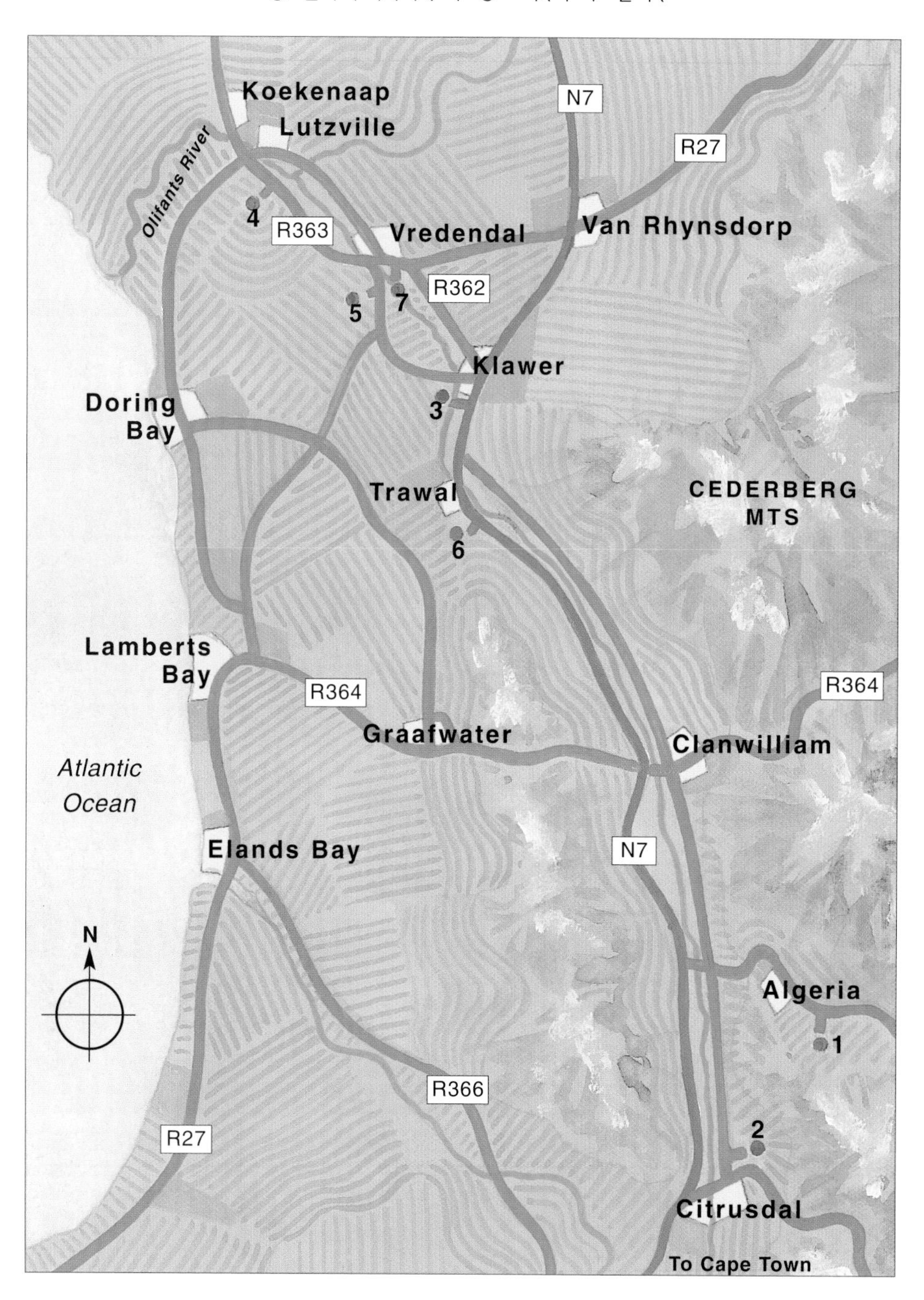

1. Cederberg
2. Citrusdal (Goue Vallei)
3. Klawer
4. Lutzville
5. Spruitdrift
6. Trawal
7. Vredendal

OPENING PAGE: Vineyards around Klawer are watered by the Olifants River, with fertile alluvial soils yielding large crops for mainly bulk and distilling wine.

CEDERBERG

OWNERS

Ernst and David Nieuwoudt

KEY WINES

Cabernet Sauvignon, Pinotage, Cederberger, Sauvignon Blanc, Chardonnay, Chenin Blanc, Bukettraube

Among the rugged red sandstone rocks and Cape fynbos of the Cederberg range, at an altitude of over 1 000m, lie some 23ha of vines planted to classic wine varieties. The Nieuwoudts have owned Dwarsrivier farm since 1835, converting a sheep station to mixed farming – apples, peaches, pears, vegetables and tobacco. Grandfather Pollie introduced Barlinka table grapes to the mix in 1967 and then planted his first Cabernet and Pinotage in 1973. The first certified wines came in 1977 and the new-generation Cederberg label was relaunched by David Nieuwoudt in 1997. He maintains he has simply fine-tuned the essentially cool-climate wines, obtaining a fresher, fruitier character and greater complexity from fermentation and maturation in small French-oak barrels instead of large vats.

The Cederberg is snowbound in winter and the average summer temperature is some 10°C lower than Clanwilliam. Though ripening grapes may be exposed to temperatures of up to 35°C (Paarl is often higher), coolth comes from the height of the vineyards and a little south-east zephyr that pops up in the late morning. The largely Malmesbury shale soils contain enough red clay to retain water and the naturally low-vigour soils result in yields below 10 tons/ha, though bunches are dropped to ensure fruit with greater concentration.

Nieuwoudt starts harvesting at least two weeks after the rest of the country.

Despite pioneering red wines in the district and still devoting some 60% of its land to red varieties, the farm's cool-climate, reductively made grassy Sauvignon Blanc can be impressive. The off-dry, melony Chenin is of a similar style and is also wooded. Likewise the Chardonnay, finely balanced between citrussy freshness and buttery fatness.

The reds all exhibit good fruit, with the Cabernet probably the best. The more mature, 14-year-old vineyards give it a complexity and ripe tannin structure that will reward with bottle-age but take nothing away from its early drinkability. Recent investment in the popular Schleipp clone should soon make a mark. Some of the Cabernet also goes into the accessible red blend, Cederberger, predominantly Ruby Cabernet fleshed out with Merlot. Nieuwoudt is particularly excited about the Merlot, which may take over from the Pinotage. A new Shiraz vineyard has been planted, perfectly placed in low-vigour rocky shale soil combined with some clay on one of the farm's warmer slopes. Current production of 5 000 cases is set to increase to nearly 15 000 from some 40ha.

TOP: David Nieuwoudt is exploiting cool, high-lying sites in the Cederberg mountains for fine-wine cultivation. The farm Dwarsrivier (**ABOVE**) is overlooked by the Sneeuberg peak, snow-capped in winter.

VREDENDAL

OWNERS
160 wine growers

KEY WINES
Maskam Cabaret, Maskam Classic Red, Maskam Sauvignon Blanc, Maskam Special Late Harvest, Maskam Sweet Hanepoot, Maskam Red Muscadel, Maskam Port; Gôiya G!âan, Gôiya Kgeisje; Vredendal Sparkling Wine (Dry, Semi-sweet, Spumanté)

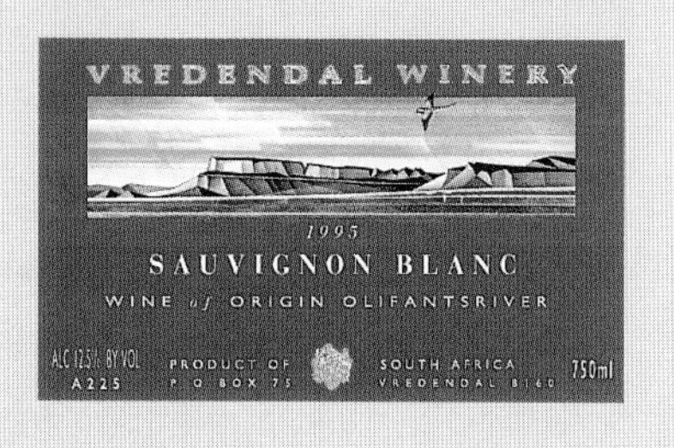

From humble origins as a mere co-op in 1947, Vredendal is now the largest single winery in South Africa, moving 60 000 tons of grapes sourced from over 2 000ha. Fundis first sat up and took notice in 1994 with the launch of a hot new, award-winning blend of Ruby Cabernet and Cabernet Franc called Cabaret. It showed that, given good material, viticultural application and careful cellar treatment, Vredendal could produce the goods. The massive 'factory' cellar was subsequently given a R25-million facelift and viticultural consultants were called in to help select the best blocks and advise on canopy management and optimum ripeness levels.

As more attention is paid to reds, the poorer, low-vigour soils have been sought out. Growers plant fewer vines per hectare to ensure a natural balance in the growth of the vine; correct directional placing of rows protects against from the sun; cutting back the canopy allows for cooling aeration; early-morning picking combats any jamminess. The results are seen in the Maskam range of premium wines.

The elegant, flavoursome Maskam Cabaret now combines Ruby Cabernet with Cabernet Sauvignon. The Classic Red blend of Merlot, Ruby Cabernet and Cabernet Franc is seriously wooded and can be quite tannic, needing time. Ruby Cabernet is an important variety here, doing well in the heat and providing a rich ruby colour, pronounced fruit and typical grassy, herbaceous character. Pinotage as well as the newly planted classics such as Cabernet Sauvignon, Merlot, Cabernet Franc and Shiraz, up until now mostly used in blends, are being honed to appear as varietal wines soon.

Vredendal's greatest export success has been the Gôiya G!âan and Gôiya Kgeisje red and white. (They commemorate the Kung language of the San people who first discovered the fertile Olifants River Valley, and mean 'red wine' and 'white wine'.) The 62 000 cases of the just off-dry Sauvignon Blanc and Chardonnay blend in '96 doubled its sales in the UK in '97. The spicy, very ripe, quaffable G!âan melange can consist of anything from Ruby Cabernet and Cabernet Franc to Pinotage and Shiraz.

Winemakers Pieter Verwey and Alwyn Maass make no bones about 'producing wines for immediate drinking: fresh and fruity and not lengthy or heavy on the aftertaste'. Wood

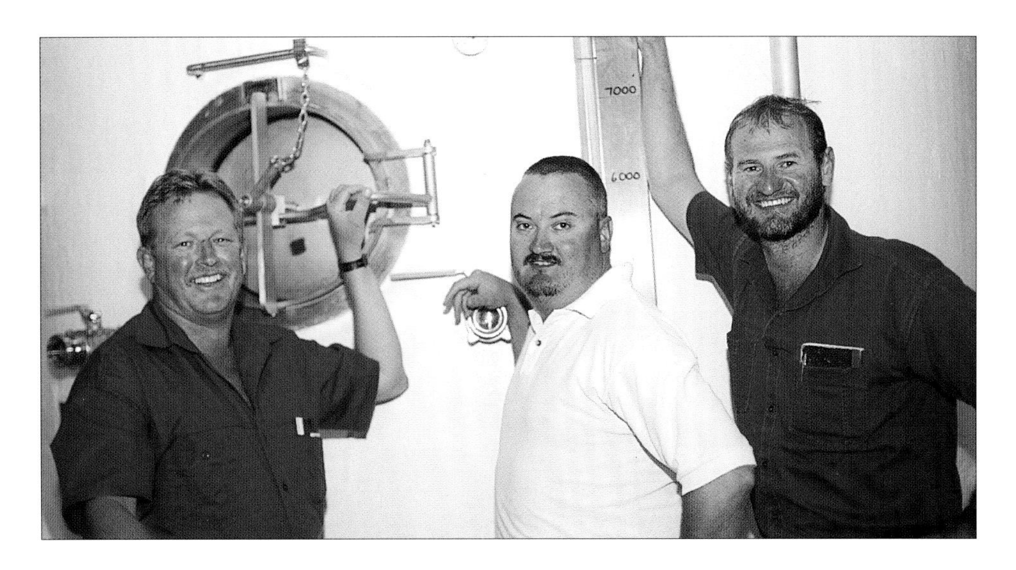

on limey soils. A flavoursome Chardonnay and semisweet Blanc de Noir from Grenache appeal. Experienced winemakers Sias du Toit and Len Knoetze are new appointees.

LUTZVILLE

This co-op's Fleermuisklip range contains good varietal wines from specially selected vineyard blocks. The Sauvignon Blanc surprises with its cool-climate-like green pepper, nettley astringency, while the barrel-fermented Chardonnay is rich with fruit and buttery fatness. There's even a grassy Sémillon. The unwooded Robyn blend of Cabernet Sauvignon, Merlot and Ruby Cabernet exhibits rich, ripe fruit, auguring well for later releases of single-varietal reds. Cellarmaster Jacques du Toit handles grapes from nearly 1 900ha of vineyards belonging to over 100 member-growers in what is the Cape's second-largest winery.

treatment on the reds is circumspect – mostly French barrels, and always with some second-, third-, or fourth-fill to tone down the effects of new wood.

CITRUSDAL

This co-op markets its wines under the Goue Vallei label. Winemaker Bennie Wannenburg sources nearly 14 000 tons of grapes from his 120 member-growers, who, between them, cultivate about 800ha of vines. There are still a lot of Chenin, Palomino and Muscat grapes coming into the recently upgraded cellar, but premium varieties such as Sauvignon Blanc, Chardonnay, Cabernet Sauvignon, Merlot and local cultivar Pinotage are on the rise. For the sweet tooth, both the Hanepoot Jerepiko and Red Jerepiko are good buys.

KLAWER

This 80-member co-op is renowned for its dessert wines, especially the value-for-money Hanepoot and White Muscadel. Good things are expected from reds such as Merlot, Pinotage and Ruby Cabernet, recently planted

TOP: Winemakers Pieter Verwey, Len Knoetze and Alwyn Maass handle 60 000 tons of grapes at Vredendal, the Cape's largest winery drawing on more than 2 000ha of vines (**LEFT**).

SPRUITDRIFT

The reds impress most, though Chenin Blanc and Colombard still make up 60% of the total crop, which amounts to over 28 000 tons, supplied by some 85 members. New plantings of Merlot, Pinotage, Shiraz and Chardonnay show a shift towards more serious wine grape cultivation. Winemaker Erik Schlünz's soft, fruity, gently wooded Cabernet Sauvignon is charming and works well in a blend with Merlot. The Pinotage has a wonderfully typical nose and the honeyed, raisiny Muscadels are bargain buys.

TRAWAL

With only 47 suppliers, Trawal is one of the smaller co-ops in the region, yet winemaker Alkie van der Merwe still processes over 7 000 tons of grapes from about 450ha. Most of this gets exported – a lot of it in bulk – with a small amount bottled locally as the Travino range, including the only Shiraz in the region. (That's until Cederberg gets going with its new plantings of this classic variety.)

BIBLIOGRAPHY

Phyllis Hands and Dave Hughes, *Wines and Brandies of the Cape of Good Hope*, Stephan Phillips, Somerset West, 1997

Dave Hughes, Phyllis Hands and John Kench, *The Complete Book of South African Wine*, Struik, Cape Town, 1988; *South African Wine*, Struik, Cape Town, 1992

John and Erica Platter, *John Platter's South African Wine Guide*, Stellenbosch 1982–1997; Creda, Cape Town, 1998–1999; *John Platter South African Wines*, Andrew McDowall, Kenilworth, 2000

Jancis Robinson, *Vines, Grapes and Wines*, Mitchell Beazley, London, 1994

WINE (SA) Magazine, Ramsay, Son & Parker, Cape Town, 1993–2000

WINE Magazine's Pocket Guide to Wines & Cellars of South Africa, Ramsay, Son & Parker, Cape Town, 1999–2000

INDEX